D0623409

CONCEPT
TESTING

CONCEPT TESTING

How to Test
New Product Ideas
Before You Go
to Market

David Schwartz

American Management Association

This book is available at a special
discount when ordered in bulk quantities.
For information, contact Special Sales Department,
AMACOM, a division of American Management Association,
135 West 50th Street, New York, NY 10020.

Library of Congress Cataloging-in-Publication Data

Schwartz, David, 1940–
  Concept testing.

  Includes index.
  1. New products. 2. Marketing research. I. Title.
HF5415.153.S42 1987   658.8'3   86-47987
ISBN 0-8144-5905-6

Printing number

10 9 8 7 6 5 4 3 2 1

Preface

In the last few months several thousand American companies did some form of concept research to help develop new products or reposition existing ones. Much of that research was flawed, some of it quite seriously. Many of those products ultimately will fail, in spite of rather massive concept testing efforts. The total cost of these failures will be in the billions of dollars.

Some failures are relatively quiet but carry price tags in the tens of millions of dollars. Others are more public, like Coca-Cola's infamous reformulation and quick about-face. The price? Damage to a reputation of trust and confidence that took almost a century to build. In many cases the failed product simply gets withdrawn from the marketplace, and life goes on. But some new-product failures, like Western Union's Easy Link electronic mail service, are so disastrous that a company's survival and ability to do business are threatened.

On the other hand, just as poor concept research can severely hurt a company, the effective use of concept research can immeasurably help it. Look at Campbell Soup Company. For many years it was a slow-moving, production-driven company. But soon after Gordon McGovern became president and CEO, things began to change. A heavy emphasis on new-product development was encouraged. Many new-product successes emerged, including Le Menu frozen entrees and Prego sauce (which grew so fast that it doubled revenues for the total sauce category*). Even Campbell's sleepy soup division, which had not grown for years, suddenly began to expand. Concept research did not do all this, but it played an important role.

To my knowledge, this is the first book ever written about concept research. Because concept research is so important in the development of new products, and because new products contribute so significantly to

---

* A *category* consists of all brands of the same type of product that compete for sales.

America's economic growth and health, I believe such a book is sorely needed.

During the course of my career I have conducted more than a thousand concept tests. My clients have included private and publicly owned companies on three continents, government agencies, and political candidates. In serving their needs, I have had an opportunity to see, firsthand, which techniques work best and which ones do not work at all. The ideas and many of the examples included in this book are drawn from these experiences.

Who will benefit from *Concept Testing*? Anyone involved in the process of concept research, from those who execute the research to those who must interpret the findings and apply them to a highly competitive and, at times, quite unforgiving marketplace. Since the book contains lots of practical information on how to execute and correctly interpret a concept test, researchers with responsibilities in this area will find it valuable.

But researchers are just a tiny part of the audience. For every researcher involved in a concept test, there are dozens of executives at different levels of management and with different specializations who need to competently use the results of a concept test. These nonresearch executives—in marketing, advertising, sales, manufacturing, and financial disciplines—share the responsibility for their company's or their client's new-product development. While they may not wish to master all the minute details involved in executing a concept test, they must know how to interpret test findings and what to do with the information once it is uncovered.

For these nonresearchers, this book aims to provide technical research information in an extremely nontechnical fashion. It is my hope that by reading this book, they will become more meaningful contributors to their company's new-product development process.

Acknowledgments

Some years ago I met Philippa Dunkley, a brilliant researcher whose insightful analysis of raw research data and ability to convert stark computer printouts into perceptive and profitable marketing recommendations were a continued source of amazement to me. As I think back on it now, I realize that about the only time her good judgment could have been questioned was when she married me.

I know it is often said, but in this case it is quite true: This book could not have been written without her active support and encouragement. Her suggestions on the content, my organization of it, my language, the examples I included and the ones I omitted helped me to convert a dry research treatise into a readable and hopefully enjoyable source of information for the reader.

I would also like to thank several individuals who were enormously helpful in the development of the book:

Dick Turkisher and Neil Katz of Revlon, Inc.: Dick for always pushing to extract that last insight and extra morsel of value from assignments we worked on together; Neil for showing me how to apply concept research to real-world marketing problems.

Jim Vanek of Miles Laboratories, who helped me see the value of norms as diagnostic tools, not just evaluative ones.

Pat Custis and Dick Nelson of Campbell Soup Company, for wanting only my very best work and causing me to stretch myself.

Fred Baker and Paula Drillman of McCann-Erickson, for sharing many of their good ideas with me.

Jack Grossman of William Esty, for frequently serving as a sounding board for some of my "bright ideas" and for having sufficient grace, wit, and sensitivity to allow me to feel great while being told my idea was too bad even to be called terrible.

Concept Testing

My editor, Adrienne Hickey, who led me by the hand around the reefs that sink many first-time authors. Her suggestions on where and how to expand or clarify key passages immeasurably improved the value of this book.

And finally, my thanks to *Advertising Age*. As I wrote this book, I found myself constantly needing to check facts and turned to *Advertising Age*, which bills itself as the "newspaper of marketing." This opinion is truly deserved. As a resource of which company did what and when, I found this publication a lifesaver. My special thanks to Debbie Krell of the New York office for her generous assistance.

Contents

Contents

I.

Concept Testing: What It Is and What It Does

1
An Introduction to Concept Testing

This book is about concepts—how to write them, how to test them, and how to improve them. The techniques described here will help you improve your company's system of developing new products and revising or restaging existing products. These tricks of the trade are easy to apply. Aside from inertia, there is no reason why your company cannot use them.

SOME KEY TERMS

There is a great deal of talk in today's marketing world about concepts and concept testing. Unfortunately, many of the people talking are miscommunicating with one another because they are talking about different things. A good starting point for a book on concept testing is to describe just what a concept and a concept test are.

What Is a Concept?

The term *concept* means different things to different people. To make sure we are thinking about concepts in the same context, I offer this definition:

> *A concept is a printed or filmed representation of a product or service. It is simply a device to communicate the subject's benefits, strengths, and reasons for being.*

A concept allows individuals who have not previously seen the product to understand what it is, how it will work, and what benefit it will provide. It is a road map showing all members of the corporate team the direction the product will take. It guides advertising, packaging, product formulation, pricing, and distribution strategies.

What Is a Concept Test?

Companies evaluate their new-product ideas many different ways: management review committees, new-product experts, interviews with the trade, and concept tests among consumers. Each of these techniques contributes something to the new-product development process. This book focuses on one technique—concept testing.

> *Concept testing is a quantitative market research technique used to evaluate a concept's potential and to discover ways of improving it. A concept test involves exposing a product idea to consumers and getting their reaction to it, using a predetermined series of questions designed to measure various emotions, reactions, and opinions.*

Analysis of this data gives marketers 1) information about the product's sales prospects; 2) tools to improve the product's positioning; and 3) ideas for advertising copy.

TWO KINDS OF CONCEPTS

There are two different kinds of concepts. Industry lingo refers to them as *core idea concepts* and *positioning statements*.

A core idea concept is usually quite short, just a few sentences or brief paragraphs. The core idea concept focuses directly on the product's main benefits, and puts very little emphasis on secondary features. It is relatively emotionless, making little effort to persuade the consumer to buy the product. Occasionally, core idea concepts are supported by rough artwork to help communicate how the product might look or function.

A positioning concept statement, on the other hand, is much longer. Print versions usually run several paragraphs. A positioning concept lists *all* the product's main benefits and various secondary benefits. While it may not be as blatantly sales-oriented as an advertisement usually is, a positioning concept often includes some "sell" as the writer tries to explain what makes the product advantageous compared to other products. Often it is supported with a photograph or illustration, many of them high-quality.

Occasionally positioning concepts are filmed, rather than written. These films use visual *and* verbal stimuli to describe the product, its benefits, and its end-use applications. Filmed concepts differ in complexity and degree of polish. Some are roughly filmed animatics and photomatics, and some are much like 30-second and 60-second commercials, using live actors and high-quality photography showing the product in use.

A Concept Is Not an Ad

At times, advertisements and positioning concepts are confused for one another. Experienced marketers understand that a positioning concept is designed to communicate information realistically and an advertisement is designed to attract attention, be memorable, and *persuasively* communicate information. But even marketers sometimes have trouble when they try to decide whether a specific execution is an ad or a concept.

Here's the primary difference: Most advertising is designed to sell something. There may be an occasional exception, but, for the most part, companies spend money on advertising to increase sales. Ad messages are designed to break through competitive clutter, be remembered, and, above all, persuade. A positioning concept, on the other hand, does not have to break through competitive clutter or be remembered by the consumer over a long period of time. The most important purpose of a positioning concept is to present the product idea realistically to learn whether consumers will eventually buy the product. The focus is on clear and forthright communication rather than persuasion. The goal is to portray the product as it will eventually be presented in order to determine its sales potential.

Positioning concepts usually explain more and contain more information than ads. But sometimes ads and positioning concepts are very similar, so close, in fact, that occasionally positioning concepts can be used later for advertising purposes.

The secret to preparing a successful positioning concept is to have a clear sense of what you want to accomplish. If concept writers do not have a firm grasp of their objectives, the unfortunate result is a product that tests well as a "concept" but fails in the marketplace.

Examples of Concepts

Let's look at some examples. Figures 1-1 through 1-4 are core idea concepts. Remember that core idea concepts are quite short. I was particularly interested in consumer reactions to the "Trees of the World" concept shown in Figure 1-3. I was concerned that the test would be wasted, that many consumers would reject the idea because the concept did not give enough information. The client's marketing representatives figuratively patted me

Concept Testing

Figure 1-1. Vaseline Intensive Care lotion core idea concept.

VASELINE INTENSIVE CARE LOTION MAKES YOUR SKIN FEEL SOFT *AND* SMOOTH.

Treat your rough, dry skin with Vaseline Intensive Care Lotion. It causes your skin to heal fast and makes it smooth *and* soft.

Vaseline Intensive Care Lotion penetrates fast into your skin. And it doesn't feel greasy.

I had the opportunity to test the Vaseline Intensive Care lotion concept in two formats: once as a core idea and once as a positioning concept (see Figure 1-8). Both concepts communicated similar information although the positioning concept focused more attention on its appropriateness for use on hands and its therapeutic value.

---

on the head and told me not to worry. They believed the concept contained more than enough information to allow coin collectors to evaluate the idea. It turned out they were absolutely correct.

Figures 1-5 through 1-11 show various types of positioning concepts. As you can see, they run the gamut in terms of medium (film and print), length, and use of illustration. Figures 1-5, 1-6, and 1-7 are all print statements, with no artwork or photography. Figures 1-8 through 1-10 make extensive use of artwork and photography.

Figure 1-5 is the positioning version of the core idea concept portrayed in Figure 1-4. Comparing the two vividly shows that there are wide differences between a core idea and a positioning concept even when the positioning version is, itself, quite short. Note also the differences between the core idea and the positioning concept in Figures 1-1 and 1-8.

Figure 1-9 is of particular interest because of the heavy emphasis on the product's package. Although the product failed, its concept remains of interest today because of its extensive use of the product package. Since packaging plays so important a role in the decision to purchase a cigarette, especially for the first time, R.J. Reynolds chose to prominently feature the package in many exhibits shown to consumers including this one. Back in

Figure 1-2. ZapMail core idea concept.*

ZapMail is a new service from Federal Express. ZapMail will deliver a high quality copy of a letter, report, or any document to another city within 2 hours.

All you have to do is call Federal Express to arrange for a pick-up or bring your document to a Federal Express manned facility. The document is electronically transmitted from the Federal Express office in your city to a Federal Express office in another city. It is then delivered to the recipient by Federal Express.

This entire process is completed within 2 hours after you call Federal Express to arrange for a pick-up or within 1 hour after you bring your document to a Federal Express manned facility. The material delivered to the recipient will be printed on high quality plain paper.

Writing concepts for complicated product ideas is very difficult to do. You must provide enough information so that a true sense of the product is communicated. But at the same time, you mustn't go so far that the reader feels inundated with detail and loses sight of the big picture. The task is even harder when a core idea concept is being tested. Federal Express did an excellent job of writing its core idea concept for ZapMail. Unfortunately for Federal Express, doing a good job of describing a product does not guarantee that customers will want to buy it. ZapMail ultimately failed in the marketplace. (See Chapter 7.)

*Courtesy of Federal Express Corporation.

1976 when Real cigarettes were first tested by R.J. Reynolds Tobacco Co., the low-tar category was considerably smaller than it is today. Consumer preference for items not containing additives and artificial ingredients was growing. The company attempted to meet these needs with Real.

Real's positioning concept was to tell consumers the product was all-natural, with no artificial ingredients. Unfortunately, the issues of naturalness and artificialness were health claims that apparently did not motivate cigarette smokers at the time the product was introduced. The product failed and was withdrawn from the market. As *Advertising Age* said in its post-mortem on Real's failure, "RJR constructed a sales proposition based on a non-problem."

Figure 1-3. Trees of the World core idea concept.

The United Nations announces

Trees of the World

A collection of 12 sterling silver collector coins

Important new issues from Germany, Canada, China, France, United Kingdom, Italy . . . Commemorating the International Year of The Forest

Even though this core idea concept is quite brief, with little explanation or fleshing out of the basic idea, coin collectors had strong reactions to the idea.

WHICH SHOULD YOU TEST: CORE IDEA OR POSITIONING CONCEPT?

According to some product development programs, once the decision is reached to begin work on a new product, the first step is to prepare a core idea concept and test it. If the test fails, you have lost very little, since you have not spent a great deal of time discovering subtle differences and unique elements that will separate your product idea from competitors. But if the core idea tests well, one of the immediate next steps is to flesh out the idea with a positioning concept that captures all these benefits and special features, and then test it.

Figure 1-4. Secret Solid antiperspirant core idea concept.

Secret Solid Antiperspirant is comfortable to apply to the body because it goes on dry.

It contains a pleasant feminine scent and provides the wearer with effective, all-day protection.

Figure 1-5. Secret Solid antiperspirant positioning concept.

Secret Solid Antiperspirant

Goes on drier than roll-ons, so it feels good on a woman's underarm.

Secret Solid Antiperspirant is different. It goes on drier than wet, sticky roll-ons, so it feels more comfortable when a woman puts it on.

And Secret Solid gives you effective, all-day protection that's strong enough for a man, yet its pleasant, feminine scent tells you it's made for a woman. Secret Solid Antiperspirant.

In theory, the plan seems sound enough. But in my experience the theory works only for unique, breakthrough products. In the case of the "me-too" product, trying to win its share of an already developed market segment, the plan does not often work. For these products—and they are far more typical—core idea concepts may serve an internal corporate purpose, but they are not useful for consumer testing.

Why? Because the consumer often already has a preconceived notion of what the products in the category are like. A core idea concept that focuses only on these standard major benefits, shared by all the products in that category, could cause the consumer to reject the idea because there is nothing unique about it.

Let us assume you try to avoid this problem by writing a core idea concept that primarily stresses its difference from other products in the cat-

9

Figure 1-6. Meal Relishers positioning concept.*

MEAL RELISHER

Open the door to a new world of side dishes that will add an extraordinary touch to all your meals. And they're easily found in your grocer's dairy case. New Meal Relishers are a unique variety of side dishes specially blended to enhance any dinner you've planned.

There's *Roasted Tomato Salsa* and *Onion Marmalade* that elevate ordinary flavors into delightful new tastes. *Vegetable Chutney, Pickled Baby Vegetables* and *Marinated Vegetables* add spice to any meat or fish entree. And *Herb Jellies* or *Special Flavored Ketchups* enhance a variety of your favorite foods.

Each Relisher is packaged in a 12 oz. container—enough for a family dinner. Prices range from $1.75 to $2.20 depending on which one you choose.

Meal Relishers was tested exactly as shown in a simple verbal format with no supporting artwork or illustration. Yet consumers had no trouble understanding the concept.

*Courtesy of Campbell Soup Company.

---

egory. Now you run the risk of having consumers reject your product because you did not adequately explain that it also provides all of the basic benefits and features offered by other products in the category.

Take home permanents, for example. Assume that a new home perm will be marketed that offers women all the basic features and benefits that other perms offer, plus several special benefits. If the core idea concept just talks about the basic features—easy to use, keeps hair soft, safe for the hair—consumers have no compelling reason to want to try it. On the other hand, just stressing its special benefits, without addressing the basic issues of safety, softness, and ease of use, will also result in disappointing scores. And if you talk about both basic *and* unique benefits, you begin to move your concept away from a core idea approach to a positioning approach.

There is another problem associated with testing a core idea concept. It often stimulates a lower level of buying interest than the positioning concept, which contains all the extra "goodies" that cause some consumers to want to

Figure 1-7. Financial services positioning concept.

Owning a home has become a necessity. It's not a luxury. It's the way most people protect their savings and their earnings. It's probably your most important single investment. And in today's rapidly changing world, first with inflation, and then with recession, unemployment, and deflation threatening, it's becoming more and more difficult.

We arc one of the nation's largest financial institutions. We feel very strongly about this problem. So strongly that we are creating a new company, committed to assisting people like yourself who are home-owners or want to be homeowners.

We believe that people like you should be able to obtain a home mort-gage. Even if you are starting out, don't already own a home, and don't have a lot of cash. We will help you to save and when you are a customer in good standing, we will guarantee you mortgage money when you need it. Bigger mortgages. Smaller down payments. Faster approvals. Even in times of tight money. Even if you move to another state. Anywhere in the whole country.

In addition we will do everything you need relating to buying, selling, insuring, finding a home. Engaging movers. Our efforts don't end once you get your mortgage. One account executive will coordinate it all for you. At no extra cost.

Some concepts contain more justification and emotion than others. The financial insti-tution preparing this concept felt that the emotions and values of homeowning had to be addressed by a concept or else the basic benefits of its service would never be heard by consumers. For this reason, they staged their offer in the opening two paragraphs to set the reader up for the basic benefits to follow.

try your idea. If you do test a core idea concept, be sure that you compare the results with other core idea concept scores, not positioning scores. Otherwise, it is the equivalent of racing your Volkswagen Beetle against a finely tuned Maserati. You may win, but the odds are not in your favor.

Testing a core idea is theoretically a fine first step. But on a practical basis it often is difficult to do. Furthermore, you still must do a positioning concept test to develop final ads. Since this next step is needed anyway, the

(text continued on p. 15)

Figure 1 8. Vaseline Intensive Care lotion positioning concept.

Figure 1-9. Real cigarettes positioning concept.

The makers of Real cigarettes developed what was thought to be a product with a unique difference, a low-tar cigarette with nothing artificial added. Because the package plays so important a role in the decision to purchase a cigarette product, the concept made extensive use of Real's package. Here the concept itself was used as the finished ad.

Concept Testing

Figure 1-10. Cordon Rouge Collection positioning concept.*

You are invited to an extraordinary dining experience. Announcing the Cordon Rouge Collection of super premium gourmet meals, unlike anything previously available frozen.

Proudly, the Cordon Rouge Collection presents the ultimate pleasures of classic cuisine.

If filet mignon is your cut of beef, there are elegant Tournedos Rossini. For seafood lovers, Lobster Thermidor, properly presented in its own scarlet shell. Imported morel mushrooms flavor the Chicken Breast Forestiere–or perhaps tonight you would prefer Roast Pheasant with wild rice stuffing?

Cordon Rouge prepares each classic dish faithfully. Selects appropriate accompaniments to complement your meal. Serves it graciously on a handsome ovenable plate suitable for microwave or conventional ovens. Only a few select restaurants offer a comparable dining experience (and certainly no other frozen dinners.)

Cordon Rouge invites you to enjoy a truly memorable meal. Tonight. At home.

CORDON ROUGE SELECTIONS

*Lobster Thermidor - Chunks of tender lobster baked in cream, beautifully presented in its own scarlet shell, with whole fresh-parsleyed potatoes and slender haricots verts.

*Tournedos Rossini - Sliced filet mignon topped with foie gras and truffles in Madiera sauce, with piped Dutchess potatoes and tiny peas with pearl onions.

Dilled Salmon - Whole baby salmon in dill sauce with parsleyed rice and asparagus spears.

Pheasant Classique - Roast pheasant with wild rice stuffing, sautéed mushrooms and braised endive.

*Chicken Forestiere with morels - Boneless breast of chicken sautéed with imported morel mushrooms, served with tarragon rice and julienne of summer vegetables.

Noisettes of Lamb Beatrice - Delicate fillets from loin lamb chops. Served on croutons with mushrooms, quartered artichokes, glazed baby carrots and new potatoes.

Priced from $6.00 - $8.00

*Included in photography

The Cordon Rouge Collection is a more complete print concept. A good-quality photograph was used to communicate the specialness of the product and its fine taste. A series of specific menu selections gave consumers a feeling about the kind of items that would be in the line.

*Courtesy of Campbell Soup Company.

Figure 1-11. First Glass positioning concept.*

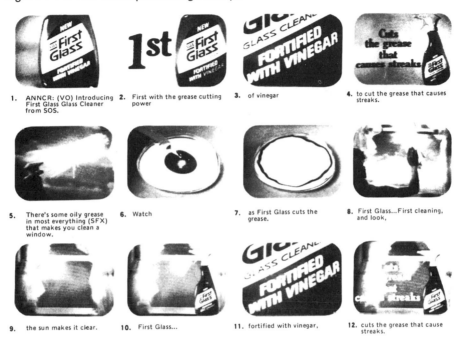

1. ANNCR: (VO) Introducing First Glass Glass Cleaner from SOS.
2. First with the grease cutting power
3. of vinegar
4. to cut the grease that causes streaks.
5. There's some oily grease in most everything (SFX) that makes you clean a window.
6. Watch
7. as First Glass cuts the grease.
8. First Glass...First cleaning, and look,
9. the sun makes it clear.
10. First Glass...
11. fortified with vinegar,
12. cuts the grease that cause streaks.

The developers of First Glass glass cleaner believed the grease-cutting power of vinegar required a visual presentation to properly communicate the message. A 30-second film was shown to respondents. Figure 1-11 is the storyboard version of that film. Panels 6 and 7 illustrate the product's grease-cutting power with a demonstration showing a drop of grease getting dissolved by the product.

*Courtesy of Miles Laboratories.

core idea concept seems superfluous. In fact, I have only once seen a core idea concept be completely and fully translated into an advertising campaign that caught the essence and all the nuances of the concept.

The concept was for Mern's Mart, a small chain of men's clothing stores in the New York Metropolitan area. The company, formerly known as Mern's, elected to change its name and strategy in the late 1970s. The core idea concept is shown in Figure 1-12.

The concept was translated into a very successful advertising program (see Figure 1-13). The customer count increased by 25 percent after a print

Concept Testing

Figure 1-12. Mern's Mart core idea concept.

PAY LESS FOR MEN'S CLOTHING

Why pay full price for up-to-the-minute men's fashions? You can look exactly the same while paying a good deal less.

We carry all the same famous labels that you'll find at full-price stores. But our price is much less.

---

and television campaign ran for just two weeks, and sales doubled after the first year.

The Mern's Mart example is atypical. For the most part, it is quite difficult to move from a core idea concept into a real-world marketing action. The experience of Arm & Hammer baking soda's management team is a case in point.

The explosive growth of Arm & Hammer baking soda sales in the 1970s was one of the major marketing successes of the decade. Its makers, Church & Dwight, converted a sleepy brand with flat sales into one of the nation's most rapidly growing brands, primarily by showing the consumer new uses for a trusted and reliable product.

Before 1972, baking soda was primarily used as a cooking ingredient. However, its ability to absorb odors was also well known to Arm & Hammer management. In fact, over the years untold shipments were ruined because the odor of foul-smelling railroad cars was absorbed into the product. The idea of using the product in the refrigerator as a deodorizer had been around for many years. In the 1930s instructions on the package itself recommended this as a secondary use.

In the early 1970s Church & Dwight began a concerted effort to improve product sales. Many ideas were tested, including the old standby of using the product as a refrigerator deodorizer. This idea, tested as a core idea concept, was of some interest, but did not overwhelm the research team as the Big Idea they were seeking. Repeated testing, with the core idea fleshed out a bit, continued to encounter some problems. Members of the team hypothesized that some consumers rejected the product in this context because they felt refrigerator odor reflected on their ability as homemakers.

Figure 1-13. Mern's Mart advertisement.

Mern's Mart advertising closely followed the core idea concept. In fact, the company's slogan "Look the same for less" came right from the concept.

17

Concept Testing

Chart 1-1. Tracking Research Results.

Period	Used Baking Soda as a Refrigerator Deodorizer
February 1972	19%
June 1972	38
October 1972	43
March 1973	57
May 1973	63

Eventually, they hit upon one positioning concept version that managed to extol product benefits without making the consumer feel deficient. Consumer reaction to this positioning concept was extremely positive. Because of the test, Church & Dwight developed an ad campaign featuring Arm & Hammer baking soda as a refrigerator deodorizer and, in 1972, gave it a test run on the West Coast while the rest of the country saw the then current campaign. According to Jack Honomichl, who is the writer of *Advertising Age*'s well-regarded research column, the results of this test market turned out to be absolutely eye-popping. The percentage of West Coast housewives who reported that they had ever used baking soda as a refrigerator deodorizer had risen rather dramatically during the period of time that the test had run. (See Chart 1-1).

Eventually, penetration leveled off at 80 percent and the company's West Coast brokers began complaining about extensive out-of-stock problems up and down the coast. The campaign was quickly moved nationally, with similarly impressive results. From a 1971 level of 2.3 million cases, sales rose 72 percent to 3.9 million cases by 1974, largely because of this campaign.

The moral of the story, from a concept tester's point of view: Positioning concepts are better vehicles with which to test an idea. Core idea concepts may be helpful management tools for internal usage, but when the consumer is involved, spend the time and effort required to develop the complete idea more fully. Mern's Mart's execution of its core idea concept was a smashing success, but this is quite rare.

WHEN DO YOU DO A CONCEPT TEST?

Developing a concept and testing it occur quite early in the product development cycle. But a number of critical actions must precede them.

Preliminary Steps

The starting place for any new-product development program is to determine if there is a marketing opportunity or a consumer need. Is there a gap between what consumers would like and what various manufacturers are currently offering? Do consumers have a need that no one is adequately satisfying? Are society's values and attitudes changing in some new direction that opens the door to new marketing opportunities?

Answering questions like these is step one of a new-product development program. The answers usually come from the experienced judgment of senior executives, from strategic consumer research, secondary or library research, qualitative research (focus-group discussions, for example), or a combination of these elements. Concept preparation or testing is not required at this point in the cycle.

The second step is to examine the fit between the need or opportunity uncovered in step one and the sponsoring company. Is there a reasonable chance that the company can provide a product to satisfy the need (even though no one has, as yet, carefully defined its specifications), either through in-house resources or by acquisition of machinery, qualified management, or other companies? Do the need and the tentative product fit the company's image, style, and philosophy?

Step three is an initial financial review. The finance department's involvement occurs, of course, through all phases of the development cycle. Each time additional information is obtained or various elements of the program change, the finance department must be invited to contribute its point of view. But here is the first occasion of its involvement. Based on the rough information available, some of it simply guess and hunch, the finance department should be measuring the potential cost and possible payout associated with satisfying the need in question.

Step four is the final major preliminary step—an evaluation of the competition. Who are they likely to be? How well financed are they? How fast are they likely to respond? What might be their response? A high-tech company can gamble on a new product or service with a feeling of security in at least one area: It knows that a competitor cannot easily, quickly, and inexpensively replicate it. On the other end of the continuum, in industries like toys, cosmetics, and foods, competitive products can be introduced to the marketplace featuring "new" and "improved" benefits before the originator even completes its own introduction.

A case in point is Sealtest Light n' Lively brand of ice milk. When the product was first developed, its reason for being was that it was like ice cream but with less fat and fewer calories. Sales soared when it was first introduced to the market. But soon after, competitive products arrived, and sales of Light n' Lively plummeted. Eventually the product was repositioned with a "good taste" claim, and sales again rose. One moral of the story: Not enough thought was given to competitive reactions when the product was initially marketed.

At this point, when all four preliminary steps have been completed, the time is right to begin developing the concept (see Chapter 2) and testing it.

Follow-up Steps

Once the concept test is successfully completed, you will—if you use the ideas contained within this book—undertake five follow-up steps.

1. Revise the concept to incorporate changes and improvements suggested by the concept test.

2. Develop final specifications for the actual product, making use of input from the concept test.

3. Define the target group in a manner that allows the concept to reach its full potential. Companies often make the serious error of defining the target group *before* the concept test, and fail to use the test to assist them with that decision. The results could be disastrous.

For example, a few years ago Weight Watchers introduced a line of low-calorie frozen dinners, aimed directly toward the nation's dieters. It rapidly became a profitable line within the frozen food category. A short time later, Lean Cuisine entered the market with a low-calorie line of foods aimed at all calorie-conscious *and* health-conscious individuals.

By focusing on a broader slice of the population, nimbly including Weight Watchers' dieter segment plus the larger segment of people who would like to lose weight but are not actively dieting plus those who are generally interested in the quality and quantity of the food they eat, Lean Cuisine more than tripled the size of its potential market.

Within a few years, Lean Cuisine became the category leader, swamping Weight Watchers with a strategy that rightfully could have belonged to Weight Watchers. It is a vivid example of why a final decision on the target group should be made after concept testing, not before.

An Introduction to Concept Testing

4. Concurrent with product development, work should begin on the product's advertising, promotional, and marketing plans.

5. During this same time period, various legal, financial, manufacturing, and administrative professionals should be contributing their skills to the development process.

Clearly, concept testing is just one step in the lengthy process of developing and successfully introducing a new product.

WHY SOME CONCEPT TESTS FAIL

When concept tests fail to perform properly, there are usually two reasons: poor executional techniques, and unrealistic expectations. We will spend a great deal of time discussing the executional steps required to correctly conduct and interpret a concept test. But the problem of an unrealistic expectation is more subtle, more insidious, and more destructive, and deserves our attention here.

People often want the wrong things from a concept test. Some expect too much from a test. They try to use it to help them make strategic decisions: "Let's see if there is enough interest in this kind of product so we can decide if we should market a product in this category." Concept tests are *tactical* aids to help you market the best possible product. They are not designed to address strategic issues such as whether you should be in a category. People who use concept tests in this manner often fail.

An example is provided by the makers of Formica laminated countertops. The Formica name is well known to most Americans. Its high awareness led the company to test the idea of Formica floor shine a few years ago. Their thinking was that the hard, scratchproof image of Formica countertops would be a wonderful umbrella under which to market a floor shine product. Concept testing confirmed this thinking: Consumers liked the idea.

But the product flopped when it was brought to market. The major problem was that it was sold through building-material distributors who handled the company's laminate sales. They did not gain sufficient distribution in supermarkets, where the bulk of this category's sales occur. Nothing could have helped this product. Let's face it: You cannot buy a product if you cannot find it in the store.

Some people err in the opposite direction—they expect too little from a concept test. They use it merely to see if there is a sufficient level of consumer interest in a concept, in effect, using it as a go/no-go decision aid.

WHAT GOOD CONCEPT TESTING WILL DO

A well-planned, well-executed, and well-analyzed concept test can provide you with several important pieces of information.

• It can tell you if your concept has sufficient sales potential. If potential is high, it should help you to pinpoint the segments of the population that are most responsive to your idea. If results are disappointing, the test should let you determine whether there are any potential targets of opportunity if the population were to be segmented into different or narrower demographic, behavioral, or attitudinal groups.

• It can help you determine the degree to which the message that consumers receive from the concept (both factual, direct statements, and subjective hints or implied suggestions) is the same one you think you are sending. This will tell you if the concept's level of success or failure comes solely from the inherent value of your idea, or is compromised in some way by a biased or inaccurate execution. This is especially important in the case of a poor-performing concept when you must decide whether to kill the idea or make another attempt at describing it.

• It should allow you to pinpoint the individual strengths and weaknesses of the concept. It should tell you which concept elements played a major role in making the concept succeed, and which ones played a minor role or provided no help at all. On the negative side, the test should tell you which elements of the concept held back acceptance. As a result of these data, you should have a clear picture of what must be said louder, better, or not at all. By identifying all appropriate changes, improvements, or modifications, a well-designed concept test should allow you to strengthen your concept.

• And finally, a concept test often provides morsels of information about the product and the consumer that can help you create a better product, as well as improved advertising, packaging, and promotional programs. While it is not the primary job of a concept test to provide information in these areas, a well-designed test almost always provides this valuable "fallout" in the normal course of fulfilling its other objectives.

2
The Art of Concept Writing

You have uncovered a major market opportunity: You found out that consumers are dissatisfied with the widget they currently use. You also have concluded that the widget business is compatible with your own company's interests, skills, and financial strength. The initial financial analysis suggests there is money to be made.

Or perhaps you are already in the widget business, selling a brand that is producing disappointing sales. You learn that consumers prefer the category leader because of perceived benefits that your product also provides. The only trouble is, you never told consumers about this aspect of your product.

In both cases the time has come to prepare a concept statement for test purposes. But where do you begin?

It's a good question. Concepts look deceptively easy to write but are devilishly difficult to write well. In fact, I suspect that poorly written concepts are the number one reason potentially good ideas are killed off prematurely.

GENERATING THE IDEAS

The starting point is to prepare a list of benefits and features that the product will contain. Some are "standard" benefits that all products in the category possess. Others might be unique to your product. The standard ones are pretty easy to identify by studying the category and individual companies currently participating in it. The unique benefits are sometimes harder to pinpoint. The very fact that they are unique means no one else is offering them. In other words, you are breaking new ground, not copying someone else's thinking.

Concept Testing

Here are some places concept writers can turn to for stimulation:

1. Brainstorming sessions among corporate staff members as well as interested outsiders such as advertising agencies and creative consultants.
2. Advice from retailers, distributors, and sales staff.
3. Focus-group discussions among consumers who have a need, are users of the category, or express some interest in it.
4. Problem analysis research and related forms of consumer research. Consumers are given lists of problems that the product is designed to resolve and asked to rank each problem on several dimensions, including its seriousness and the frequency with which it occurs.
5. Analysis of the marketplace as it currently exists, to seek out unique opportunities.

EXAMINE EXISTING PRODUCTS

With the last item—analysis of the marketplace—the idea is to create a point of uniqueness by looking at the product in new ways. What would happen if something about the product was changed? What if there was a new way to use it, or if something was added to it or subtracted from it? The process is simple. The ideas are all around us. All you have to do is open your eyes to see them. Let's consider this approach in detail, with a few examples. You might:

1. Add something to an existing product.

- A manufacturer of gardening and farming supplies has a line of weed, insect, and slug control devices. It learns that many gardeners leave a saucer of beer in their garden overnight to catch slugs. It asks its technical staff to work on an antislug spray that contains beer.
- A marketer of canned tomato juice learns that many consumers spice the juice with pepper, lemon juice, and various other seasonings. It produces a spiced juice line suitable for drinking as is or for use in making Bloody Marys.

2. Change something about an existing product.

- A shoe manufacturer learns that 100 million people wear running shoes, but many of them do not run or jog and have no intention of ever doing so. After eliminating buyers who are responding to fashion, there are still more than 50 million people who wear running shoes simply because they are more comfortable than traditional shoes. But many of these people are dissatisfied with the fabrics and colors that running shoes are made with. The manufacturer responds with a line of regular, everyday walking shoes that look like traditional shoes but contain some comfort features formerly found only in running shoes.

- A jeans manufacturer learns that dark blue jeans are bleached by some consumers before the first wearing to give a lighter, older, used look. It begins to sell prebleached jeans.

3. Subtract or substitute something from an existing product.

- A local package delivery company learns that one of its customers, a midtown New York City company, has sent a package to nearby Fort Lee, New Jersey, a distance of eleven miles. The customer paid $18 for overnight delivery. The local company could have delivered the package to Fort Lee in just two hours, but at a cost of $35. It begins to offer a next-day service, just for the New York area, for $10 per package.
- Some consumers dilute their wine with carbonated water. An alert winery begins to test a light wine. Another experiments with dilution and added flavoring.

4. Look for new ways to use an existing product.

- A cracker manufacturer learns that a popular cheesecake recipe calls for a crust to be made of 12 graham crackers. It introduces a pie crust product made from broken crackers and crumbs.
- In a business crisis, four executives rent a nearby hotel room for the day to get away from office interruptions. The hotel begins to offer meeting rooms to local businesses.

5. Reorganize the components of an existing product by re-engineering, rearranging, or combining them in some way.

- A manufacturer of small kitchen appliances and gadgets learns that virtually every household owns a garlic crusher but most consumers do not use it because it is too difficult to clean. It asks R&D to design a more functional crusher.

- In localities with pet feces cleanup laws, plastic food storage bags are substituted for "pooper-scoopers" to clean up dog droppings. A manufacturer tests the idea of plastic bags (under a new brand name) in the pet supply section of the supermarket.

At this point you may be thinking that the entire process of concept creation is a colossal waste of time. Why not, you may wonder, follow the practice of so many other manufacturers and simply copy an existing product, distinguishing the knockoff by making minor alterations or modifications?

Because, in general, this knockoff approach does not work very well. One exception is in a new or rapidly expanding category, where a growing dollar volume and an increasing number of customers provide high sales potential for a new product. A second exception is in a category that does not completely satisfy the need—wrinkle removers and acne prevention aids, for example.

Without question, some companies do succeed with knockoffs, especially if they are large and well financed enough to *buy* awareness and distribution. Knockoffs also succeed if the company is already in the category or a related one and can use existing production lines, marketing skills, and distribution networks. But in general, knockoffs are typically not big profit producers. And in your heart I know that you agree. Otherwise you would not be reading this book.

BE REALISTIC

A poorly executed concept does not clearly communicate the nuances of the product idea. Realism is often a major deficiency. So here's a simple reminder: Be realistic. Your concept statement must reflect the real-world environment that will exist when you market the product or service being tested. Control your zeal. Remember that a concept test should help you to estimate the product's potential and figure out how to maximize its performance in the marketplace—given the real-world constraints that exist. If your product has four major benefits but will eventually be promoted in a 15-second commercial that can use only two of them, don't give equal prominence to all four in your concept test; instead, let the test help you to select the best two. If a regulatory agency will not let you refer to a key product benefit, keep it out of your concept test, even if it will help your score. If it takes three paragraphs of copy to explain how the product operates or how the end result will please the consumer, but real-world promotional plans will not allow you to spend this much time, shorten the description in the concept test.

The importance of being realistic is so obvious, yet the error occurs again and again. The trade press is full of examples. One was a new-product launch attempted by one of the major companies in the women's personal product field. The company is a highly skilled marketer with a proven track record of developing and profitably marketing new products.

A few years ago it investigated the viability of a new woman's body lotion. The company concluded the category had high potential, so its new-product experts moved to the next product development stage—a concept statement describing the proposed product. The concept writers did a very fine job. Their body lotion was a unique product idea, containing several desirable benefits. Consumers liked the idea; a concept test found that Purchase Interest was well above average.

Based on the high-scoring concept test, the product and package were developed, media plans were prepared, commercials were made, and the product was introduced into a small group of test markets.

The commercials were skillfully prepared. It was not possible to stress all benefits equally in 30 seconds, but the agency did an excellent job of stressing one key benefit and supporting others.

The product failed because of low consumer trial rates. The company assumed there was some problem with the concept's execution or with the level of marketing support. It believed the opportunity still existed. So it took a second shot in the category, substantially revising various elements of the marketing mix. It relaunched into another group of test markets with new packaging and new advertising. The advertising, again skillfully prepared, stressed a different combination of benefits.

Again the product failed—at a total cost of more than $1 million.

In retrospect, the reason for the failure was quite clear. There was no way to address all the unique features of the product in a real-world TV commercial. In a forced-exposure concept test, where you can cause the consumer to see or read about each feature, no problem. But in a 30-second commercial, with lower viewer attention levels and less time to tell a story, the task was impossible. The result: a very expensive failure.

There are lots of lessons to learn from this example. And at the top of the list is simply this: Don't develop or test a concept that cannot be replicated in the real world.

27

COMMON ERRORS IN BODY COPY

When researchers prepare a print concept for test purposes, they place a great deal of emphasis on the headline and illustration. Body copy, which is also a very important part of the concept, often gets much less attention. The result is a concept which does not achieve its full potential.

The problem, I suspect, is that they are writing an ad to attract attention, not a concept to communicate an idea. Three frequent body-copy errors are: making the concept too long, using valuable time and space to state the obvious, and being unclear in describing the product or its benefits.

Being Too Long

Actual length is often not the problem—it's the *perceived* length that affects the level of interest, or lack of it. I have tested three-paragraph concepts that bored the respondent and could have communicated the same ideas in one paragraph. I have also tested eight-paragraph concepts that held consumer interest throughout.

Length can cause serious problems. An overly long concept can bore respondents or reduce emphasis and impact of a key benefit. The result is a concept that scores lower than its true potential.

I recently tested a concept for a new brand of antiperspirant that was formulated to appeal to males 25 to 49 years of age. The hook, or reason for being, was efficacy *and* gentleness—it was strong enough to keep a lumberjack dry but would not irritate his skin. Only 12 percent of all those interviewed thought gentleness was a valuable benefit in spite of the fact that it was stressed in the headline and played a dominant role in the first two paragraphs.

The problem was caused by an excessively long concept statement that stressed wetness prevention, longevity, and odor prevention, in addition to gentleness, during the course of its seven paragraphs. A followup version of the same concept with sharper, more hard-hitting body copy, shorter and more focused on gentleness, communicated its point of strength to a significantly better degree.

Unfortunately, in some complicated, technical product categories, a lengthy or time-consuming description is required to explain how the product is used or how it benefits the consumer. The writer's task is to communicate these benefits in an interesting manner. It's a difficult task, and not everyone succeeds.

When MCI Mail was first conceived, its developers viewed it as a rather

The Art of Concept Writing

simple computer-to-computer communications system that used available office-equipment technology. But from the prospective user's point of view, the decision about whether to use MCI Mail was far more complex, involving dozens of considerations. Precisely how does MCI Mail work? Can I use it if I do not own computer equipment? Do I need a special computer? How is my letter entered into the system? Can my secretary handle the task or does it need a computer operator? Does use of the system require special training? Can charts or pictures be transmitted?

Prospective users also wondered about reactions of those on the receiving end. What does the recipient's copy of my letter look like? How does MCI Mail handle letterheads and corporate logos? What happens if the recipient does not have a computer or word processor, or has a different make or model? What happens if the recipient's equipment is malfunctioning or not plugged in? Do I have to waste some of the money I saved by telephoning to make sure my letter arrived?

In the emotional, "softer" aspects of the product concept, prospective users wondered: What does use of MCI Mail say to the recipient about me? Am I getting involved in some new technology that will boomerang or take too much time or effort? What happens if I need a copy of the letter after 5:00 P.M. when my secretary has left for the day? Is this a suitable vehicle for private or confidential messages?

To address *all* the key issues of a product like MCI Mail, a concept statement might be more like a small book. Unfortunately, a book-sized concept statement has some obvious drawbacks.*

Figuring out if the length of a concept affected its performance is difficult. Asking respondents to rate the length on an appropriate scale and compare those results against norms will pinpoint a length-related problem about half of the time. Here are two other ways you can gauge whether the concept's length may have hurt performance.

First, if the concept is considered uninteresting or boring by an above-average number of consumers, it may be a signal that it is too long. Second,

---

* The problem with technically oriented new-product concepts that require lengthy explanations is not limited to concept testing. These products often encounter significant problems in the marketplace. Advertisers often find them hard to explain in advertising. They require much more time and effort to stimulate purchase. The failure rate for these products is high because companies often overestimate the speed of the sales curve buildup, no matter how conservative they think their projections are.

The marketing problems of technical breakthrough products are well beyond the scope of this book, but here is one poor man's rule of thumb: If a new product cannot be easily described in concept form, prepare yourself for a long and expensive introductory phase of the product's life cycle. Why a *poor* man's rule of thumb? Because ignoring the rule makes you poor.

if the percentage of people who think the concept is hard to understand is higher than usual, that is also a clue about length, especially if the things they didn't understand are widespread and diffuse instead of focused on one or two specific aspects of the concept.

But be careful. It may also be that the test concept is boring, uninteresting, or hard to understand. Subjective judgment is required. The thing to do is to look for patterns of response. Are consumers complaining about a specific element or are their complaints all over the lot? The more varied and uncorrelated their complaints are, the more likely the problem is caused by excessive length.

Stating the Obvious

Another common problem is wasting time and space to state the obvious. Let me illustrate with an example from the frozen food category. The very mention of "frozen dinner" connotes ease and convenience, so why waste valuable space reporting what the reader already knows?

Yet the newly emerging microwavable food category perpetuates this error. Many new-product concepts stress that the food product can be microwaved in just a few minutes. Why bother? Consumers already know this—that's why they bought a microwave oven in the first place. Why not use the available time or space in the concept to convince potential buyers that the product tastes good? Or what about marketing the product more effectively with shorter but more frequent advertising support instead of wasting money promoting the obvious?

Occasionally a category does require a bit of reassurance. The safety and ease of use of home permanents is one case in point. But if your concept requires this type of reassurance, relegate it to a less dominant place in the copy. Don't make it your lead benefit.

Being Unclear

A third common problem is the tendency of writers to be unclear as they attempt to describe the product or its benefits in some special way. A few years ago one food manufacturer went into test market with Frozen Fruit Bars, like an ice cream bar in size and shape, available in five fruit flavors: pineapple, banana, strawberry, coconut, and watermelon. The two major benefits of the product were its delicious taste and the fact that it contained no artificial preservatives.

Unfortunately, body copy talked about a "nutritious quiesently frozen confection on a stick." What exactly, I wondered, is a frozen confection? Is it like an ice cream? Is the strategy to sell the product as a non–ice cream, by being different, better, or more special? For that matter, precisely what is a confection on a stick?

And what does *quiesently* mean? Do you know? Does anyone? I turned to my trusty Webster's. No *quiesently*. Could they have mean *quiescently*, that which is at rest or motionless? Probably not. Could they have meant *quintessence*, the highest essence of quality or class, or its derivative *quintessential*? Not with that spelling! Just what is going on? Are these just words to fill up space, or are they intended to communicate something special about the product?

All three concept-writing problems are very serious, because they serve to reduce the concept's appeal. It all goes back to the basic problem: The writers forget what the assignment is. They think they are writing an attention-getting advertisement, rather than a concept description of a product and its unique benefits.

EMOTIONALLY LOADED WORDS

There is considerable controversy over the use of emotionally loaded words in concepts—expressions like "great taste," "best," "engineering breakthrough," "the first," and "great looking."

Do they belong in a concept statement? Some researchers believe emotionally loaded words are "selling" the respondent and therefore should not be allowed. Others think emotion is part of a product and should be part of its description. In my opinion emotionally loaded words *should* be allowed because they can be important tools to help communicate key benefits or points of difference. If you are trying to communicate that the product tastes great, don't be afraid to say it.

The problem comes with idle, uninformative superlatives that are just puffery and may even get in the way of your message. But a clear statement describing a real benefit in language that the customer knows and understands can only help the concept to be evaluated fairly and accurately.

When using emotionally loaded words you must watch out for the word that acts as a lightning rod, causing lots of negative reaction and getting in the way of positive communication. Here are some examples.

- A new financial service might not be perceived as "sophisticated" and "elegant." The language might be so powerful or inappropriate that consumers focus on this issue and fail to perceive other benefits.
- Home gardeners might not believe a headline for a gas-driven tiller

concept that promises that the tiller will let them "start your best garden ever."
- A supermarket ice cream brand could be "luscious," "rich," and "thick." But "gourmet" might not fit with a supermarket image.

On balance, the issue to consider is whether the *right* emotionally loaded words are being used, not whether emotion should be allowed in a concept.

CONCEPT HEADLINES

Marketers spend a great deal of time and effort writing concept headlines. In my opinion, they overdo it. The extra effort often has no significant influence on a concept's overall performance.

The secret to a successful concept headline is clear communication. The major problem, again, is that some concept writers, while they give lip service to the fact that they are writing a concept, are unconsciously writing an ad. Their headlines become punchy and short. This style may be terrific for advertising, but it doesn't always help a concept test. In fact, it sometimes hurts. My research shows that jazzy headlines are often bypassed by respondents. They dive into the body of the concept, treating the headline as—you guessed it—an ad claim. They are racing past the sizzle to get to the steak.

In a study for a small-business office product, I observed that purchase interest was just average and communication of the main sales point was low. I wondered if the headline might be causing the problem. The concept was retested with the headline written as an informative lead-in to the concept, not as a cutesy advertising headline. The improvement was striking; see Chart 2-1.

It's worth repeating: Write a headline that is a lead-in to the body of the concept; don't try to write a grabber. Remember: We are not testing the ability of an advertisement to attract attention or stimulate interest. We are simply conducting a forced-exposure test, with respondents being asked to read everything placed in front of them.

The most important thing is to convey the core idea clearly and concisely. Worry more about clear communication, and less about punch and pizazz. You'll wind up with a concept headline that gets better attention and increases the chance of your idea receiving a fair hearing.

Sometimes print concepts attempt to communicate the main benefit better or more persuasively by treating the headline in a graphically different manner: headlines set in radically different type, large lettering, small let-

The Art of Concept Writing

Chart 2-1.* The importance of a headline.

	"Ad" Headline	"Lead-in" Headline
Had high Purchase Interest in product	16%	(22)%
Understood main benefit of product	41	(59)

tering, a few words, very wordy, above the photo, below the photo. In my experience, it simply does not matter *how* you present the key idea as long as you do it clearly. The concept's performance is based on values inherent in the concept itself, and not in the graphics of the headline.

Most concepts use one single headline, but some use two. The lead headline usually carries a major benefit, and the second usually contains another benefit or explains an application or advantage.

I have tested double headlines in a number of different formats: large lettering, small lettering, both headlines above the photo, both below the photo, one above and one below the photo. But regardless of the format, double headlines add nothing to the concept's performance. Purchase Interest is not higher. Communication of the main benefits is not increased. Believability, Uniqueness, Importance, and other diagnostic ratings are not helped. A well-written single headline could have done precisely the same job.

SHOULD YOU ILLUSTRATE A CONCEPT?

The visual aspect of a concept's presentation is also an issue to consider. Some researchers like their concept to be filmed or, if printed, to contain an illustration of the product. Others think a film or illustration adds nothing to the success of the test. Who is right? Probably they both are, at different times. It depends on your concept.

If the concept contains a major product benefit that cannot be communicated adequately without visual support, then an illustration, film, or photograph is strongly recommended. But if a written description can do

---

* Throughout this book, I have circled some numbers on various charts in order to highlight them.

the job, you don't need an illustration. It will not help your concept and could even hurt if it's done poorly.

For example, suppose you are testing a concept for a new lipstick and you want to communicate its iridescent look. A high-quality film or illustration may help accomplish your goal, but it could cost thousands of dollars. Compromise to save money, and you might produce a so-so visualization. And if it fails to capture the nuances required to communicate a beautiful product, what have you saved?

The bottom line? Don't do things halfway. If you are absolutely convinced your concept needs illustrating, make the investment in time and money to do it right, or don't do it at all.

By the same token, using an illustration just because "we always have artwork in our concepts" adds nothing to your results. Art for art's sake has no place in a concept test. This lesson was graphically illustrated in a recent concept test for an electric frying pan with an automatic timer and shutoff switch. The concept produced disappointing scores when tested in print form. Management believed that consumers would like the idea more if they could see how it worked, so another version of the concept was produced, this time with the automatic timer illustrated. The new version was tested, and produced a similar score.

When an illustrated concept tests poorly, the researcher must question if the visual played any role in its poor performance. An inexpensive way to test for this problem is to give respondents a self-administered checklist of different words and phrases that describe consumer reactions to advertisements or commercials, and ask them to select the words that apply to the exhibit just viewed: "clever," "offensive," "silly," "informative," "friendly," and a host of other adjectives.

Often it is not even necessary to analyze this data. If your concept is successful, why bother? On the other hand, suppose your concept performed poorly. Suppose it elicited very little Purchase Interest even though data from all the communication questions suggested the concept communicated its benefit clearly, previous research showed that the benefits being communicated were important, and various diagnostic questions revealed no problem. In such an instance the visual execution might be the problem.

One of my clients discovered this during the course of a test to evaluate a new food processor with a very large bowl capacity. The bowl was filmed in a manner that deliberately exaggerated its capacity. In addition, an on-camera spokesperson made many funny comments and facial expressions as the machine's capacity was demonstrated. The concept was unsuccessful. The manufacturer wondered if the visual execution caused the concept to

The Art of Concept Writing

Chart 2-2. Commercial characteristics.

	Total Sample	Respondents with:	
		High Purchase Interest	Low Purchase Interest
Description			
Insincere	47%	38%	(56)%
Exaggerated	27	29	25
Silly	21	8	(34)

fail. If so, was it the exaggeration of the capacity, or the funny comments and expressions of the spokesperson?

Chart 2-2 gives us the answer. It shows the percentage of respondents with high and low Purchase Interest who selected each adjective. The exaggerated bowl capacity is clearly not the problem. It is true that 27 percent of all respondents think the demonstration exaggerated the bowl capacity, but on this issue there was very little difference between those with high and low Purchase Interest. But look at the number of individuals who think the on-camera spokesperson is silly or insincere. Look especially carefully at the differences between individuals with high Purchase Interest and low Purchase Interest. Clearly, low Purchase Interest is associated with more frequent perceptions that the on-camera spokesperson is silly and insincere. We can conclude that the performance of this new-product concept was hurt by its on-camera spokesperson.

To me the evidence is quite clear. Illustrating a concept is a two-edged sword. It can hurt you as easily as it can help.

As you can see, the process of creating a concept is not a simple task. You must first generate the ideas and then commit them to paper. Many decisions must be made along the way regarding the content and format of the headline as well as the body copy. Issues relating to length, clarity, degree of realism, and emotion must also be addressed. Clearly, a concept is not a quick or simple task to be thrown together in a few minutes.

II.

Tools for Successful Concept Testing

3
All About Purchase Interest

The Purchase Interest question is the tool most frequently used to measure concept success, both as a decision-making variable and as a key element in various volume-prediction models. It is far from flawless, but it is extremely useful. Unfortunately, its full potential is often not realized by research practitioners. Some researchers have problems with Purchase Interest, both in how they word the question and in how they interpret the results. Many do not properly use it as a diagnostic tool. This chapter addresses all these issues.

HOW TO WORD THE QUESTION

There is no generally recognized single correct way of asking the Purchase Interest question. One acceptable question format, which I often use, employs a five-point answer scale. The respondent is asked to select the item on the scale which best describes his interest in the product. Here is an example:

[Hand respondent Purchase Interest scale.] Based on the description you just saw, which phrase on this card best describes how likely you would be to buy this product if it were available at your local store?

Definitely would buy it	☐
Probably would buy it	☐
Might or might not buy it	☐
Probably would not buy it	☐
Definitely would not buy it	☐

Concept Testing

Most researchers use a five-point scale similar to this one, although some use a six-point scale. Their theory is that since most consumers generally give positive responses to this question, a scale with three positive levels is more discriminating than one with two levels. One of my clients, in the personal products business, prefers the following format. (Notice that they also changed the question slightly.)

[*Hand respondent Purchase Interest scale.*] Which phrase on this card indicates how likely you would be to buy this product the next time you were to go shopping for a product of this type?

Definitely would buy it   ☐
Very likely would buy it   ☐
Probably would buy it   ☐
Possibly would buy it   ☐
Probably would not buy it   ☐
Definitely would not buy it   ☐

I don't think there is anything sacred or magical about one answer scale or the other and I applaud this company's attempt to make the question work better for them. I also don't think one question's wording is significantly better than the other. It's all a matter of personal comfort. The one important problem to consider if you customize or drastically change an answer scale is that most available normative data are based on a five-point scale. By changing the scale you are effectively turning your back on these norms. (For a detailed discussion of norms, see Chapter 9.)

In addition to scale revisions, some researchers alter the focus of the question to suit their specific needs. I have seen questions measuring possible purchase interest, interest in trial, interest in visiting a showroom, in tasting a product one time, in getting additional information, or simply general overall interest. In my opinion, this is a good thing. Different questions probably work better in different categories. More attention should be given to customizing the Purchase Interest question to the need of the category under investigation. But keep in mind that you are dealing with a double-edged sword. The more you revise the question, the less industry experience and norms can be of use to you.

Here is how one organization used a Purchase Interest type of question in a situation that did not involve a "purchase" at all. I tested a concept in 1980 for New York City's Metropolitan Transportation Authority, a government agency whose responsibilities include running the city's subway and bus system.

All About Purchase Interest

The public's opinion about the transit system had been declining for many years and had reached a very low point by 1980. Years of neglect, partially caused by New York's fiscal crisis during the 1970s, resulted in a significant deterioration of tunnels and equipment. The public's perceptions of poor service and fear for their personal safety made daily riding an issue of high concern for millions of New Yorkers.

Not surprisingly, the safety issue was overwhelmingly important. Daily newspaper articles, extensively reporting on the issue, fanned public fear to the point that it began to feed on itself, growing bigger with each passing day. By 1980, an unbelievably high 30 percent of all New Yorkers claimed they personally had been robbed, bothered, or hassled on the city's buses or subways one or more times, 8 percent within the last three months. An additional 23 percent claimed that they personally had not experienced a problem but knew someone who had. These figures were even higher among citizens who used the public transportation system on a daily basis. Of course these were opinions and perceptions, not necessarily reality. Also, the data did not distinguish between violent incidents and relatively minor ones. Nevertheless, the data reflected a truly shocking state of affairs.

The Metropolitan Transportation Authority began a series of actions designed to improve the system and riders' perceptions of it. One part of this program was a proposed safety campaign showing subway riders how to protect themselves. The campaign was designed to save lives, protect property, and increase public confidence in the system. Although all interested parties agreed that it definitely was needed, there was one issue of major concern. Could the campaign boomerang, causing riders to think the system was so out of control that its management was publicly admitting it could no longer protect them?

A concept test was conducted on consumer reactions to the rules shown in Figure 3-1. Unlike most concept tests, which measure success by responses to such questions as desire to purchase a product or visit a showroom, this survey used its own version of the Purchase Interest question. Here a unique battery of questions was designed to measure whether:

1. Riders thought this kind of campaign was a good thing to run.
2. The campaign provided them with useful information on how to protect themselves.
3. They felt better able to protect themselves after exposure to information contained in the campaign.
4. Their opinions about the Metropolitan Transit Authority had fallen because of its implied admission that it could not solve the crime and safety problem by itself.

41

Figure 3-1. Safety rules used in Metropolitan Transportation Authority's concept test and newspaper ad campaign.

SIMPLE TIPS TO HELP YOU RIDE SAFELY.

There are about 2600 Transit Police that patrol the New York City Transit System. Obviously, there can't be a police officer or a transit employee everywhere, at all times. You can help by following these simple rules.

1 Each bus, train and token booth has radio or phone contact to the Transit Police. Report crimes or emergencies to the operator, dispatcher, conductor, motorman, or token booth attendant for police assistance.

2 If you carry a handbag, keep a firm grip on the bag—avoid using the handle. Under no circumstances wrap the handle around your hand or wrist as this is likely to cause you to be pulled down if the bag is grabbed.

3 Ride the center car, near the conductor, during non-rush hours.

4 Wait near the token booth on empty subway platforms.

5 Don't fall asleep on the bus or subway.

6 Don't invite trouble by a needless display of money or jewelry. Keep chains out of sight; turn rings around so stones are on the palm side of your hand.

7 Don't stand near the edge of the subway platform as a train approaches. Ever.

8 Whenever it is possible, travel on the subways with a friend.

In an emergency only call 911, or call the New York City Transit Police direct: 330-3333

To report a crime call the New York City Transit Police: 330-4944.

For non-emergency assistance call: 330-3881.

WE'RE WORKING TO MAKE THINGS SAFER. YOU CAN HELP.
 Metropolitan Transportation Authority

All About Purchase Interest

The results of the test were extremely positive. The campaign was not intended to make riders feel good about the system, merely to acknowledge that problems did exist and to help them protect themselves. And help them it did. The concept test showed that riders thought the campaign was a good thing for the Metropolitan Transportation Authority to run and that it provided them with good help to deal with the crime and safety problem.

- 85 percent of the riders interviewed thought this kind of campaign was a good thing to run.
- Several minutes after exposure to the rules (for just a few seconds) the average rider recalled, verbatim, three of them.
- 79 percent felt able to protect themselves after exposure to the campaign (up from 73 percent before concept exposure).
- 71 percent felt the Metropolitan Transportation Authority was interested in stopping crime (up from 61 percent before concept exposure).

Based on the results of the test, the safety campaign was authorized, and commercials and car cards were prepared. Two examples of the concept's translation to actual subway car card advertising are shown in Figures 3-2 and 3-3.

The results were quite impressive. The public was pleased that the Metropolitan Transportation Authority was taking the first step toward a solution by admitting the problem existed. Newspaper editorials were also quite positive. The number of chain snatchings (one focus of the campaign) decreased by an astounding 40 percent after a four-week television and print campaign. The advertising agency won one of its industry's advertising effectiveness awards for its work.

As you can see, the idea of an overall Purchase Interest question is usually quite useful, but sometimes a little ingenuity is required to maximize its usefulness.

INCLUDE THE QUESTION IN EVERY SURVEY

It continues to amaze me that anyone would decide not to include a Purchase Interest measure (or some variation of it) in a concept test. It's clearly the decision of someone who wishes to avoid being evaluated quantitatively. But if you don't want to be evaluated, why bother to do the concept test in the first place?

One advertising agency research director I know disagrees. He says that the purpose of some tests is solely to evaluate the ability of different strategies

Figure 3-2. Subway car card version of newspaper ad campaign.

HOW TO RUIN A PICKPOCKET'S DAY.

You can stop most pickpockets by following these simple tips:

1 Avoid crowding near car doors when entering or exiting the subway.

2 If you're jostled in a crowd, be aware that a pickpocket might be responsible.

3 Use handbags that close tightly, and carry them securely.

4 If your pocket is picked, call out immediately to warn the driver or conductor and everyone else that there's a pickpocket on board. Don't be afraid to shout.

5 Beware of loud arguments or commotion. Incidents are often staged distractions.

6 Carry wallets inside coat or side pants pockets —never in back pants pockets.

WE'RE WORKING TO MAKE THINGS SAFER. YOU CAN HELP.

Ⓜ Metropolitan Transportation Authority

Figure 3-3. Highly successful subway car card warning riders about chain snatching.

Chart 3-1. Average Purchase Interest scores in selected categories.

	Definitely Will Buy
Category	
Fragrance (no price)	9%
Detergents	12
Fragrance (with price)	18
Food	20
Cleaning products	28

to communicate clearly. Therefore, no Purchase Interest question is needed. My response: Every concept test needs a Purchase Interest score, even if the survey objective is merely to evaluate the ability of the concept to communicate clearly. After all, how do you determine the significance of a communication problem unless it is correlated with overall interest? For example, if just 3 percent of those with high interest have some problem with a copy point while 21 percent of those with low interest have that same problem, we can assume the issue is important, since it is highly correlated with the concept's overall performance.

WHAT IS A TYPICAL SCORE?

People often ask what constitutes a high or low Purchase Interest score. My answer, unfortunately, is "It depends."

On average, the typical concept stimulates a "definitely will buy" score of 19 percent among target group consumers and a *total* positive interest score ("definitely will buy" plus "probably will buy") of 65 percent. But there is a great deal of variation, depending on the category; see Chart 3-1.

Because of the range of scores between categories, an analyst cannot look at a Purchase Interest score by itself. The number must be related to others within the same category. Even scores from allied categories are not always useful. Take the cleaning and detergent categories as an example.

Cleaning products usually score high. It may be that products like oven cleaners, toilet bowl cleaners, and furniture polishes are used for cleaning tasks that are not enjoyable, and so any product that promises a reasonable benefit is of interest to consumers. Detergents are also used for unenjoyable tasks, but over the years many manufacturers have marketed many products that claimed to offer unique benefits. Unfortunately, they turned out to be parity products, that is, they were not substantively different from other products. Eventually the public caught on. Today, a new-product concept in the detergent category has a lot less credibility and generates a lot lower Purchase Interest score.

Since we are discussing scores, here's a bit of minutiae that probably will not make the next edition of Trivial Pursuit. The highest-scoring concept I ever tested received a 61 percent "definitely will buy" score. The lowest-scoring concept received a 0 percent "definitely will buy" score. The same company tested both concepts—which proves that even a talented concept writer isn't a winner every time!

COMMON MISTAKES IN ANALYZING SCORES

Purchase Interest is a critically important research tool. Unfortunately, many analysts use it improperly. They make three common errors:

1. Relying too heavily on it, to the exclusion of all other questions.
2. Using one number from the answer scale, not the entire scale.
3. Not making proper use of Purchase Interest as a diagnostic tool.

Overrelying on One Question

Some marketers simply place too much value on Purchase Interest. Product ideas often live or die on the basis of the Purchase Interest score. Blind reliance on any single question is dangerous, and Purchase Interest is no exception.

A few years ago I tested a concept for a new wine product. The idea was well regarded by consumers who examined the concept statement. Compared to appropriate benchmark data, the product idea had some very unique elements. Consumers thought the main benefit was very important. Their ratings on various other product attributes were very positive. They also indicated they would use the product differently from other wines. The only problem was with Purchase Interest. The "definitely would buy" score was 2 percent below average for the category.

In my judgment, it was a winning idea, in spite of the peculiar Purchase Interest score. I argued that in this case Purchase Interest should be downplayed. At worst, it signaled some flaw that needed to be identified and corrected. I also pointed out some minor and easily fixable problems with the concept that would help to improve the Purchase Interest score. My

47

Chart 3-2. All other things being equal, which concept
has the most potential?

	Concept A	Concept B
Definitely will buy	23%	28%
Probably will buy	39	27
Might or might not buy	30	19
Probably will not buy	4	15
Definitely will not buy	4	11

arguments were unpersuasive. The idea was not developed further by the
company.

A short time later a similar concept—a wine cooler—was successfully
marketed by another company. The sales curve grew so rapidly that one
industry observer likened it to the presence of a fifty-story skyscraper in a
neighborhood of one-family homes. Sales are still skyrocketing. Eventually
category growth will flatten, but only after a period of rapid profit growth
for those companies that got in early.

Not Using All the Data

Unfortunately, industry practice often makes the problems associated
with Purchase Interest worse by relying on a single number. This number
goes by lots of names: "top box," "definitely will buy," "DWB"—names that
imply a high degree of accuracy and precision. But no matter what you call
it, it is still just one number.

Have you ever witnessed someone saying with a smile, "We got a 27"?
And what about the manager who's disappointed with a high Purchase Interest score of 13 percent? It's bad enough that our industry places so much
emphasis on one question. Let's not make the problem worse by ignoring
most of the data that the question produces. As a first step, look at data
from the entire question, not just the top item of the scale.

Chart 3-2 shows Purchase Interest for two new-product concepts. Concept A has a 23 percent "definitely will buy" score and virtually no negative
reaction (only 8 percent). Concept B has a top score of 28 percent, but an
additional 26 percent tell us they will not buy it. All other things being
equal, which concept do you think has greater potential for improvement,
one with a few rejectors or one with *many* active rejectors?

Concept A has the greater long-term potential. Sure, it misses the boat
when it comes to the highest level of Purchase Interest. However, it does

generate some interest. The marketing problem is to discover what factor is holding back interest, causing mild rather than strong appeal. Other questions and cross tabulations can help solve this problem.

If I were testing an *ad*, not a concept, I would probably make a different decision. Since I would have several executions to choose from, I would be more interested in the execution that generates the *strongest* positive response, and I would vote for B.

However, we are testing a concept, not an ad. Our goal is to optimize long-term sales and our focus is on the strategy that promises the most long-term potential. It's an important point, worth remembering.

Using Purchase Interest Ineffectively

The third critical mistake some researchers make is to underutilize Purchase Interest. Often they focus their analysis upon the total sample, and neglect to look under the surface at various subgroups.

As a starting point, compare Purchase Interest scores among consumers with different demographic, attitudinal, or category-usage characteristics. Discover which segments of the population are most and least turned on to your idea. (See Chapter 8.)

Take the time to delve into the data more deeply. For example, compare Purchase Interest scores among consumers who understand your message with those who do not. This comparison allows you to determine if the problem with a concept is a lack of persuasiveness or an unclear communication of the main benefit.

I recently tested a concept for a manufacturer of telecommunications products. Only 14 percent of the target group had high Purchase Interest, well below the client's action standard.* But further analysis showed that, among target group consumers who heard and understood the full message, 31 percent were interested in purchasing the product (see Chart 3-3). Consumers who didn't fully understand the unique benefit being provided were much less likely to wish to purchase the product.

Clearly, the problem was not an unpersuasive concept, but one that did not adequately communicate to enough people. The solution was not to kill the concept, but to reword it so that it transmitted a more easily understood message.

Another diagnostic angle emerges when you consider this simple marketing fact of life: No company can convert *every single consumer* to become a user of its brand, no matter how good the product, its distribution, price,

---

* The minimum level of acceptability is called an action standard by many companies.

Concept Testing

Chart 3-3. Purchase Interest by receipt of main benefit.

	Total
Definitely Will Buy	
In total sample	14%
Among those who understood the product's unique benefit	㉛
Among those who did not understand the product's unique benefit	9

or advertising. Some consumers are very satisfied with their current brand, and there is not much anyone can do to change their opinion.

Since new products are often purchased by consumers who are dissatisfied in some way, why just examine overall interest scores for the total target group? Broaden your analysis. It's easy. Simply add a question to measure the degree of dissatisfaction respondents have with their existing brand. Then analyze Purchase Interest for your concept among those who express low satisfaction for their existing brand. The marketing decision you make can be strikingly different.

Chart 3-4 shows the percentage of respondents with high Purchase Interest in two different concepts. Interest is approximately the same for the total sample. However, among those having low satisfaction with their existing brand—the real potential market—Concept A outperforms Concept B.

When you isolate individuals with high Purchase Interest in your concept *and* low satisfaction with their existing product, you have zeroed in on a highly committed group. Their reactions to the test concept are often quite unique and contain useful clues on how to improve the concept. The secret is to examine responses to other questions among consumers in this committed group and compare their opinions and reactions against those of other consumers in your sample.

Chart 3-4. Purchase Interest for a new detergent.

	Concept A	Concept B
High Purchase Interest within total sample	22%	19%
High Purchase Interest among those with:		
High satisfaction with existing brand	19	18
Low satisfaction with existing brand	㉗	19

All About Purchase Interest

Chart 3-5. Problems associated with a new service for interior decorators.

	Total Sample	High Interest in Concept	High Interest in Concept and Low Satisfaction with Present Alternative
High cost	(22)%	(20)%	11%
Range of photos provided will not be adequate	(19)	(23)	(25)
Poor quality of individual photos	(15)	11	7

Chart 3-5 illustrates this point. The data come from a study that identified problems associated with a new product to be marketed to interior decorators. The total sample pinpointed three major problems with the product, but among people with high Purchase Interest (see second column), just two problems were important—a sufficient number of photos and their high cost; photo quality was less important.

Among people with high Purchase Interest *and* low satisfaction with their current alternative—the most likely purchasers—only one problem was of prime concern: the range of photos. High cost was less important. This, of course, makes sense; people with an unsatisfied need would be less concerned about price if a new product offered the hope of addressing this need.

The underlying point is that by zeroing in on your true prime target group—individuals stating they are likely to purchase your product *and* are not being satisfied with existing alternatives—you have an analytic tool capable of revealing new and powerful marketing implications.

This special analysis deals with the interaction between Purchase Interest in the concept and overall satisfaction with the respondent's usual brand. But it could just as easily have been the interaction between Purchase Interest and price, flavor, size, or anything else that is key in the category of interest to you. Be clever on this point. Use your imagination. Don't go blindly ahead and always analyze by degree of satisfaction. In some categories, your hook is not "low satisfaction" but identifying those with a high likelihood of trying a new product.

Take wine, for example; some wine drinkers have a dozen favorites and are happy with all of them. Analyzing Purchase Interest by degree of satisfaction with their current brands would not be productive. To enhance the usefulness of Purchase Interest in the wine category, examine scores of individuals who like to try new wines.

A different situation exists in the financial industry, where consumers' willingness to use a new service is partially related to their perceptions about how appropriate it is for a financial institution to offer new and nontraditional services. In this industry, a key analytic step is to cross tabulate Purchase Interest by responses to this attitudinal dimension.

In the consumer electronics category, the key population subgroup to study is what I call the ESPs (Electronically Sophisticated People). ESPs are individuals who have integrated consumer electronics into their everyday lives; electronic products wake them in the morning, cook for them, entertain them, and help them study or perform work tasks. This segment is growing. A few years ago just 1 out of 100 people fit this profile. Today, this segment is about 10 percent of the population, and it seems to be growing at a rate of 2 or 3 percent per year. If you are marketing a new consumer electronic product, you would be wise to study this group as part of your analysis of Purchase Interest since they tend to be the first buyers of a new product. Without their support, the bandwagon never gets rolling.

Regardless of your category, I hope you agree that a complete analysis of Purchase Interest results can reveal many insights about your concept and how to improve it. All it takes is an additional question. Then it's just a matter of using the data cleverly and to the fullest extent possible. Regardless of the industry, the benefit of improving your analytic system is obvious.

DO PRICE AND PURCHASE INTEREST GO HAND IN HAND?

Some researchers prefer to ask the Purchase Interest question after the retail price is given to the respondent. Their position is that price is an important purchase determinant and that Purchase Interest scores not based on price are less meaningful.

In principle this is true. However, on a practical level, providing price information often affects the quality and quantity of responses to various diagnostic questions. Apparently, price is so important an issue that it gets in the way of other aspects of the concept, and they do not get a fair hearing.

To get around the influence of price, you can use two alternate procedures for determining Purchase Interest, depending upon the purpose of the concept test. If your primary objective is to predict actual volume once the product is introduced to the marketplace, make sure to tell respondents the price *before* asking about their interest in purchasing the product. The resulting information is then entered into a predictive model (described in Chapter 7).

But if the primary purpose of the survey is diagnostic—to learn whether

All About Purchase Interest

the basic idea of the product has merit or needs improvement—modify the system by asking the Purchase Interest question two times in the same survey. Near the beginning of the interview, ask Purchase Interest in the traditional manner, with no price. Toward the end of the interview, after all the diagnostic questions have been administered, tell respondents the retail price (even if it's only a tentative price point) and then ask Purchase Interest again. The results can be quite illuminating.

In most instances, the level of interest will be about the same or slightly lower once price is introduced. Probably consumers are generally aware of competitive prices and have a good sense of what your concept's price will be, even when it is not stated. This is why Purchase Interest scores often remain substantially unaffected by price.

In those instances where exposure to the price *does* cause interest to drop significantly, it's a clear signal that you have a price problem on your hands. The converse is also true. If Purchase Interest rises after price is revealed, this is a powerful research finding. It opens the door to many marketing opportunities such as raising profit margins, or keeping the price low and promoting the low price heavily.

In one test, interest in purchasing a new household cleaning product increased dramatically after price information was provided to respondents. This indicated an opportunity to build market share by telling a price story. In the personal products category, Pfizer found it had a low price story to tell with its Barbasol men's shaving cream brand. Sales immediately began to grow after the low price of Barbasol was publicized.

The key point to keep in mind: The introduction of price *usually* causes no major difference in concept Purchase Interest. When a difference does occur, treat it as an important signal.

4
Six More Key Indicators

As you've seen, it's unwise to rely on Purchase Interest alone to evaluate the success of your concept. There are six other key indicators that can make a big difference in the value of your test data.

1. The concept's uniqueness.
2. The concept's appropriateness or relevance to the consumer's needs.
3. The main idea being communicated by the concept.
4. The importance of the main idea.
5. The expected frequency of purchase.
6. The reason that consumers offer to explain their level of Purchase Interest.

This chapter discusses each of these six measures, in terms of their ability to help you make go/no-go decisions and their use as a diagnostic aid for revising and improving deficient concepts.

UNIQUENESS

Uniqueness is, I believe, the most useful of the Big Six.

Let's see how it works. A recent concept test for a new over-the-counter medication revealed the concept to be quite weak. Investigation showed that the concept communicated its main benefit extremely well. The majority of consumers considered the benefit quite important and quite relevant to their needs. But the concept failed to generate high trial interest. Why? Only 7 percent thought the product was *unique*.

This is not a unique event (pardon the pun). Uniqueness of a concept, or more correctly, lack of uniqueness, is frequently a major problem. Marketers have a tendency to develop new-product ideas that are aimed at knocking off the category leader. Consumers often reject the idea; after all, why buy an imitation if you are satisfied with the real thing? Even when a company tries to develop a product with a unique twist, consumers increasingly tell us it's the same old stuff. As a result, frequently a concept scores very strongly on many key survey questions, yet receives low Purchase Interest scores. The cause is its perceived lack of uniqueness.

Marketing a product that stimulates low Purchase Interest because of low uniqueness is a difficult task. Obviously, a skilled sales force or large promotional budget can cover a multitude of sins. But a better approach might be to change some aspect of the product to drive up perceptions of uniqueness. Clever thinking can make the difference.

Take a commodity product like milk, for example. A concept test on any new milk brand would probably produce a very low Uniqueness score. After all, what can you do to make your product different or stand out from the crowd? For one thing, you could look at other consumer data showing that milk's perceived major benefit is that it supplies lots of calcium for good health, and experiment with a new calcium-enriched milk. Or another commodity: chlorine bleach. If you were the Clorox Company, you could combine bleach's low Uniqueness score with other data showing that many consumers dislike the strong smell of bleach, and develop a nice-smelling product called Fresh Scent liquid bleach.

Clearly, a low Uniqueness rating is a serious problem, but innovative thinking can overcome it. Concept research can help to solve the problem by helping to identify it.

In some categories, Purchase Interest is virtually useless as a predictor of sales success, and Uniqueness ratings become even more valuable to the analyst. Take the ice cream category, for example. Most concepts for new ice cream products score very strongly on Purchase Interest. Furthermore, the range between high scores and low scores is much narrower than what is witnessed in most other categories. As a result, Purchase Interest is less useful as a predictive tool. The problem can be overcome once the product is made available for the consumer to examine and taste. But if the product is not yet available, other concept testing tools must be used to supplement Purchase Interest. Experience suggests that Uniqueness fits the bill.

In the past few years I had opportunities to test several different new ice cream product ideas. Some were basically "me too" premium products, high in butterfat and pricey. A few were novelty products, including something akin to today's DoveBar. In Purchase Interest, there were small differences between the "me too" premium products and the novelty products. But the Uniqueness question produced very high scores for the novelty items and lower scores for the "me toos."

If you are a student of the ice cream category, you would know that the explosive growth of its premium segment flattened a bit in the mid-1980s, while novelty items like DoveBar and its clones grew rapidly. And Uniqueness did a better job of highlighting these differences than did Purchase Interest.

Ways to Measure Uniqueness

There are a number of ways to measure Uniqueness. Here are two questions that many researchers use. The first makes reference to the category being tested, the second doesn't. They also use different answer scales. Both questions work well. I usually use the first one, mostly out of habit.

How different is this product from other frozen meals? Would you say it is . . .

Very different	☐
Somewhat different	☐
Slightly different	☐
Not at all different	☐

Overall, how would you rate this product on uniqueness? Would you say it is . . .

Extremely unique	☐
Very unique	☐
Somewhat unique	☐
Slightly unique	☐
Not at all unique	☐

You can analyze Uniqueness data by examining either end of the scale. When working with the top of the scale (in the first question), I use the "very different" rating. In the second question, I combine the "extremely unique" and "very unique" ratings. When working with the bottom of the scale, I find that combining the "slightly" and "not at all different" ratings together works best. But in either case, comparing scores between the various concepts being tested or against previously developed norms is a useful way to make this data come alive.

As a valuable followup to the Uniqueness question, ask those who do think the product is different this probing question:

Six More Key Indicators

In what way do you think this product is different from other frozen foods? In what other ways is this product different?

If the Uniqueness score is low, you have an insufficient number of consumers responding to the probe question and you need not even bother to analyze the results. But if your concept gets high Uniqueness ratings and there are lots of possible benefits that might be driving Uniqueness up, this question can produce valuable insights.

I once tested a concept for a men's shampoo that proported to offer special benefit to hair that was damaged by various excesses, be it overexposure to sun, heat from a hairdryer, or too much perspiration. Even though consumers didn't go for the idea, many thought it was quite unique. And when they were asked the special probe question about *why* it was unique, we learned that they thought it was appropriate for people with an outdoor lifestyle. In other words, they heard all the benefits but rejected the product because it was not congruent with their own self-perceptions. Without this special question, we might have concluded the problem was with one of the benefits.

Two Aspects of Uniqueness

Keep in mind that there are two elements to uniqueness: uniqueness of the overall product and uniqueness of a single product element. Both should be studied.

In the consumer market, think of a standard facial moisturizer with the added benefit of a special "skin rejuvenator." In the business market think of an overnight delivery company that offers special assurance that its delivery promise will be fulfilled. Two different industries, two different "typical" products. But in each case the company offered a unique benefit to set its product apart from the competition. In both cases, ratings on overall Uniqueness would be a slightly above-average score. But ratings on Uniqueness of individual product elements would be well above average.

Can the uniqueness of one product element affect the success of a concept? The answer is a resounding *yes*. In a recent test of a new financial services product, the Uniqueness rating for the overall product was just slightly above the category norm. But as Chart 4-1 shows, one element of the concept really popped on Uniqueness when compared with available norms—a clue that while the overall product was "me too," it contained an element that was quite promotable.

When exploring the two aspects of Uniqueness, you may wish to exper-

Chart 4-1. Two aspects of uniqueness.

	Test Concept	Category Norm
Uniqueness Rating		
Of the total product	39%	36%
Of one product benefit	(63)	41

iment with the following self-administered seven-point bipolar scale. I have used it frequently and with great success.

An ordinary product	☐ ☐ ☐ ☐ ☐ ☐ ☐	A unique product
Saying something unique	☐ ☐ ☐ ☐ ☐ ☐ ☐	Saying nothing unique

In most instances you will find that the ratings for each question are similar. But when differences occur, it's often a clue that your product has one very unique feature. And you can use that feature to open the door to more effective advertising and higher trial in the marketplace. Not a bad result for one additional question, don't you think?

Uniqueness as a Diagnostic Aid

In addition to helping you to decide if a concept is worthy of further development, Uniqueness is an excellent diagnostic tool to help pinpoint how to fix a deficient concept. Cross tabulating Uniqueness by Purchase Interest is an incredibly sensitive analytic approach. It can help you pinpoint subtle issues that are holding back concept success.

I recently tested a new food product concept. The product's reason for being was a special ingredient that improved the taste, and the concept scored very well on most measures, including Purchase Interest. However, the percentage of those who thought the product was unique was well under the norm. Without cross tabbing of Uniqueness by Purchase Interest, I would have simply concluded that we had a successful product concept, and that in this case Uniqueness was not the driving force behind the concept's strength.

Tabulating Uniqueness by Purchase Interest revealed a different picture. Respondents with high Purchase Interest had an acceptable Uniqueness score. But the Uniqueness score for low Purchase Interest individuals was very, very low—much lower than the norm for Uniqueness among low Purchase Interest individuals. Clearly, uniqueness was an obstacle holding back higher performance. Even though the concept was already strong, poor perceptions of uniqueness among some respondents affected their interest in the product.

A reverse twist occurred in a household appliance concept test. Virtually everyone understood that the product contained a special feature, and that it was the only product on the market that contained this feature. Yet a below-average number of consumers thought the product was unique. The reverse twist was this: Respondents with *low* Purchase Interest were especially likely to think the product was unique.

After scratching my head for a while over this one, I retabulated some open-end data, and found my answer. High Uniqueness individuals clearly understood that the product contained a unique feature—but not much else about the product. Those with low Uniqueness scores were much more likely to tell us that the product worked well; clearly they had made the connection between the special feature and superior performance. Equally clear: Many consumers did *not* make the connection, and that held back product success.

The point of these examples is to encourage you to use Uniqueness to help figure out how to fix a deficient concept. Try this the next time a concept fails because of a low Uniqueness score. Retab all your key diagnostic questions among respondents with high Uniqueness ratings. Look for clues as to what caused these consumers to consider the product unique. The sample size may be small and the results may be qualitative feelings, not solid fact. You may even be on a wild goose chase. But you just might find the key that lets you bring a dead product idea back to life.

Another value of Uniqueness was vividly illustrated in a concept test for a financial services product (see Chart 4-2). A very large number of respondents believed the product concept offered a unique benefit. Furthermore, respondents with high Uniqueness ratings also had very high Purchase Interest in the product and were especially likely to focus on one specific product advantage (Benefit C). Because of this diagnostic insight, the concept was rewritten. Instead of having a concept *liked* by many consumers, we developed a tighter strategy, with a concept *loved* by a smaller segment. And, best of all, it became possible to market the product at a slightly higher price.

The point of the story? Uniqueness is a valuable tool, both as a diagnostic aid and as a decision-making tool.

Concept Testing

Chart 4-2. Uniqueness as a diagnostic tool.

	Total Sample	Those Who Think Product Is Very Unique
Overall Performance		
Very unique product idea	40%	100%
Definitely will buy	21	(32)
Main Idea of Product Communicated by Concept		
Benefit A	63	51
Benefit B	49	43
Benefit C	41	62

RELEVANCE TO THE CONSUMER'S NEEDS

Relevance, the second of the Big Six key indicators, is sometimes more valuable than Purchase Interest. One of the key advantages is that it is a very sensitive indicator, more so than Purchase Interest.

Chart 4-3 shows the performance of two concepts for a new financial services product. Concept B is about as strong as Concept A, on the basis of Purchase Interest. Yet A is much more relevant to the respondents' own needs, and that makes A the winner.

One way to measure relevance is to ask the question in a bipolar format with the respondent having seven points to choose from, as shown here:

Relevant to my needs   □ □ □ □ □ □ □   Not relevant to my needs

Chart 4-3. Comparison between Purchase Interest and Relevance.

	Concept A	Concept B
High Purchase Interest in a new financial services product	16%	14%
High ratings for same concept on "relevant to my needs"	(62)	49

60

Six More Key Indicators

Chart 4-4. Relevance of prospective TV program.

			Interest in Viewing the Program	
	Relevant to My Interests	Not Relevant to My Interests	High Interest	Low Interest
Characteristics of Perceived Viewer				
Enjoys watching most TV shows	7%	13%	12%	15%
Enjoys watching movies	7	11	11	14
Wants more from TV	28	11	21	17
Is open-minded, inquisitive	31	17	24	17

Naturally, there is more than one way to pose a question. Other ways of asking the question would probably prove equally good. Experiment and decide for yourself.

But regardless of the format, you will find Relevance quite useful as a diagnostic tool, to help you strengthen a sick concept. As a first step, compare your Relevance score to appropriate norms. If your concept scores below the norm, retabulate key diagnostic questions among those with high, then low Relevance scores. Watch for different consumer responses in the two Relevance groups. This can provide you with rewarding information that Purchase Interest might not turn up.

In a concept test on TV programming, a number of consumers thought the programming idea was relevant to their interests. Believing that a consumer who considers a program personally relevant would be more likely to watch it than other consumers, I did a special diagnostic analysis on this high Relevance group. An interesting pattern emerged; see Chart 4-4. High Relevance people described the prospective audience for the program as more discriminating and wanting much more from TV programming. This is the type of actionable data that allows you to tighten your positioning, plan an appropriate promotional strategy, and develop a better product. What could be more relevant than that?

MAIN IDEA

Some researchers think open-end questions are very valuable diagnostic tools that can be used to identify why a concept is weak or discover ways to improve consumer acceptance.

But many others disagree. They believe that a combination of problems with interviewing (improper probing, inconsistent probing, and incomplete recording of responses) and with coding makes all open-end data suspect.

Although much of the criticism is valid, I believe open-end questions are valuable diagnostic tools. The value is created by the analyst, not the interviewer. In other words, it's what you do with the data generated by the question that creates value. The Main Idea question is a case in point.

Virtually every concept test questionnaire includes a question that asks respondents what they consider to be the main idea of the product. Here is the wording I often use.

Other than trying to sell you the product, what do you think was the main idea in the description you just read? That is, what was the main thing they were trying to communicate to you about the product?

While almost everyone asks the question correctly, few analysts interpret the answers properly. The main problem is that many analysts merely *look* at answers to the question. They do not *analyze* them.

Try this analytical approach on your next concept test. Before examining any data, reread your concept's strategy. Using your own personal judgment, pick out the sales points or benefits that are the product's main reasons for being. Then select benefits that are of lesser importance (some marketers call them the secondary benefits). Finally, list the benefits that are window dressing, the kinds of things you say to provide credibility or support for a more important benefit: "new" or "convenient."

Now you are ready to look at your concept findings. Are the benefits you judged to be most important the same ones that consumers mention as the main idea of the concept? If not, your concept may need some revision. Are the minor points like "new" or "convenient" perceived by consumers to be the product's main reason for being? It may be a signal that something is wrong.

The key to this analysis is making personal judgments, in advance, about what to expect. Then, if the actual data are different, you have the basis for your analysis. If Purchase Interest in the concept is very high, you always have the option to look the other way in spite of surprising Main Idea results. But if Purchase Interest is low, this analysis might give you a possible explanation as well as a clue on how to fix the problem. The cost? Just a few minutes of logical thinking.

Correlation to Purchase Interest

A simple cross tab can make the Main Idea question even more valuable. After examining the answers from the full sample, look at the data among those with high Purchase Interest and those with low interest. Identify the ideas that each group mentioned a different number of times. This easy analysis is a powerful tool to help explain why a concept succeeds or fails.

A few years ago, a concept test for a chain of low-cost Italian restaurants found just average interest among target group consumers. As part of the analysis, the main idea communicated by the concept was compared among those with high interest in eating at the chain versus those with low interest. There was little difference in their playback of three benefits: tasty food, a good variety of menu choices, and reasonable prices. Both groups of consumers mentioned each benefit a similar number of times.

But one interesting difference did emerge. Those with high interest were much more likely to mention one feature that was given very little attention by the concept: the promise of a quick delivery to the customer's home. Those with low interest referred to home delivery much less often—a clear correlation between liking the idea of home delivery and having a high interest in eating this restaurant's products.

Unfortunately, the client company's arrangement with its franchises meant that it could not offer quick delivery from all its outlets, and so it could not use the claim on a national basis. For this reason the claim had been relegated to a secondary position in the concept, a feature that *some* branches might be offering.

But Domino's pizza chain did use the very same idea, and with great success. In just one decade Domino's has grown to become one of the major players in the pizza segment of the Italian restaurant business. And rapid delivery to its customers' homes played a major role in fueling this growth.

Sometimes correlating the Main Idea question and Purchase Interest can help identify why a concept succeeds or fails. A household cleaner concept built its reason for being around a unique ingredient. Analysis of the Main Idea question among consumers with varying degrees of Purchase Interest found that those with positive Purchase Interest heard the "unique ingredi-

Concept Testing

Chart 4-5. Main Idea communicated by cleaning product concept.

	High Purchase Interest	Low Purchase Interest
Reference to Product Cleaning Well	(51)%	32%
Cleans easier/means less work	19	12
Cleans better/does a good job	27	14
Leaves no streaks/smudges/grease	19	11
Reference to Product's Special Ingredient	41	(70)
Contains special ingredient	28	49
Cleans because of special ingredient	13	21

ent" story and translated it into a "cleans effectively" sales message. Unfortunately, many of those with low Purchase Interest heard the same special ingredient message but did not translate it the same way (see Chart 4-5).

Analysis of the Main Idea question can do more than just identify why some concepts fail. It can also identify high-scoring concepts that are troubled *in spite of* their high Purchase Interest score.

As an example, picture a cosmetics concept with overtones of glitter and glamour and with high Purchase Interest among all respondents, even those who did not understand the product's unique benefits. The problem is quite serious. It means the concept is working because of the glamour and excitement of the *category*, not because of a skillful execution of the product's strategy. It is a pretty good reason to abort the product's development until the concept gets rewritten into a format that communicates its unique reason for being. A product with no special or unique reason for being is especially vulnerable to any competitor that comes along with the same benefits plus a little something extra.

This type of analysis is easy to do. Merely count the number of respondents with high Purchase Interest among those who understand the main product benefits, and those who *do not* understand the main benefits.

Chart 4-6 shows results from three concept tests. Purchase Interest in Concept A is higher among individuals who played back the main sales point. This is to be expected if the test concept is a good one. Theoretically, the concept is based on solid marketing thinking, satisfies a significant con-

Six More Key Indicators

Chart 4-6. Correlation between overall interest and playback of main sales point.

	Total Sample	Played Back Main Sales Point	Did Not Play Back Main Sales Point
High Purchase Interest After Exposure to			
Concept A	18%	(26)%	14%
Concept B	21	22	21
Concept C	14	8	(19)

sumer need, and is clear and well written. Those who "heard" the message should be more readily persuaded than those who didn't get the full message.

But look at scores for Concepts B and C. In Concept B, those who played back the main sales point have the same level of interest as those who did not. Clearly, communication of the main benefit did not stimulate additional interest. Furthermore, Concept B's main benefit is not as persuasive as Concept A's, a point not clear if you examine results for the total sample without doing this analysis.

In the case of Concept C, the communication of the main benefit resulted in *lower* Purchase Interest. In other words, those who played back the main sales point were turned off by it. *Something* about the concept interested consumers; you see this by the relatively high interest in trial among those who did not play back the main benefit. But it wasn't the *main* benefit. Concepts B and C are examples of poor concepts. Either the main benefit was off target, or the concept was poorly executed.

The only problem with this analysis is that you must decide *in advance* what the main benefits are. Surprisingly, many companies are unable or unwilling to commit to this up front. They often hedge their bets by expanding the list of possible concept benefits that are proof of understanding the concept. Expanding the list of acceptable answers increases the number of respondents who are classified as understanding the main benefit. Unfortunately, it also increases the likelihood that this sensitive indicator will signal your communications strategy is not working. After companies have several experiences like this, they often decide not to do the analysis again—the twentieth-century version of killing the messenger who brings bad news.

Increasing the Value

Still another way to increase the value of a Main Idea question is to compare responses to it with responses to the question on Reason for Purchase Interest. In making this comparison, keep in mind that the main idea communicated to consumers by a concept statement and the reasons they give for wanting to buy the product should be related. If consumer responses to these two questions are not similar, the data are sending you a very big signal that something is wrong with the concept and an even bigger clue on how to fix it.

Suppose your concept promises good taste, but the most frequently mentioned reason for high Purchase Interest is nutrition. Have you got a problem? Or what about the concept that uses half its time to talk about construction quality but virtually everyone who wants to buy it is interested primarily in its ease of use. It may be that they didn't hear the construction claim. This means you have to deliver it louder or better. Or maybe they heard it but felt something else was more important. This should cause you to rethink and revise your strategy. Or perhaps they heard the construction claim but were not persuaded by it. Perhaps you should take another crack at describing the benefits.

Comparing the Main Idea with Reasons for Positive Purchase Interest will not tell you why the problem is occurring. Other cross tabs will answer that question. But it will tell you that a problem does exist, and that is the first step toward solving it.

IMPORTANCE

Purchase Interest may get all the glory, but to me, the unsung hero on many concept tests is a question measuring the Importance of the idea. Knowing how important consumers think the concept is can make concept data come alive, providing researchers with information they can act on.

An Importance rating is particularly valuable when you are testing a concept for a breakthrough product—something completely different from what consumers generally use or have even dreamed of. Such a product idea is sometimes difficult to test. Even though it may have high appeal, it could score low on Purchase Interest because it has low credibility—consumers don't think the product can really deliver the promised benefit. Imagine, for example, a detergent that promises to prevent shrinkage or a ballpoint pen that claims the ink will last at least ten years of normal usage.

If you are testing a concept with a very novel benefit, the Importance rating might be a better indicator of how much the benefit really matters to consumers. Here are three examples.

1. The concept for a product in the financial services area stimulated relatively low trial interest. Various diagnostic questions identified a number of specific reasons that caused the concept to bomb. The problems were quite severe and the improvements needed to fix them were substantial. But consumers thought the concept's main idea was very important. So the company had to decide whether additional efforts should be made to improve the product. When 74 percent of all consumers interviewed said the main benefit was very important to them, the answer had to be yes, even though the concept scored poorly.

2. In another concept test, this time for a frozen food product, Purchase Interest was disappointing, but it was not difficult to figure out why. Virtually every single survey indicator produced an average rating. The only exception was the Importance rating—which was well below average.

3. A concept for a new office product failed to stimulate any Purchase Interest. Although it was rated as unique, interesting, and persuasive, few thought the idea was very important.

The bottom line on Importance: It's a valuable tool and should be included in every concept test. There are a number of ways to collect this information. A standard one is to have consumers rate the concept on a seven-point bipolar scale.

Not saying important things ☐ ☐ ☐ ☐ ☐ ☐ ☐ Saying important things

Or you could ask this question:

Considering everything, how important is this product idea as far as you are concerned? Would you say it is . . .

A very important idea	☐
Of some importance	☐
Of little importance	☐
Of absolutely no importance	☐

Concept Testing

Importance of Main Idea

Still another approach is to ask consumers to rate the Importance of the Main Idea, not the Importance of the total concept. You can do this by modifying the Importance question to read:

Considering everything, how important is the main idea of this product, as far as you are concerned?

In my experience, you get similar results either way. But if you prefer this second question, take the following three steps to make the results even more valuable to you.

1. Start by asking respondents what main idea is being communicated by the concept.
2. Follow with a second question measuring the Importance of this main idea.
3. Next, milk this data further by tabulating the Importance rating for each specific response to the Main Idea question; that is, among all those who thought the main idea was Point A, Point B, and so on.

The results are often interesting. In a concept test for a new food product, most consumers thought good taste was the main idea. Fewer people thought the unique mix of ingredients was the main benefit, but those people were more likely to consider this a very important benefit (see Chart 4-7). This raised the question of whether there was room in the market for a second product with a different positioning strategy: a special formulation using unique ingredients. The idea would not have been uncovered had the Importance question been tabulated in the "normal" way only.

The point of this story relates to Importance, but a second message is also apparent. Sometimes a little twist in how you tabulate the data can reveal secrets that would have remained hidden if you looked at data the same old way.

Interpret Other Questions

Importance is also a good diagnostic tool to help you interpret responses to other questions. A good place to start is to compare your score to the norm for the category. If your concept is below norm, retabulate various open- and closed-end questions against high and low Importance scores.

Six More Key Indicators

Chart 4-7. The importance of Importance.

	Total	
Base	(200)	
Main Idea		
Good taste	66% ──────┐	
Unique blend of		
ingredients	41	
	↓	↓

Importance of Each Main Idea Mentioned	*Unique Blend of Ingredients*	*Good Taste*
Base	(82)	(132)
Very important	㉗ %	18%

Look for the issues that seem to separate the two kinds of people. All it takes is a few additional tabulations. The results might pleasantly surprise you.

I recently tested a concept for a new vitamin-enriched entree. The product stimulated low Purchase Interest scores and was rated poorly on Importance. I went back through the data and reexamined the Main Idea question among those with high and low Importance ratings. Widespread differences were apparent. Those who thought the product was an important idea were more likely to report the main idea related to good taste and nutrition. Those with low Importance scores dwelled most of all on ease of preparation (see Chart 4-8).

Similar patterns were evident for other open-end questions. The data clearly signaled the need to portray taste and nutrition in a more persuasive manner.

Sometimes a simple tabulation produces extremely important data!

Chart 4-8. Main Idea communicated by concept.

		Importance Rating	
Major Mentions	*Total Sample*	*High*	*Low*
Good taste	34	㊼	26
Easy to prepare	23	11	㉛
Healthy/nutritious	16	㉗	10
Fancy/elegant	11	3	10

FREQUENCY OF PURCHASE OR CONSUMPTION

Another valuable issue to explore is the frequency with which consumers think they would purchase the product.

In the mid-1970s, the national media began to report that Americans were becoming more conscious of health and nutrition. During the next few years, several marketers responded with products that would appeal to this population segment. The products tended to be low in fat, starch, or sugar.

Various marketing strategies were followed. New evidence suggested that the average American gained 30 to 40 pounds between the ages of 25 and 45. Consequently, many of the companies trying to develop this business segment targeted their products directly toward this population group, with advertising, packaging, and menu items designed to appeal to young adults.

The Nestlé Foods Corporation, with its 30-item New Cookery line, broadly targeted an entire family of products toward people who wanted to eat properly, sensibly, and healthfully but not give up too much taste. Nestlé cut back somewhat on the amount of fat, starch, and sugar to a level about halfway between a standard food and a low-calorie substitute, in an effort to minimize the change in taste.

Unfortunately for Nestlé and many of the other players involved, concept testing repeatedly showed a high Purchase Interest for many of these products but a low projected Frequency of Consumption. Consumers were clearly signaling that they were not yet ready to accept this kind of product into their everyday constellation of food products. They apparently viewed these foods as diet-oriented, so their projected usage was limited to occasions of a need or desire to diet.

The data were telling us that the emerging interest in health and fitness had not yet translated into broadscale diet changes. Many of the companies, including Nestlé, went to market anyway. For the most part, they encountered disappointing sales. In Nestlé's case, the New Cookery line had to be withdrawn from the market. Eventually, in the 1980s, this segment of the food business finally began to grow. However, the Frequency of Purchase and Frequency of Consumption data showed that a high-volume market did not exist in the mid-1970s, in spite of newspaper and magazine articles.

Using the Data

As this story indicates, the frequency with which consumers think they will purchase a product described by the test concept is important information for a new-product development team.

70

Six More Key Indicators

Sometimes this information kills new-product concepts. Sometimes it saves them. A concept rated average on Purchase Interest and low on Purchase Frequency may not be worth marketing. But the same concept with an above-average Purchase Frequency may indicate a high-volume opportunity.

A major food company recently tested a line of children's foods to be marketed to mothers with young children. Purchase Interest in the concept was average, suggesting the idea had to be revised and improved. However, the frequency with which mothers with high Purchase Interest planned to serve the product was well above average. It was a very clear signal that the line had high profit potential in spite of average scores on other dimensions.

Another example is tied to consumer concern about osteoporosis, a weakening or brittleness of the bones that begins to affect women as they reach middle age. Several companies have entered the market with calcium-enriched products specifically designed to address this health concern. The Norcliff Thayer division of Beecham attacked this market opportunity from a different angle. Instead of developing a new product, they repositioned an old one, promoting the presence of calcium in Tums, an antacid product for more than half a century. Research revealed that publicizing the calcium encouraged significantly more frequent usage among target-group women. Apparently, women took Tums as a calcium substitute regularly, but they only used it as an antacid sporadically. Norcliff Thayer moved fast, before other companies could launch their own new products, and were immediately rewarded with higher sales.

The bottom line from a concept tester's point of view: Frequency of Purchase is an important concept testing tool. It is also easy to administer, because it takes just one question:

Which statement best describes how often, if ever, you think you would buy this product if it were available where you shop?

Once a week or more often	☐
Once every two or three weeks	☐
Once a month/every four weeks	☐
Once every two or three months	☐
Once every four to six months	☐
Once or twice a year	☐
Less often than once a year	☐
Never	☐

Concept Testing

Adjusting for Overstatements

Surprisingly, questions that measure intended Purchase Frequency are often omitted from concept tests. The problem is that consumers often significantly overstate their intended Purchase or Usage Frequency, sometimes by as much as 50 percent. But eliminating the question is a poor response to the problem. Better to ask the question and use some care in interpreting the results. One approach you might consider is to use the data in a relative sense, comparing your results with category norms or with another concept.

In the late 1970s Riviana Foods, then a division of the Colgate-Palmolive Company, introduced Success instant rice. According to reports in *Advertising Age*, the rollout followed classic Colgate new-product introduction practices: a heavy introductory advertising campaign, supported with lots of samples and coupons. Industry observers concluded that the new-product introduction was not very successful. After three years of heavy advertising and coupon support, Success had won considerably less than 10 percent of the instant rice market.

The rice business is not like the detergent or toothpaste business. One major difference: The Frequency of Purchase and Frequency of Usage are a lot lower. So rules of thumb used to evaluate the potential of special promotions in some of Colgate's other main categories did not apply here. The lesson to be learned from a concept tester's point of view is that if you ask the question, be sure to use care in interpreting the results. Using the data in a relative sense, comparing them to norms from that category, is a good approach to follow.

Another way to correct consumer overstatement of usage frequency is to develop a "deflation factor." For each brand in a category, ask users how often they purchase it. Then compare their perceptions with reality by inspecting available diary panel data.* Use the resulting ratio to adjust your concept test's Purchase Frequency data.

If your sample size is large enough, you should analyze responses to the Frequency of Purchase question by different population segments. The results can be quite surprising. Take pasta, for example. Per capita consumption of pasta has skyrocketed more than 50 percent in the last decade, more so among upper-scale consumers. A concept test for a new pasta product would reveal lots of intended purchase and usage in all popula-

---

* A diary panel consists of a sample of consumers who report their purchase behavior in categories of interest on a continuous basis. The diary panel enables the researcher to measure consumer behavior along such dimensions as brand loyalty or number of days between purchases.

tion segments, with an especially high frequency among wealthier, trendy consumers. Quite a change from the image of pasta as an inexpensive way to feed your family.

What is a marketer to do with this information? Lots of things. Develop new pasta varieties of interest to upper-scale consumers. Show consumers new and trendy ways of serving pasta. Advertise in different media vehicles. Or follow the lead of the Prince Company, a Boston-based regional firm, and launch a new product, the President's Silver Award brand, incorporating all three elements.

REASONS FOR PURCHASE INTEREST

The reasons consumers give for having high or low levels of Purchase Interest often provide valuable insights about a concept's strengths and weaknesses. Reasons for Purchase Interest is another question that can help you spot the winners and losers, and understand the factors responsible for their performance.

- If most consumers who see a concept for a cleaning product think its main reason for being is that it removes rust, but the reason they give for wanting to buy it is that it removes grease, something is wrong with the concept.
- If an office machine concept promises a low purchase price but those who intend to purchase it do so because it is inexpensive to operate, something is wrong.
- If a private mint sells a collectible with the promise of long-term capital appreciation but rejectors claim to have no Purchase Interest because they don't believe there is a potential for appreciation, it is clear that the mint did a poor communication or persuasion job and something is wrong.

The best way to identify the reason influencing consumers' level of Purchase Interest is to ask the following question immediately after the Purchase Interest question:

Why do you say that you [insert answer from Purchase Interest question]? [Probe:] What other reasons do you have for feeling this way?

Concept Testing

Chart 4-9. Reasons for Purchase Interest of a new cleaning product.

Major Mentions	Total	Positive Purchase Interest	Neutral/ Negative Purchase Interest
Positive Reasons			
Convenience (Net)	52%	69%	29%
Easy to use	18	12	㉖
Fast/quick to use	17	㉖	4
Disposable	17	㉒	10
Does several tasks and replaces several products	13	㉑	1
Effective cleaning (Net)	27	39	10
Cleans well	11	16	3
Good for between major cleanings	10	13	4
Negative Reasons	21	13	33
Too costly/wish it cost less	10	12	4
Prefer current brand	7	—	16
Would rather use sponge and water	4	—	10

Interpreting Responses

Since the question is open-ended, the answers will range all over the lot. In general, people with high Purchase Interest give positive reasons for wanting to purchase a product. Those with little or no Purchase Interest usually give negative reasons. But there is a lot of crossover. It is quite common for someone who has just finished saying he definitely will buy your product to tell you his reasons for wanting to buy it are A and B although he wishes the manufacturer would fix C and do a better job on D.

Because of the crossover effect, you run a risk of drawing inaccurate conclusions if you analyze the results of the Reason for Purchase Interest question by examining the responses from the total sample. The problem is vividly illustrated by Chart 4-9. If you examine the results from the total

sample (left-hand column) you would conclude that all four of the convenience-related reasons for wanting to purchase the product are similar in
importance. However, if you look at the second and third columns, you can
see that "ease of use" is not a very important purchase influence among those
with high Purchase Interest. Most of those comments are being made by
individuals with little likelihood of buying the product.

In effect, if you look at the data differently you reach a completely
different conclusion. Without looking at the data in this way, you might
have been tempted to use the "ease of use" benefit as one of your promotional points, instead of stressing speed, disposability, and applicability for
several different cleaning tasks. And you would have wasted a valuable promotional opportunity.

Similar problems exist on the bottom part of the chart, which lists the
negative responses. If you study only the responses of the total sample, no
distinction is made between negative comments by people with very high
Purchase Interest and negative comments by those who have absolutely no
interest in buying the product.

A case in point: 10 percent of the total sample complain about the high
cost of the product. Cost is the most frequently mentioned inhibitor of purchase. Yet analysis by the degree of Purchase Interest shows that cost is
mentioned mostly by people who have already stated they plan to buy the
product. Clearly, they are griping; they wish it were less costly. But equally
clear is that the high cost is not keeping them from wanting to buy it.

Separating by Purchase Interest

This crossover effect pops up in virtually every concept test I do. For
this reason, it is a good idea to analyze the Reason for Purchase Interest data
separately among individuals with positive or negative Purchase Interest.
But how should they be divided up? Should you combine into one group
those who indicate they definitely will buy the product and those who probably will buy it, or keep the two groups separate? Should you throw the
neutral people (those who may or may not buy the product) into the positive
group, the negative group, or keep them separate? And what about the
negative people? Should the responses of someone who probably will not
buy your product be combined with the responses of someone who definitely
will not buy it?

When I first considered Reason for Purchase Interest data, I experimented by analyzing the data in different ways. Over time, I continued to
observe that the answers of the "definitely will buys" and the "probably will
buys" were usually very similar, and that there was nothing to be gained

75

Concept Testing

analytically by studying each group separately. However, the same is not true for respondents with neutral and negative Purchase Interest. Their reasons are often quite different. Respondents with neutral Purchase Interest are often fence straddlers; they like the product on some dimensions and dislike it on others. Often the things they dislike are different from the things disliked by those with negative Purchase Interest.

These neutral respondents should be analyzed separately. The problem is that the number of people who fall into this neutral group is usually too small to be useful analytically. To have enough neutral respondents, you would need a total sample size of 300 or 400, which is often unaffordable. You can handle this problem either by combining the responses of the neutral and negative individuals into one group, or by totally ignoring the neutral responses. Neither solution is perfect, but thus far I haven't found anything better.

Responses to the Reason for Purchase Interest question can by analyzed in two ways. One is simply to read the responses by themselves. The second way is to compare responses to this question against responses to the Main Idea question. Answers to the two questions should be somewhat related. In other words, one of the more frequently mentioned main ideas of a concept should also be one of the more frequently mentioned reasons for a respondent wanting to buy the product. If the responses are out of balance, the data may be sending out a signal that the concept is troubled. This kind of problem occurs relatively frequently.

For instance, a competitor to AT&T tested a concept stressing the lower cost of its long distance calls. Many consumers heard the message but also indicated on the Reason for Purchase Interest question that clarity and quality of the sound were very important to them. And a ski resort stressed the large number of slopes on its property and the availability of snow-making equipment to help nature along whenever necessary. All respondents played back these points in response to the Main Idea question. However, expert skiers were quite likely to mention the length and challenging nature of some of the slopes as a reason to visit the resort. Novice skiers tended to talk about the availability of instruction and rental equipment. The data were indicating that in an effort to be all things to all people, the concept missed some points of critical interest to various target-group segments.

As you can see, the Reason for Purchase Interest question as well as five other key indicators—Uniqueness, Relevance, Main Idea, Importance, and Purchase Frequency—are important concept test indicators. To maximize the potential of your concept, it makes good sense to consult each one of these valuable indicators.

5
Imagery

In addition to the Big Six, there are a number of other diagnostic questions that can help you evaluate the strengths or weaknesses of test concepts. Three of them may be grouped under the heading of Imagery: Product Imagery, User Imagery, and Use Occasion Imagery.

When I talk about image, I am referring to feelings and impressions that consumers have about a product. An image is the consumer's perception of a product, not necessarily the reality of it.

The problem with Imagery data is that a poorly worded question, poor analytic procedures, or both, can negate the value of the data in terms of helping you resolve the marketing problem at hand. The purpose of this chapter is to show you how to collect various types of Imagery data in a useful, action-oriented manner.

PRODUCT IMAGERY

I suspect that every marketer has, at one time or another, reviewed a series of product attribute ratings for a test concept, noting which attributes scored high, and which scored low.* It's a useful analysis, telling you at a glance how to rectify problems with the concept or suggesting new product ideas. For example, consumers often give a poor rating to the freshness and the amount of pulp present in frozen orange juice concentrate. Apparently, the bits of pulp are associated in some way with perceptions of freshness, nat-

---

* For concept testing purposes, the terms *image* and *attribute* are used interchangeably. That is, both refer to the *perceptions* of the consumer. The terms *image rating* and *attribute rating* are also interchangeable in this context.

uralness, and less intensive processing. One solution suggested by these data is to market a frozen concentrate with added pulp.

Here's an example of how product imagery can be critical to the success or failure of a concept. In 1979, Minnetonka, Inc., successfully introduced Softsoap, a liquid soap, and virtually overnight created a large and rapidly growing category. Soon after, many other manufacturers jumped in with their own version, and the market quickly became quite crowded. This caused some of the newer players to go after small segments of the total market to isolate profitable niches for themselves.

One company investigated the idea of a heavy-duty liquid soap for heavy dirt like grease and gardening dirt. The concept tested poorly. Product attribute ratings showed low scores for the product's perceived ability to clean heavy-duty dirt. According to reports in *Advertising Age*, Minnetonka itself ultimately tried to segment the liquid soap market with work soap, which it pitched to consumers as being for heavy dirt in the home. The product was not successful.

Apparently, consumers do not associate this type of product with heavy-duty dirt in spite of the concept's effort to make this point. The reason is undoubtedly that all other liquid soap brands, including Minnetonka's own Softsoap, are cosmetically oriented toward the hands and face. The idea of an industrial-strength cleaning product in a cosmetics-linked category and a cosmetics-linked package just does not work.

Applying What You Learn

Clearly, product attribute ratings can be very useful in pinpointing why concepts succeed or fail. Unfortunately, there are times when the results of this attribute analysis are confusing or hard to apply to the real world. The major problem is that all attributes receive equal weight, even though some matter more to consumers. In other words, if a concept is rated high on Attribute A and low on Attribute B, you cannot always determine whether this is a serious problem. Is it a problem, for example, if your food concept is rated strongly on every attribute except "fresh ingredients"? What about a concept for a new hand-held tool that has very good ratings except in "good value for the money"? In each case, you must judge how serious the problem is—doing cross tabs and weighing various positives and negatives—before reaching a conclusion.

Most analysts ultimately look to Purchase Interest for help. If the Purchase Interest score is high enough, they don't worry too much about a low-scoring product attribute. In the reverse situation, the low-scoring product attribute rating receives greater attention and concern.

The problem with this system is that you don't always know for sure if the low-scoring attribute is the one that is causing the problem. The data do not tell you if the attribute is *very* important or of marginal concern. To handle this problem, you can use this three-step system.

1. Measure the perceived image of the product on a series of specific product attributes.
2. Measure the importance the respondents give each of these same attributes.
3. Chart the relationship between the attributes that are important to respondents and their rating of the product on these same attributes.

The procedure is easy and inexpensive to implement since the data can be collected with a self-administered questionnaire. Start by handing respondents a list of appropriate product attributes. These attributes will vary from product to product; you should build your own list based on the strategy of the product.

The questioning process has two parts: having the respondents rate their impressions of the product's attributes, after reading the concept, and then rate how important each of the same attributes is to them. You can use ten-point numerical scales, five-point "excellent to poor" scales, or any others you are comfortable with.

Here is one series of questions you can use to measure both the reactions to the product and the importance of each attribute.

1. I would like you to rate this product on several different characteristics. Although you have evaluated the product on an overall basis, you may feel differently about it on some of these characteristics. Since you may not have used this product before, please base your answers on your impressions from what you've just read.

    After you read each characteristic, rate the product either as excellent, very good, good, fair, or poor. Pick the choice that best describes how well you think the product would perform on that characteristic.
2. Now I'd like to find out how important each of these characteristics is to you. After you read each characteristic, rate it as either very important, somewhat important, neither important nor unimportant, somewhat unimportant, or very unimportant.

Concept Testing

Importance and Rank: The Quadrant Analysis

You can easily analyze the scores produced by these two questions by plotting them on a two-dimensional scale like the one shown in Figure 5-1, taken from a recent food product concept test. The vertical axis carries the Importance score. The more important to the respondent, the higher up the attribute is plotted. The horizontal axis plots the concept's rating. The better the product is rated, the more to the left it is plotted. You need not be particularly interested in actual percentages; your main interest is to see the relative performance of each attribute, that is, its position relative to the others.

The upper left quadrant contains attributes that are important to the respondent and that the test concept scores well on. The upper right quadrant contains attributes that are important but low-rated.

The concept being tested describes a frozen dinner product. It is obvious from the chart that the concept delivered a very strong "convenience" message, an issue of high importance to the target group. This conclusion is based on the fact that both "ease of preparation" and "speed of preparation" are at the very top of the chart and as far to the left as is possible to go. Other important issues, such as the product being viewed as well-balanced and nutritious, are also adequately communicated by the concept.

But look at the problems being signaled in the upper right quadrant. It is clear that the concept does a poor job of communicating good taste, high-quality ingredients, and good value for the money—all very important issues.

This graphic presentation can be an excellent tool to aid analysis of attribute data. It lets you easily see relationships and, more important, it helps nontechnical marketing people visually grasp the various strengths and weaknesses of the concept.

A case in point: When Equal (G. D. Searle's aspartame-based sweetener) was first marketed, management grappled with positioning it several different ways. Should they stress that it contained no saccharine, or that it tasted as good as sugar? Research showed that the proposed product was well rated on both of these dimensions. However, the fact that it tasted as good as sugar was much more important to consumers. This relationship is noted in Figure 5-2, which shows both attributes tied on the rating dimension, with taste rated higher on Importance.

As a result, Equal took the high ground with a position that appealed to sugar users as well as users of low-calorie sweetener. Rather than competing with other low-calorie sweeteners, it took aim at winning a share of

(text continued on p. 82)

Imagery

Figure 5-1. Importance and ratings of food product attributes.

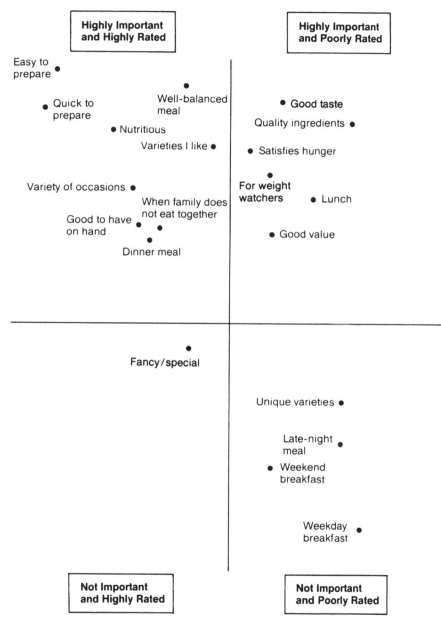

Figure 5-2. Importance and ratings of sugar-substitute attributes.

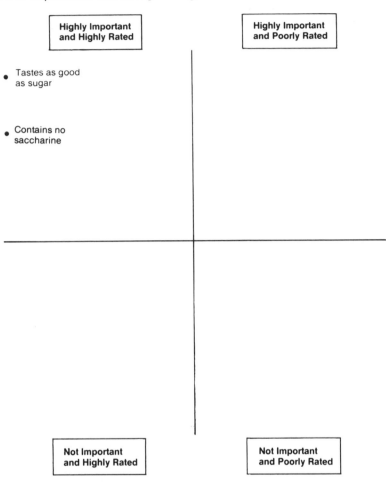

the total sweetener market. So far, the product has been quite successful in the marketplace.

Putting the Analysis to Use

Once you complete the quadrant analysis, pinpointing highly rated attributes that consumers say are important, you are still stuck with the task of applying these findings to the real world. A concept test often contains

10 or 15 highly rated attributes that are important to consumers. However, advertising and packaging can usually address just two or three. Which ones do you use?

One approach is to stress those few benefits that are not being currently stressed by competition. If Benefits A and B are equally important, why stress Benefit A if everyone else in the category is promoting the same thing and no one is stressing Benefit B?

Here is a simple method to pinpoint attributes that you should stress. Isolate all attributes that your concept is rated highly on *and* that are important to consumers. Have consumers compare the test concept with other products in the category on these special attributes. In other words, if consumers tell you safety is an important food processor attribute and your food processor concept receives good safety ratings, you should determine just how safe you are perceived to be versus the competition. Your goal is to isolate attributes for which your product is thought to outperform competition.

An eye care retailer was planning to offer consumers a one-stop "supermarket" approach to eye care. A customer could get an eye exam by a qualified physician, get fitted for glasses, select frames from a large assortment, and receive the finished product within one hour, at a very low price.

The quadrant analysis of the concept test found five areas on which consumers rated the concept highly: professionalism, speed of service, location of the store, range of merchandise, and prices. For each attribute in these five areas consumers were asked if the concept was thought to be better, the same, or not as good as other eye care retailers. The results are illustrated in Chart 5-1.

The results were quite interesting. Compared to the competition, the concept performed strongest on the issue of professionalism. The comprehensive eye examination and the availability of the latest equipment were points that best differentiated the concept from competition. Other attributes dealing with speed, location, merchandise, and pricing were also important, but consumers did not think the new concept offered something substantially better than the competition. As a result of this analysis the retailer was able to hone in on a specific product benefit with high leverage potential.

Other Information in the Data

While the quadrant analysis (with appropriate followup questions) is a terrific tool, valuable information can often be milked from the data merely by looking at Importance scores by themselves. Just ranking each attribute

Concept Testing

Chart 5-1. Comparing new eye-care concept to competition.

	New Concept Rated "Better"
Attributes	
Professionalism	
Comprehensive eye exams	(57) %
Qualified eye doctors	40
Latest equipment for eye exams	(63)
Speed	
Quick service on prescriptions	48
Location	
Located in or near shopping mall	44
Merchandise	
Wide variety of styles	31
Latest, most current styles	41
Prices	
Fair, reasonable prices for glasses	21
Reasonably priced eye exams	25

in descending order of importance can reveal valuable insights. For example, isn't it useful for an overnight package delivery firm to know that guaranteeing a 10:00 A.M. delivery is more important to consumers than offering to refund their payment if the delivery promise is not kept?

Comparing Importance scores against scores from previous concept tests is another way of uncovering useful information. Take the men's skin care category, for example. Compared with women's skin care sales volume, men's sales are tiny. And when we exclude shaving-related products, the size of the market is positively puny.

Why is that? Years of advertising by skin care marketers have made women well educated about the idea of beautifying the skin and caring for it as a standard part of their daily personal hygiene regimen. Virtually none of this advertising has been aimed toward men. Not surprisingly, concept testing reveals that daily skin care is not especially important to men. And this perception has not changed much in the past few years. It's a tough environment within which to develop a male skin treatment line. So far, despite enormous effort and substantial dollar expenditures, no one has succeeded. And the Importance ratings tell why.

Another example of values changing over time: A few years ago, a concept test on color television found that issues such as picture quality and styling were much higher in importance than sound quality. But recently, because of engineering advances and aggressive promotion of stereo sound, the issue is rising markedly in importance. This issue, though not the primary reason for doing a concept test on television sets, is a wonderful morsel to uncover. It sets a whole sequence of thoughts into motion:

1. Sales of TVs with stereo sound are rising. The promotional efforts of companies marketing stereo TV seem to be working well.
2. Since stereo is a valuable TV sales tool, other manufacturers will probably jump into this market soon.
3. With more competitors, the ability of stereo sound to generate higher profit margins will fall. Instead of stereo being a balloon to help raise profits, it may become a drag on profits, with everyone offering it but no one able to price it properly.

USER IMAGERY

Equally important to your analysis of a concept's strengths and weaknesses is the need to identify the type of person that respondents associate with your product. What is their image of a user? In general, this is useful information. But in emotionally oriented categories (fragrances, cosmetics, beverages, tobacco) where the sizzle is as important as the steak, it is absolutely imperative.

At its simplest level you need only to determine who in the household is perceived to use the product or service being tested. Compare findings from your concept test with data from larger-scale strategic studies that have usage data. A survey for Gerber Products Company, a leading baby food manufacturer, would show that up to 10 percent of the consumption of some of its products is adult-oriented: people who want smooth or whipped foods, those interested in small portions, and those on low-salt diets. Contrasting perception with reality provides new product opportunities for the alert marketer.

In addition to demographic characteristics associated with a new-product concept, it is also useful to identify the personal values, self-perceptions, and perceived lifestyle of the prospective user. The best way to collect this

Concept Testing

Chart 5-2. User imagery of two concepts.

	Concept A	Concept B
Type of Person Who		
Would Use This Product		
Thinks skin appearance is		
important	82%	83%
Takes care of herself	81	81
Fashionable	60	59
Practical	49	54
Working woman	63	76
Confident/self-assured	55	65
Contemporary/modern	51	66

information is to give respondents a list of applicable image attributes and ask them to select the ones that are most associated with the user of the product. Here is one way of asking the question that works quite well.

Now I'd like to know your opinion about the type of person who would use this product, based on what was said and shown in the description.

    To do this, use the numbers from 1 to 10. 10 means you agree strongly that the person described by the phrase would be a product user. 1 means the person described by the phrase would definitely not be a user. Of course you may pick any number in between.

Using the Data

    The simplest way to use the resulting data is to compare ratings between Concept A and B, or between those with high Purchase Interest for a concept versus those with low Purchase Interest. The data are incredibly discriminating and sensitive, and often tell a powerful story.

    In a concept test of a line extension for a major product in the cosmetics business, there were widespread differences in User Imagery among various versions of the concept, in spite of the fact that all concepts used the same heavily advertised brand name and all respondents were current users of the parent brand. Chart 5-2, which notes the percentage of respondents who agree strongly with the statements, shows how two concepts compare. Concept B was associated with modern, working women to a larger degree.

    Sometimes the answer is not this apparent, and you must delve a bit deeper into the data. A good next step is to compare ratings between those with high versus low Purchase Interest in the concept.

Imagery

Chart 5-3. User imagery correlated to Purchase Interest.

	Concept A		Concept B	
	Positive	Neutral/ Negative	Positive	Neutral/ Negative
Type of Person Who Would Use This Product				
Thinks skin appearance is important	71%	76%	(77)%	69%
Thinks skin care is important	70	74	(81)	71
Takes care of herself	73	69	(77)	69
Fashionable	54	48	(57)	47
Appreciates value	(60)	51	55	56
Practical	(54)	39	42	36
Traditional	(48)	34	39	37

Another skin care concept test revealed no differences in User Imagery between two concepts for the sample as a whole. But when data for each concept were tabulated by Purchase Interest, an interesting pattern emerged (see Chart 5-3). Those with high Purchase Interest in Concept A thought its user would be a practical, value-oriented person. Those with high Purchase Interest in Concept B associated the product with fashionable women who were oriented to skin care.

Can this type of analysis be used to increase sales? You bet it can. For years, Almay, a hypoallergenic cosmetic line, plodded along with small year-to-year sales gains. Consumers thought it was a high-quality product for individuals with serious skin problems. In 1983 the company changed Almay's direction, positioning it as a product for everyone, not just for those with skin problems. Interest in the brand rose. Why? User imagery changed. Women began to believe that the product was for everyone, not just a few.

Positive or Negative Image?

User Imagery data is generally easy to analyze merely by using the techniques described in these examples. But occasionally, an analytic problem emerges: You cannot always tell if the user image you so accurately measured is positive or negative.

Concept Testing

If your concept is frequently associated with snooty or pushy people, you could assume these are negatives. But what about a product strongly associated with sophisticated women or fashion leaders? Is this good or bad for your product? Cross tabbing by Purchase Interest will not always give you the answer. Just because many consumers with high Purchase Interest think your product is for sophisticated women doesn't tell you if this individual attribute is a good one or not. Maybe your concept could have done even better if it was not associated with this type of user. And even if the attribute is potentially positive, perhaps your concept executed this issue poorly or too heavy-handedly.

To solve this problem, try using the following improved approach to measure User Imagery.

1. Measure the image of the product user that is suggested by the concept on a series of specific attributes.
2. Measure the type of person that the respondent admires (or wishes to be like) on these same attributes.
3. Chart the relationship between the two, using the same quadrant graphing procedure described earlier.

For example, in a test for a personal care product, User Imagery ratings were correlated with the degree of admiration respondents had for people with those same characteristics. The degree of warmth and friendliness suggested by the concept was very low and these characteristics were highly admired. This pointed to a key barrier to high Purchase Interest: a cold, aloof, user image.

On balance, charting User Imagery data in this manner takes a bit of clerical time and effort, but in certain circumstances the time and effort are well spent.

Open- or Closed-End?

You probably have noticed that this User Imagery section makes no reference to open-end questions. The reason is that I have had no success with open-ends in this subject area. I've made many attempts to measure User Imagery with open-end questions, asking respondents to describe the concept user's demographic and psychological characteristics. These approaches never led to actionable results. I suspect the problem is twofold: improper or incomplete probing by the interviewers, and the inability to construct codes that are sufficiently sensitive to identify nuances.

After being continuously dissatisfied with the efforts of skilled code

Imagery

builders, I once made an attempt to build codes by myself. The result was quite humbling. I simply couldn't build a code that captured the multitude of shadings and subtleties I encountered while reading respondent answers. The English language is too rich and too imprecise.

Open-end questions are poor image measuring devices for another reason. Sometimes respondents have difficulty expressing the underlying issues that affect their feelings. An example is a concept for a facial cleansing product that tested poorly. One problem was that respondents did not perceive the product as appropriate for their personal use. It didn't seem to fit their lifestyles, their values, or their ways of dealing with the world around them. The trouble was, we couldn't get this insight from direct questions. Had we asked a respondent why she was not interested in purchasing the product, it's highly unlikely we would get an answer like this: "This product is not for me. It's for a different kind of woman. I do not have her values, her desires, or her style of living."

I recommend closed-end rating scale questions to measure User Imagery. The results are satisfactory most of the time. But there is one problem that you must continuously remind yourself of. Responses to an attribute question are only as good as the attributes that you start with. If you inadvertently omit a key personality dimension, you are simply out of luck.

USE OCCASION IMAGERY

A third Imagery area is the measurement of the usage occasions associated with the test product concept. How do the respondents imagine the product would be used? In what kinds of situations?

Putting the Data into Action

This kind of diagnostic data can help in five ways.

1. It can help the analyst fine tune a concept. A case in point comes from the hot sauce category. A major brand in the category is Tabasco, which controls about 30 percent of the market. A concept test for Tabasco shows a great deal of usage is related to making Bloody Marys. The implication of this finding is that showing the wider applicability of Tabasco—as a flavor enhancer or salt alternative for all foods—could expand sales.

2. It can give the analyst a new product clue. Let's go back to the liquid soap category for a moment. The category, less than a decade old, has already grown to $100 million in annual sales. Research shows most usage is related to washing hands. Various line extensions, such as those for cleaning

Concept Testing

Chart 5-4. Occasion most likely to eat product, by Purchase Interest.

	Positive Purchase Interest	Neutral/ Negative Purchase Interest
Breakfast	4%	7%
Lunch	㉝	17
Afternoon snack	4	—
Dinner	20	㉚
Late supper	8	12
Late-night snack	7	12

heavy-duty dirt and for shower use, have gone too far afield and have not done well on the market.

One implication is to do what Minnetonka, the founders of the category, did: introduce a new line. The Softsoap Boutique Collection has added skin conditioners for hand *and* face use. The goal was to cause the consumer to use liquid soap more often, without going so far afield.

3. Sometimes the Occasion of Use question helps the analyst decide whether or not a concept is in trouble when other indicators are sending more muddled signals.

To illustrate: A concept test for a new food product was well received by the target group, and achieved high Purchase Interest scores. Several variations were tested, including a "lunch" positioning, which suggested the product was most appropriate for midday consumption, and a "brunch" positioning, which slanted usage in a slightly different way. The brunch concept stimulated slightly higher Purchase Interest than did lunch.

At first glance brunch appeared to have won over lunch. But when we asked respondents how often they ate brunch at home, we learned that very few did so, mostly on weekends. A much larger number served lunch, and they did so six or seven days of the week. Clearly, brunch was preferred (possibly because of its novelty value) but lunch had much higher volume potential.

An additional tabulation made data from this question quite useful in improving the lunch concept. We measured when consumers with high and low Purchase Interest were most likely to serve the product. The results are in Chart 5-4. Those with high Purchase Interest were especially likely to associate the product with lunchtime consumption. Those with neutral or negative Purchase Interest were especially likely to associate the product with dinner consumption. This finding suggested the possibility of strengthening the concept further by convincing some rejectors that the product was appropriate for lunchtime consumption.

4. The Occasion of Use question also ensures that the concept does not accidentally cause consumers to limit their use of the product. The problem inadvertently comes about because of category segmentation. As companies develop tight little niches for their new products, they run the risk of reducing potential consumption by narrowly defining when or how the product should be used.

The problem is more frequent than you might think. Take, for example, a chocolate-covered mint that is individually wrapped within a very fancy outer package. The wrapping causes consumers to think of the item as a special gift or dinner party item. Unfortunately, the limited number of gift occasions and dinner parties doom this product to a low-volume niche. Yet the product itself could be used almost daily if it were positioned as a means of dressing up an everyday meal. Or take a beverage concentrate for piña colada, a drink often identified with sunny beaches and exotic climates. Why settle for a warm-weather vacation positioning if a slight concept adjustment could provide you with a year-round market?

To determine if your concept has this problem, ask respondents two questions: when they currently use products from the category, and when they would use the test product? By comparing the ratings, you can determine if you have a special-occasion product problem.

Applying the results of this analysis to one of your marketing problems can be incredibly profitable, as the makers of Pretty Feet learned. This product, a rough-skin remover for women's feet, yielded disappointing sales to Norcliff Thayer, at the time a division of Revlon. Research showed that while most women used the product primarily on their feet, many potential users were not especially concerned about rough skin on their feet because that part of their body was often hidden by shoes. In addition, research also showed that an even greater number of women were interested in removing rough skin from other parts of the body, like their hands.

A concept test found that Purchase Interest rose when the product was portrayed as a rough-skin remover for both hands and feet. The product was repositioned, renamed Pretty Feet & Hands, and the new product went to market. Sales quadrupled!

The Pretty Feet & Hands example may be dramatic but it is by no means rare. Another concept test, this time for a new line of long underwear, tried to demonstrate that it was appropriate to wear the product for many different occasions. The concept test revealed that the concept inadvertently moved the product image away from everyday use and toward several special occasions (see Chart 5-5). Once the problem was uncovered,

Concept Testing

Chart 5-5. Reasons product is worn.

	Current Long Johns	Weak Test Concept
For everyday use to keep warm	(72)%	63%
For specific activities	28	(37)
Outdoor work	17	27
Hunting/fishing	8	16
Watching outdoor sports	7	13
Jogging/running/hiking	9	14

it was quite easy to revise some sections of the concept to broaden the occasions for which wearing the product was appropriate.

5. And finally, the Occasion of Use sometimes provides surprising marketing insights that are well beyond the issues of positioning strategy and copy development that caused you to do the test in the first place. Take the popcorn industry. Something like 94 or 95 percent of all popcorn consumed at home is eaten while the person is sitting and watching television. If you were a popcorn marketer, where would you advertise your brand? In newspapers? In magazines? Any other thoughts—evening television, maybe?

Phrasing the Question

The Occasion of Use issue can be addressed in two ways. You can give respondents a list of different occasions, such as this one for a food concept test, and ask for their opinion of appropriateness.

Chart 5-6. Is this compact a winner?

Maybe Yes		Maybe No	
Definitely will buy	26%	Say product would cause them to carry a compact more often	11%
Understand main benefit	68		
Consider the compact to have an advantage over other compacts	81	Would continue to wear a wristwatch, even after owning product	(78)

Imagery

I'd like you to tell me how appropriate you feel this product is for various occasions. For each occasion I read to you, please tell me if you think the product would be very appropriate, somewhat appropriate, or not at all appropriate? [*Read list.*]

	Very Appropriate	*Somewhat Appropriate*	*Not at All Appropriate*
Weekday breakfast	☐	☐	☐
Weekend breakfast	☐	☐	☐
Lunch at home	☐	☐	☐
Lunch at school	☐	☐	☐
Lunch at work	☐	☐	☐
Afternoon snack	☐	☐	☐
Dinner	☐	☐	☐
Evening snack	☐	☐	☐

Or you can give the same list to the respondent and ask: "On which of these occasions would you be most likely to eat this product?"

The second alternative may be preferable simply because of cost. The first alternative really consists of eight questions, one for each serving occasion, while the second is much shorter and faster to administer.

Analytic Use

Measuring Use Occasions associated with a concept is an especially useful analytic tool when testing a unique, breakthrough product, something the consumer thinks is truly new and different. This is because it's hard for consumers to decide how they feel about a product they've never encountered or even thought about. As hard as it may be for them to visualize how they will use the product, that task is still easier than deciding how likely they are to purchase it at all.

One way around the problem is to ask respondents whether they feel the new product would change their use of the category. Assume you are testing a concept for a new product priced higher than its competitor, one that offers a benefit completely new to its category, perhaps an additional way of using the product. One example might be a woman's compact with a tiny clock built into it. Everyone loves the idea (see Chart 5-6) but they expect to continue using their compacts in the traditional way. These consumers are pointing to a problem. Put it all together and what do you have? A high-volume product or a novelty gift item that consumers might buy one time?

Concept Testing

Using the Data Fully

All the examples in this section involve the Use Occasions associated with a concept. Sometimes the data are examined alone. In some examples, they are compared with Use Occasions associated with other products in the category to pinpoint problems or opportunities. Before closing this section, I would like to point out one additional way in which a battery of Usage Occasions questions can be used. Sometimes, you need not even examine the concept-related ratings to come up with a Big Idea. Merely by examining Usage Occasions data for the category in general, marvelous new-product opportunities can be discovered.

Take the running shoe category. In a 1982 test of a running shoe concept, I asked respondents a series of Usage Occasions questions. To provide a context within which to analyze this data, I asked a similar battery of questions about the occasions when they wore their current running shoes.

When I analyzed this so-called background or context question, I came up with the Big Idea. I learned that most owners of running shoes wore them while walking, not running. And that much of this walking was part of a normal daily activity, like shopping or commuting to work, not walking for exercise. Many of these nonexercise wearers thought their running shoe competed with tennis shoes and other casual shoes in terms of how they used them. The analysis clearly suggested the need for a walking shoe designed for comfortable, everyday walking.

At the time, the running shoe category was so hot that no one was especially interested in this opportunity. But now that the running boom has peaked and sales are down, several manufacturers are jumping into the walking-shoe segment of the market.

ALL THREE IMAGE DIMENSIONS INTERTWINED

Our discussion on imagery has covered Product Imagery, User Imagery, and Use Occasion Imagery as separate topics. But when you use imagery data under actual combat conditions, you will find that the data from all three types of questions must be intertwined to give you maximum decision-making assistance. Imagery hardly ever neatly segments itself into a Product Image marketing problem or a User Image problem. Look at the marketing problem faced by American Express.

The American Express credit card is a major force in the business travel and entertainment segment of the credit card industry. If American Express

Imagery

is to increase the number of cardholders and the dollar amount charged with each card, it must continue to broaden card usage beyond travel and entertainment. It does this by encouraging cardholders to use the card for all kinds of retail purchases. However, in taking this action, it competes against VISA and MasterCard, going head to head against two charge cards with much larger bases of participating merchants, on their own turf. As it embarks upon this competition, American Express must wonder about the effects of its new approach on:

1. The kind of person who will want an American Express card in the future.
2. The image of the card itself as a high-status, hassle-free shopping tool.
3. The feeling by many consumers that travel and entertainment expenses are synonymous with an American Express card.

No one knows for sure what the long-term result will be, but testing with an extensive series of Product Image attributes, User Image attributes, and Use Occasion Image attributes is required to clarify this issue.

Another example, this time from the food industry, involves Butter Buds, a concentrate produced by the Cumberland Packing Corporation, marketers of Sweet 'n Low. Butter Buds is a dry concentrate that is extracted directly from butter. Cumberland claims its process enables it to isolate the 0.5% of the butter that represents the flavor, while eliminating the fat. To use the product consumers must reconstitute the granules by adding water.

The product was originally introduced in the 1960s but did not achieve much in the way of sales success. In the 1980s Cumberland again tried, influenced by the continued decline of per capita butter consumption because of health concerns. With annual retail sales of butter approaching $1 billion, even a small piece of this market could be of tremendous value to a company the size of Cumberland.

Will Cumberland succeed? I don't know. An analysis of consumer ratings of the product, the perceived use, and the Use Occasions for which the product is appropriate finds lots of problems, conflicts, and potential opportunities. For example:

1. *User Imagery.* A four-ounce box of Butter Buds, which contains the flavor of two pounds of butter, has just 384 calories, compared with 6,400 calories in two pounds of butter. Not surprisingly, consumers think the product is good for dieters.

2. *Product Imagery.* Unfortunately, consumers also think the product

is good for cooking and frying. However, since it does not contain any fat, it cannot be used for frying.

3. *Use Occasion Imagery*. A great deal of the butter that is consumed gets spread over bread. Because Butter Buds is liquid, it cannot easily be used as a spread.

Will Butter Buds become another Sweet 'n Low for Cumberland Packing Corporation? No one can tell. But it serves to illustrate the point that when it comes to Imagery data, the integrated analysis of all three dimensions is needed to completely define the range of problems and opportunities facing a product.

6
Other Useful Diagnostic Tools

Picking the best of several concept candidates or deciding whether or not to proceed with further development of an idea is just half the battle in concept testing. A good concept test should also help you improve the proposed concept by diagnosing weak aspects. This diagnostic process can help all concepts, weak or strong, and this is where most concept tests stumble.

Fixing an already strong candidate is a ticklish step. You don't want to go too far and weaken what you already know to be a potential winner. Yet you know in your heart that there may be some "hot buttons" you missed. Including them in the concept would stimulate even greater interest. Or maybe some of the things you believe are important motivators actually have no effect on consumers. Eliminating them and substituting other benefits could help at the cash register. Or perhaps a major benefit is not executed optimally, and fine tuning it could have a significant effect on concept acceptance.

Diagnostic data are just as important for the average or substandard concept as for strong ones. Sometimes a concept can be significantly improved by making a relatively small adjustment. All you need is a clue to tell you what is wrong or how to rectify the problem.

Chapters 3, 4, and 5 discussed the most widely used concept test questions. This chapter will outline a series of additional procedures that will help you fine tune your concepts even further.

X-RAY YOUR CONCEPT

The most serious diagnostic deficiency of concept testing is the difficulty of honing in on the specific element of a concept that is causing a negative or inadequate response. It is easier to conclude that the concept did well or

Concept Testing

Chart 6-1. Reasons for positive
Purchase Interest.

	Total
Efficacy	58%
Prevents wetness	29
Long-lasting	25
Prevents odor	17
Goes on dry	45
Gentle, not irritating	(12)

poorly than it is to identify the specific word or phrase that caused the concept to perform as it did. Most concept testing systems fall down in this area.

Even when a concept test provides some diagnostic clues, the insights are often general and unfocused. It is one thing to conclude that "good taste" was not communicated clearly by a food concept. But it is far more difficult to conclude that the first taste mention in Paragraph 1 was well executed but the second mention in Paragraph 3 was not persuasive. And it is even harder to learn that "delicious" and "mouth-watering" worked well but that "yummy" or "homemade" were ineffective.

One barrier to this analysis is the difficulty of deciding if the respondent rejected a claim or merely didn't see it. In other words, did other concept elements or sections receive most of the attention? Could the attention they received have been so strong that the benefit in question was passed over?

This point can be illustrated with a concept for an antiperspirant product. The full concept is about seven paragraphs long, but the meat of the product idea is in one key paragraph.

> Offers all-day protection against wetness and odor. You can get that
> effectiveness in a new antiperspirant designed especially for you. It glides
> on smooth and comfortably dry. And its formula is gentle enough for
> your skin.

The paragraph talks about three basic benefits: all-day protection, dryness, and gentleness. When this concept was tested, consumers repeatedly reacted positively to all-day protection and dryness claims but infrequently mentioned gentleness, either positively or negatively (see Chart 6-1). This same pattern of response occurred with questions measuring communication of the Main Idea and a variety of other open-end questions.

The research problem was to determine if the infrequent mention of gentleness was because consumers were uninterested in the benefit, positively or negatively, *or* because they merely didn't hear or see it (their attention was focused on the long-lasting or dryness claim).

Forced-Exposure Question

Address this problem by handing respondents a copy of the printed concept near the end of the interview and ask them to underline all the words and phrases that they think are interesting or important. This is rather like a forced-exposure copy test, where respondents' attention is focused onto every copy element to get them to react to each.

The result of this question is illustrated below. The concept extract shown earlier now has the percentage of individuals who selected each word indicated directly above the word. (Here the three benefits are italicized.)

```
  23   56  61      60       39      55    40   54    12  12  12   12
Offers all-day protection against wetness and odor.  You  can  get  that

      22      11  12  19      25        26        38      34  36   19
effectiveness  in   a   new antiperspirant designed especially for you.  It

  33   28     46    34        58       58    15  15    18    16    56
glides  on  smooth and comfortably dry.  And its formula  is  gentle

  39   38  40   41
enough for your skin.
```

"All-day protection" is clearly a good benefit, with six out of ten individuals reacting positively to it. This corroborates findings from the open-ended data. Similarly, about six out of ten react positively to the fact that usage of the product makes the user "comfortably dry."

Also observe the large number of people reacting positively to the "gentle" formula. Clearly, gentleness is a good benefit. The problem is that consumers just do not "hear" it as they initially read the concept. The implications for the creative department are quite significant: We should emphasize the benefit more strongly, not remove it from the concept.

99

Concept Testing

Applying the Answers

Now that you understand how this analytic approach works, let us develop it further. Here is the full concept for a product in the hair care category. Because the category is enormously competitive, and little nuances make big differences in sales, I have eliminated a few key words and phrases to protect client confidentiality. Once again, the percentage of people who chose each word as important appears just above the word.

```
  3   3  5   34     13    5    12    11   9    9      2    3
This  is  a  unique  XXX  that stands above all others. With its

  32      27     3     4     3   6   10   6   4    4    5   5
advanced formula, it represents a true first in the world of XXX.

  2    1  1   1       17
That's why it's called Emerge.

  3    5       7        13       13    6   16    22    18
A newly discovered patented molecule and special buffing action

  5    5    5    7  11 12   49    36    51   49  56   42   46
enable this product to give you exactly the amount of XXX XXX XXX

36   27   18      64      45  46   38     60   43    57     54
you want, while protecting your hair from protein and moisture loss.

18   22   25 26 33 69   52   70   26   26   24 25   25     31  61
Your hair will be as soft and shiny as before  it  was XXX—with no

77  62    75
XXX XXX damage.

  9     8  9   9    6    7   8   9     33       28     15
Emerge—a real first which will give you superior results and

34    32    32      6       6    5   7    7    6     6  6
superior hair condition—certainly worth the little more you'll have to

  7
spend.
```

Other Useful Diagnostic Tools

Consumer response reveals a very weak opening paragraph. The first sentence, announcing a unique product that stands above all others, does not elicit a strong response. Only about one-third of the audience reacts positively to the word *unique*. Other product benefits, to be discussed in a moment, elicit much more positive response.

The second sentence, proudly announcing the product's "advanced formula," also generates little interest. In fact, the second half of this sentence, which talks about the product being "a true first," puts people to sleep. And the third sentence, where the name Emerge is proudly announced, is not much better.

The concept's second paragraph gets more specific. It talks about "a newly discovered patented molecule" and the existence of "special buffing action." The low number of respondents reacting to these benefits is clearly telling us consumers are not very impressed with them. But in the rest of the sentence, it becomes clear that consumers are quite interested in the *benefits* provided by a patented molecule and special buffing action. This analysis is signaling that the benefits themselves are terrific. It is the Madison Avenue lingo—"patented molecule" and "special buffing action"—that people are turning off to.

This is a critical finding. And it never would have been uncovered with traditional market research techniques. Had you asked consumers what they dislike about this product, some would answer that they dislike a "patented molecule." Others might dislike the "special buffing action." You would therefore conclude, incorrectly, that a special feature providing these benefits is a poor idea. You would have eliminated the entire benefit. However, by looking at the data as we are doing here, it is quite clear that the product benefits themselves are excellent, but the way they are described is deficient.

Another point that emerges as we review consumer reactions to the concept in this manner is that several sentences are required before the concept begins to turn people on. In fact, it does not begin to generate strong positive response until the halfway mark. This is a signal that a very poor job was done with the first half of the concept.

The final paragraph opens with a statement that this product is "a real first." Once again, being first elicits very low positive response. The closing paragraph also promises "superior results" and "superior hair condition," both of which merely elicit mild positive interest. Clearly, these copy lines are of low interest to consumers.

As you can see, this kind of question is extremely valuable. With a thorough and imaginative analysis, it can spark many concept improvements. In the current example, this single question was the source of several recommendations that never could have been made from other data provided by the test. The recommendations included:

1. Tighten up the concept, especially the beginning, which is boring and not grabbing.
2. Revise the description of the existence of an "advanced formula." As currently written, the absence of an explanation of what an advanced formula is or what it accomplishes weakens the benefit.
3. Strengthen the uniqueness claim, or drop it. Just talking about uniqueness—especially in a bragging, exciting, announcement format (as done here)—is not working for this product.
4. If the uniqueness claim is revised or dropped, consider changing the name Emerge. Select a name that supports one of the key benefits such as protection, softness, or shininess.
5. Keep the idea of "patented molecules" and "special buffing action." In fact, strengthen them. But remove the "patented molecule" and "special buffing action" labels. They do not generate very high interest.
6. "Superior results" and "superior hair condition" are empty ad lingo terms. Their benefits must be either supported more clearly or dropped.

The concept was revised along these lines and was retested. Purchase Interest rose dramatically.

UNCOVERING MAJOR ADVANTAGES AND DISADVANTAGES

Another valuable diagnostic question is one that measures whether or not the concept communicates any *major* advantages or *major* disadvantages. When in-home pregnancy test kits were first developed, concept tests repeatedly showed several major problems, including consumers' perceptions that long or complicated procedures were required to use the product. Cost was also an important concern.

Can concept problems like these lead to opportunities in the real world? Absolutely. Two kit marketers have used this kind of information, each in a different way. Carter-Wallace, Inc., marketer of the Answer line, is now asking consumers, "Why pay more for the same answer?" The Warner-Lambert Co., maker of e.p.t., is now taking advantage of a new technology that allows consumers to do the test as early as one day after a missed menstrual period, with results determined in 10 to 20 minutes.

In the skin protection category, concept tests reveal that some people simply will not purchase sun-blocking products like tanning lotions, creams, and sunscreens. No matter what your concept states, a few continue to believe that one major disadvantage still exists: The product is not good for your skin. Some talk in terms of clogged pores. Others think blocking the sun creates skin problems. But regardless of the language, the common element is concern about the effect of the product on the user's skin. A smart analyst could use this complaint as a catalyst for a new product, perhaps a sun product with perceived "healthy" ingredients, like vitamin E or aloe.

If you ask users of packaged spaghetti sauce what they especially dislike about a concept for a new sauce, one disadvantage frequently mentioned would be that the ingredients are not fresh or that certain ingredients (basil or oregano, clams or meat) are absent or are in insufficient quantity. Consequently, many cooks either do not like to use packaged sauces (except in an emergency) or choose to modify the sauces they buy. This finding suggests several marketing actions. A company could market a basic, lightly seasoned sauce, positioned as especially suitable for doctoring by the cook. Or perhaps a premium line, with lots of extra or special ingredients that are absent from current products.

As you can see, a Disadvantage question may not always tell you what to do but it certainly helps call an opportunity to your attention. But you must use some care in how it is administered.

Administering the Question

When you ask respondents if a product has any advantages or disadvantages, the odds are they'll mention a few. Some might be significant, but others might be relatively unimportant. The problem is that the very act of asking a question creates an opinion. If you ask, "Is there something about the product you don't like?" the respondent often obliges by finding something to dislike, something that might never have been thought of without the question.

A simple clarification question can tell you exactly how meaningful those answers are. Just ask the respondent if there are any major advantages (or disadvantages) associated with the product. Depending upon the category or the specific concept, you may find it easier to talk in terms of benefits instead of advantages. Here is an example of how to ask the question.

Concept Testing

Chart 6-2. Emphasizing major advantages.

	Concept A	Concept B
Had high Purchase Interest	13%	㉘%
Played back main benefit	59	65
Named one or more advantages	47	52
Named one or more disadvantages	23	18
Found something hard to believe	14	11
Named one or more *major* advantages	26	㊹

Do you think this product would have . . .

Major benefits ☐
Minor benefits ☐
No benefits at all ☐

Another approach that also works well is to start by asking respondents what advantages they associate with your product. Then ask if any of those advantages are major.

Regardless of the question format, you will often find big differences between the kinds of things an individual thinks are a major advantage and things that are merely a minor advantage.

A detergent survey encountered the following interesting situation. Two different approaches were being considered for a new product. Concept B was very superior to Concept A on Purchase Interest, yet various diagnostic questions showed only tiny differences between the two. What caused the difference in Purchase Interest? Our Major Advantage question pinpointed the answer (see Chart 6-2). Although respondents mentioned similar advantages for A and B, Concept B communicated the benefits in a manner that better suggested they were *major* advantages. Concept A presented these same benefits in a less exciting, less dynamic manner, and fewer consumers felt the advantages of Concept A were major.

Another vivid example of the power of this question comes from the small-appliance industry. A few years ago, before the product was actually marketed, a concept test for an iron that automatically shut off received a level of Purchase Interest that was above average for its category. And so did an electric frying pan with a built-in electronic timer that shut the pan off automatically.

Other Useful Diagnostic Tools

The Major Advantage question revealed that the iron's automatic shut-off feature was a major advantage because it could prevent a disastrous accident. But the frying pan's electronic timer was not much of a major advantage; consumers reported they usually stood in the vicinity of the pan as they cooked.

Recent marketplace activity confirmed just how accurate these insights were. A newly introduced electric frying pan with an electronic timer is selling poorly, primarily as a gift item. But the automatic shutoff iron quickly captured a double-digit share of industry sales within a few months of introduction.

Here's another example. In the air freshener category, a common consumer complaint is that the product dissipates quickly. Airwick Industries responded with a time-release product that releases the fragrance throughout the day, steadily and continually.

Using the Responses

Many of the examples suggest that Major Advantage or Major Disadvantage questions are useful as diagnostic tools. But sometimes these questions can do more. Occasionally they can provide you with overall go/no-go guidance when traditional "big picture" questions like Purchase Interest cannot be used.

A case in point. Almost two decades ago, when RCA began seriously to consider if it should market a video disc player, a Purchase Interest question was of little help in making a final decision. The problem was (and still is, for that matter) that most new, expensive products initially attract a tiny segment—individuals who are motivated to be the first in their community to own the product, or extreme enthusiasts whose passion exceeds the needs and desires of most people in the mass market. So the number of people who initially indicate they definitely will buy one of these products—be it a food processor or a video disc player—is quite low. Unfortunately, there is no accurate way to measure the extent to which Purchase Interest will build up in the few years after introduction, as the mass market comes in contact with the product and begins to modify its interest in it.

In RCA's case, potential customers liked many aspects of the product, especially the quality of the sound and picture. However, a major disadvantage to the product kept popping up: the lack of a recording capability. Initially, RCA management made a judgment call and decided to proceed with developing the video disc player. This was back in the days when VCRs themselves were quite new to the market and were priced at $1,000 or more. The prevailing thinking of the time was that the two types of machines might not compete with each other; one would be used to record programming off the air for later viewing, and the other for store-bought entertainment packages. Today, smug Monday morning quarterbacks are highly critical of RCA's actions. It's easy to be brilliant after the fact. But during the early 1970s, some rather knowledgeable industry observers thought RCA's product had a chance.

Unfortunately for RCA, the level of Purchase Interest in video disc players did not rise appreciably once the product was introduced to the marketplace. Most prospective video disc player customers continued to be uninterested in buying it because of one major disadvantage, the lack of a recording capability. RCA ignored the signal and continued to market the product. During this same time period, VCR sales began to increase, prices began to drop, and sales spurted even further. According to *Advertising Age* estimates, after 15 years of development effort and a $780 million investment, RCA removed the product from the market.

Does the Major Disadvantage question provide valuable information? I say yes. But don't take my word for it. Ask RCA. There's also another point to this story: Sometimes it takes nothing more than a tiny closed-end question, buried in the back of a questionnaire, to make a survey come alive and provide actionable, useful answers.

WHAT BRAND DOES YOUR PRODUCT MOST RESEMBLE?

Another diagnostic question you can use when testing an unbranded concept or one with an unfamiliar brand name is to ask consumers which brand the concept most resembles. The fun starts when respondents don't answer as expected. In some categories there are many brands that make similar claims. Therefore an analyst might expect answers to this special question to parallel each brand's market share. If the answers differ from expectation, it's a clear signal that the positioning is communicating something different than expected.

In a recent test respondents were asked, "Which brand does this product most resemble?" We expected that the leading brand in the category would score highest on this question, if only because of its greater familiarity. But it didn't happen. Respondents associated the test concept with a lesser-used brand a disproportionate amount of the time; see Chart 6-3.

If this were your concept, you would have to decide whether you wanted

Other Useful Diagnostic Tools

Chart 6-3. Brand most similar.

	Brand Used Most Often	Competitor Most Similar to Test Concept
Competitor A	17%	14%
Competitor B	11	7
Competitor C	8	(15)

your product to be positioned so near to a less-used competitor. The question does not tell you what to do, but it does raise the all-important red flag.

Sometimes a different situation occurs. Perhaps you have deliberately aimed your concept at a specific competitor. If respondents don't associate your concept with that competitor, you should be questioning the accuracy of its execution. The question provides the necessary early warning.

"SOMETHING RUBS ME THE WRONG WAY"

It usually pays to be specific when formulating questions for a concept test. The more vague and unstructured a question is, the more likely that the response will be just as vague and unhelpful. Specific questions work best: "Is the concept unique?" (or believable, important, persuasive).

Getting at Hidden Problems

But although the benefits of being specific are significant, there is one major risk. If your question battery has not covered a key dimension (perhaps a unique one that is only rarely operative), you run the risk of not being able to figure out why a concept failed. Think of a product that consumers fear will become obsolete in the future. If we ask standard questions such as what they dislike about it or how it could be improved, this type of response might never come up.

Or think of a product concept that inadvertently gives consumers a confusing or conflicting message. Back in 1982, the Clairol division of Bristol-Myers failed in its attempt to market Small Miracle, a hair conditioner that claimed to last for as long as three washings. The product and its con-

107

cept had been well researched, and the company was admittedly disappointed about its failure.

According to *Advertising Age*'s analysis of the failure, trade sources advanced several reasons why consumers spurned Small Miracle. Consumers said, in effect:

1. "The manufacturer says it can last for three washings but I like to put conditioner on my hair after every washing. Can I use Small Miracle after *every* washing if I wish to or must I only use it after every third washing?"
2. "I don't like to use certain products on my hair, like soap for example, because they leave a film or residue. Small Miracle lasts for three washings. Does this mean there will be a residue or coating on my hair?"

Although these are important problems, they are subtle. They involve investigating nuance and shading of meaning. Unfortunately, standard direct questions do not always work well when investigating subtle issues. If you show consumers a concept statement stating the product can last for up to three washings and then ask if they think it could be used after every hair washing, most would answer "Of course." But the stated answer may differ from the more hidden feeling: "Maybe this product is not for me because I like to put a lot of conditioner on my hair after every washing."

The bottom line: Sometimes there are things about a product that trouble potential users that do not emerge from the typical open-end and closed-end questions normally included in a concept test.

Asking the Right Question

There is one way around this problem. Ask people to rate the product in terms of whether or not "something about it rubs me the wrong way." I have experimented with various methods of asking the question. The one I use most often is to include the following question in a self-administered question battery:

Something rubs me the   □ □ □ □ □ □ □   Nothing rubs me the wrong
    wrong way   way

This is a general, catchall attribute. It may not even be necessary to tabulate or analyze responses unless all else fails.

In a test for a novel small appliance, Purchase Interest was quite low, but analysis of all the key closed-end and open-end questions did not explain why. However, something about the concept rubbed 62 percent of the sample the wrong way, well above average. Cross tabulating other data revealed that those who were rubbed the wrong way had extremely high concern over issues of appliance longevity, quality, and service or repair availability. A common thread was the fear that a sophisticated element of the product, a new microchip, would fail, making the product inoperative.

In the data for Reasons for Low Purchase Interest in the total sample, none of these concerns came up very often. In the Dislike question responses, only 42 percent disliked something. And the answers they gave were widespread, not just those three reasons. But among those individuals who felt something about the product rubbed them the wrong way, practically all mentioned these complaints. Clearly, a general "fishing expedition" question can serve a useful purpose on occasion.

CHANGES AND IMPROVEMENTS

Respondents can tell you a lot about how to improve a concept. All you have to do is ask.

We've heard all the objections: The consumer is not an expert, the consumer doesn't know how to suggest changes or improvements, and so on. My answer is, "Hogwash." The analytic secret lies both in the question you ask and what you do with the answers you get.

This question has worked quite well for me:

In what ways, if any, could this product be changed or improved? I'd like you to tell me anything you can think of, no matter how minor it seems.

For established product categories, you can also try asking consumers what additional feature they would like to see in a new product that is not already available in their usual brands.

When interpreting the answers, take them with a grain of salt. Look for patterns of response, rather than at the specific solutions suggested. Which parts of the concept are evoking criticism? Which parts are respondents trying to fix?

When we ask consumers about new products in the sun care category, two problems repeatedly come up: The product is too greasy, and the product washes off or rubs off too easily and too quickly. Surely you could get at least one product idea from these complaints.

In a test for a new cleansing product, one of the candidate concepts

Chart 6-4. Ask consumers to help you improve your concept.

	First Test	Retest
Suggested changes or improvements	(32)%	19%
Prove product works as described	(18)	4
Prove price is fair	11	15
Prove product is easy to use	6	3
High Purchase Interest	13	(20)

achieved poor results. In addition, 32 percent of all respondents exposed to it recommended at least one change or improvement. That's a pretty high number and should be considered seriously.

Many respondents suggested changes in wording or graphics that would communicate in a more meaningful or believable fashion how the product works. Their specific recommendations on how to remedy the problem may not have had any practical merit, but they clearly indicated the source of the problem: Consumers didn't believe that the product was as effective as described.

The concept was rewritten, with greater emphasis on proving how the product worked effectively, and then retested. "Top box" Purchase Interest rose dramatically, from 13 to 20 percent. And the percentage suggesting changes or improvements in the revised concept fell significantly, particularly in the area of proving how the concept works (see Chart 6-4).

Another example, this time from the liquid bleach category. Consumers frequently grumble about one major problem with this category: the strong smell of the product. In concept test after test, if you ask consumers what changes they recommend, changing or fixing the smell is near the top of the list.

The Clorox Company took the advice to heart and did something about it: introduced Fresh Scent liquid bleach. It is priced about 10 percent higher than the company's other brands of bleach and is doing quite well at the cash register. Independent financial analysts expect this product to increase Clorox's total bleach business by at least 5 percent. Not bad, when the total market is $500 million a year. And not bad when responses to one question told you what to do.

Sometimes the answers are so revealing that you merely have to read them with an open mind to get a new product idea. A major problem with the maple syrup category, for instance, is the calorie content. When you ask consumers what changes or improvements they recommend, some suggest using artificial sweeteners. Others ask for products with less sugar. Still others, more straightforwardly, request fewer calories. The obvious solution: a lower-calorie maple syrup product. And the manufacturers who listened to the consumer and marketed this type of product hit paydirt; rising sales of low-calorie syrups boosted the total category by 12 percent in just one year.

In the packaged bread category, a frequent dissatisfaction voiced by consumers is the waste that occurs when the loaf goes stale before it is completely used up. The solution: a half-loaf package.

In the chewing gum category, a major complaint about chewing gum is the relatively fast loss of flavor. As many as three-quarters of all gum chewers complain of this. The solution: finding new technology that will allow the flavor to be released slowly, over a longer period of time.

As you can see, consumers can tell you a great deal about how to improve a concept—if you ask them.

HOW MUCH WILL IT COST?

At one time, the popcorn industry was strictly a low-priced commodity business. If a company attempted to market a popcorn brand that was priced a bit higher than other brands, sales response would have been quite disappointing. Then along came a premium-priced product with the incredible name of Orville Reddenbacher's Gourmet Popping Corn. It was priced higher than the competition but positioned itself as a quality product with its "pops bigger" sales message. Although interest in the concept was high, management was concerned about the effect of a higher price on sales. A series of price-related questions found price not to be a problem. The product was introduced, and within a few years, it owned more than 25 percent of the popcorn market.

The moral of the story? An investigation of consumer price perceptions can be a highly useful concept testing technique.

There are many different ways to measure reactions to price. Most fall into one of three categories:

1. *Absolute Knowledge.* How much do you think the product we have been talking about will cost?
2. *Relative Knowledge.* In your opinion, would the price of this product be less than competition, the same as competition, or more than competition?
3. *Perceived Value.* Does this product offer good value for the money?

Concept Testing

In most concept test circumstances, a price-related question can be very productive, regardless of the kind of question used. About the only situation where the pricing question is unproductive is a product in an established and frequently used category, priced similarly to competitive products. In this test environment, price reaction to the various concept candidates being evaluated usually tends to be similar; there is little differentiation from one concept to another, and most consumers think the new product will be about as costly as competitive products. As a result, the price question is useless as a means of discriminating between concept alternatives.

Existing Category: Higher-Priced Product

In the spaghetti sauce category, price questions included in most concept tests consistently show that consumers are resistant to premium-priced sauces. Many will reject the product, no matter what product benefits are being offered, and price is their primary reason. However, these same questions identify a small group of consumers who are interested in premium-priced sauces, just as long as they think they are getting added value for the added price.

Is this useful information? You bet it is. The Prince Company, with a 10 percent share of the spaghetti sauce market, according to *Advertising Age*, is introducing a line of premium-priced sauces with unique ingredients and special packaging (each unit packaged in a Mason jar). It will not be a mass-market product. The target will be cooks interested in premium-priced sauces. Pricing will be considerably higher than competitive sauces.

Existing Category: Heavy Price Discounting by Existing Brands

The wine cooler category has grown from nothing to more than $1 billion in just five years. And the growth continues. In 1986, revenue rose by almost 70 percent over the previous year. Yet problems exist for new brands attempting to enter this fast-growing market. Four-packs, originally priced as high as $3.69, are being discounted by some retailers to $1.99. On top of this, some brands are offering 50¢-off coupons and $2 rebates.

This is a difficult price environment in which to compete. A recent concept test confirmed this by producing disappointing scores for a proposed new brand. Questions measuring reactions to the proposed price helped to explain why the product performed so poorly. In spite of the category's explosive sales growth, some industry observers are expecting a major shakeout to occur shortly. And the price question explains part of the reason.

Other Useful Diagnostic Tools

New Category

Back in 1974 General Foods introduced Lean Strips, a textured vegetable protein strip that was designed to compete against bacon. Preliminary research found that consumers liked the taste and texture of Lean Strips. However, concept research found that consumers judged the price in relation to bacon. When Lean Strips was priced lower than bacon, the product did well. But if Lean Strips was priced higher than bacon, projected sales were disappointing.

When the product was tested in the marketplace, General Foods encountered similar results. As bacon rose in price, Lean Strips did well at the cash register; when bacon prices fell, Lean Strips sold poorly. Unfortunately for General Foods, retail bacon prices were based on wholesale pork prices, and pork is a commodity that can fluctuate widely in price. For a company like General Foods, with relatively high fixed expenses for manufacturing, marketing, and administration, this was a serious problem. Of course, the company still had the option of pricing Lean Strips high and marketing it toward consumers specifically concerned about high cholesterol. Unfortunately, the size of this market was too small to support the brand, and it was never successfully marketed.

Price Relative to Competition

I recommend that you include a price question in every concept test you do. I have had good results with this "relative" version:

In your opinion, would the price of this product be . . .

Less than competition	☐
The same as competition	☐
More than competition	☐

This version of the question provides opportunity for followup probes. For example, if consumers tell you the price is more than they expect to pay for a competitive product, you have a marvelous opportunity to identify the factors they believe cause the higher price. The insights you gain can be quite valuable, often giving pointers for promotional or repositioning efforts.

A case in point is provided by Goodyear's automobile tires. The company's tire image is very positive. Consumers think Goodyear tires are of high quality and last a long time. A few years ago the company had one

Concept Testing

Chart 6-5. Price information could be important.

	Concept A	Concept B
The price is		
Less than competition	⑯%	9%
Same as competition	㊻	54
More than competition	21	㊲

problem with its tire image: Research showed that many consumers thought
the price of a Goodyear tire was much higher than it actually was.

This perception of high price was costing Goodyear sales volume. Purchase Interest was correlated with price perceptions—the higher the assumed price, the lower the desire to purchase a Goodyear tire. In further
investigations, the company learned that consumers thought the high price
was because the tires were of high quality. In effect, consumers were not
refuting the quality claim; they were just unwilling to pay extra to get higher-
quality tires. The solution suggested by the data was for Goodyear to communicate to consumers that their quality perceptions were accurate but their
price perceptions were incorrect.

In a recent concept test for a product in the telephone equipment category, two concepts were tested. Although each stimulated similar levels of
Purchase Interest, respondents thought one was more costly; see Chart 6-5.

Followup questions showed that consumers thought the higher-priced
Concept B was a better-quality product that would last longer. This led me
to two conclusions. First, Concept B had the more interesting promotional
angle because of its performance on the question of price *and* quality/lon-
gevity. Second, the concept should be revised to place greater stress on product quality and longevity, key factors associated with the perceived higher
price.

Keep in mind that price is a two-edged sword. Consider the flip side of
the coin: when you expect consumers to think your concept is priced competitively, and they tell you they expect to pay *less* for it than for the competition.

HONESTY

Consumers must believe that your concept honestly and truthfully portrays
the product, or its performance will suffer.

Take the marketing of salt-free foods as an example. Virtually every

114

food manufacturer has, at one time or another, attempted to market a salt-free version of its products. From cereal to tuna fish to after-dinner snacks, most efforts have generally been unsuccessful. The problem is that consumers believe most low-salt or no-salt products do not taste very good. A promise of "no salt but the same great taste" just does not ring true. When you make this claim, some consumers will think the concept is not being honest and reduce their interest in purchasing the product.

Sometimes perceptions of dishonesty exist even when efforts are made to be completely accurate. The problem is that the concept's wording inadvertently creates doubts about the product. Not doubts about a specific operational or functional benefit, but a generalized lack of confidence in the overall product. The concept's language causes the respondent to say, in effect, "They are trying to pull a fast one on me with this product."

Concepts can fail because of this lack of perceived honesty or trust. Unfortunately, the data produced by most questions give no clues that the concept wording itself is causing doubts on such basic values as honesty, candor, and trustworthiness. Sometimes "disbelief" or "hard to understand" ratings are higher, but not always.

One way to determine if your concept's wording causes doubts on honesty, candor, or trustworthiness is to ask the respondent to rate how honest the concept is. Try a seven-point bipolar semantic differential question like this:

Description is honest   □ □ □ □ □ □ □   Description is not honest

In a test for a new over-the-counter medical product, the concept, because of government rules and restrictions, had to state product benefits in a very specific manner. The concept writer was given very little freedom.

The concept scored very poorly but there were few clues to explain why. Diagnostic data suggested consumers heard the benefits but weren't especially impressed with them. Analysis of this special question revealed the source of the problem: The Honesty rating was much lower than usual. When responses to the Main Idea, Advantages, and Changes and Improvements questions were cross tabbed by those with high and low Honesty ratings, the concept elements that caused the problem were quickly pinpointed.

This type of problem occurs infrequently. Invariably it's caused by a problem or restriction that means the writer has to choose words too carefully. Unfortunately, when the problem does occur, there is virtually no way of identifying it unless you include this type of question.

A BETTER WAY TO USE BELIEVABILITY

Believability should not be just a standard question that we always include in a concept test because it's "company policy." It is a critical issue that can affect the life or death of a proposed new brand.

In the 1970s, a task force of bright tobacco marketers employed by Consolidated Cigar Corporation tried to counter the cigar industry's declining sales trend. In addition to the public's general concern about the relationship between smoking and health, the cigar industry was further stigmatized by perceptions that cigars were smelly, strong, and offensive to others.

One idea that popped up was for a smell-less cigar that tasted like the traditional one but did not offend nearby nonsmokers with a strong, pungent aroma. Eventually a product, named Flite, was developed and placed into test market. The product flopped after being test marketed for more than one year. Consolidated Cigar executives could not convince cigar smokers that the enjoyment they derive from the smoking experience could be satisfied by smoking Flite. Clearly, these smokers did not believe that a cigar could taste as good and provide as much enjoyment if the smell was manipulated or removed.

Another example, this time from the foot care industry. A few years ago Dr. Scholl's introduced a line of six foot-care products, targeted toward women 25 to 49, under the name Foot Beauty. The line did not sell well. The company found that foot beauty is not a believable claim. When the company restaged the line, naming it Smooth Touch and moving away from foot beauty to foot care and pampering, disbelief in the product's positioning declined and sales began to rise.

The Flite cigar and Dr. Scholl's experiences have been shared by many other companies. It supports the point that believability and credibility are major features that a concept must achieve to succeed.

Because believability is so important, most researchers automatically include it in every concept survey. It gets asked by rote and analyzed by rote. As a result, it is one of the most misused of all diagnostic questions. When the Believability question fails, it most often is because of incorrect analytic techniques. In other words, the question would work fine if only we would analyze it correctly.

The typical Believability question goes something like, "Is there anything about this product that is hard to believe?" In many categories only 10 to 20 percent of the sample finds something about the concept hard to

Other Useful Diagnostic Tools

Chart 6-6. A new look at Believability.

	Total Sample	Consumers Understanding Main Idea
Base	(200)	
Main Idea of Product		
Taste	75%	
Convenience	49	
Taste *plus* convenience	31 ——————┐	
Anything Hard to Believe?		↓
Base	(200)	(62)
No	90%	68%
Yes	10	㉜
What Is Hard to Believe?		
Base	(200)	(62)
Good taste	3%	⑩%
Easy to prepare *plus* good taste	6	⑲
All other comments	1	3

believe, and some researchers mistakenly conclude this level of disbelief is not too serious.

Chart 6-6 contains data for a food concept with the twin benefits of good taste *and* ease of preparation. It shows how looking at the basic Believability data in a slightly different way can produce a very different conclusion.

Most researchers analyzing the Believability data of Chart 6-6 would never even prepare the second column. Just working from the first column, they would observe that 31 percent of all consumers understand the main concept, and that "only" 6 percent disbelieve the main benefit. Many would mutter, "Some respondents always find something hard to believe," or "The 10 percent level is really not all that high." Most would conclude there are no disbelief-related problems with this concept. I think this is a poor conclusion.

First, take one step back and think about the responses we are most interested in: those from people who grasped the *complete* message. If a consumer didn't grasp the complete message, then it's not especially surprising that something about it is unclear or unbelievable. Thus, we should be most interested in studying the 31 percent who understand our full main benefit.

Once we analyze the level of disbelief among the 31 percent who correctly understand the main benefit, we reach a different conclusion. Most of the disbelief for the concept is stimulated by the main sales point. While 10 percent of the total sample disbelieve something about the concept, 32 percent of those who comprehend the main benefit do not believe something. Furthermore, virtually all the disbelief (29 percent of the 32 percent) centers around the good taste of the product or that it is easy to prepare while also tasting good—the product's main reason for being. My conclusion: This concept has a serious deficiency.

One rule of thumb you might use is that the level of believability among individuals who understand the main product benefit should equal or exceed the level of believability among those who don't grasp the full message. If you find a higher level of disbelief among those who got the full message, it is often indicative of a communications problem.

This example concerns Believability. However, the same principles of analysis can be applied to questions measuring concept elements disliked or not understood, or for any other diagnostic you include in your concept test.

OVERALL INTEREST

In addition to Purchase Interest, you might want to add a question that measures Overall Interest. The specific form of the question can vary. I have used a 1 to 10 scale, an excellent to poor scale, and a bipolar high to low scale.

But regardless of the form of the question, Overall Interest is an occasionally useful diagnostic tool that can help you evaluate the underlying strength of the concept. Most of the time Purchase Interest and Overall Interest produce similar scores; the concept that wins on one usually wins on the other. But sometimes a concept scores well on one and is weak on the other. This signals that something is amiss; start doing cross tabs to figure out what is happening.

Some researchers think that asking two related questions is a problem. They say, "What happens if Purchase Interest and Overall Interest give conflicting results? Which one do I believe?" I say a conflicting response is

Other Useful Diagnostic Tools

Chart 6-7. Auto after-market concept.

	Percentage
High Purchase Interest in the concept	18%
High Overall Interest in the concept	5
Concept rated "very unique"	3

not a problem but an opportunity. It lets you gain specific information that could help improve your concept.

Let's assume a concept stimulated high Overall Interest and low Purchase Interest. Analyzing responses to various questions among consumers who gave a conflicting rating could prove helpful to you in determining whether:

1. They like the product but do not think it's unique.
2. They like the product but are highly satisfied with their current brand.
3. The product is attractive to the consumer, but not enough to influence purchase.

That's important information, isn't it? It gives you a clearer idea of how to begin improving your concept.

Now take the reverse situation, a concept that stimulates high Purchase Interest and low Overall Interest. It happened recently in a concept test for an automotive after-market product (see Chart 6-7). The inconsistency seemed to signal the possibility of a problem with the concept.

Eventually we found the source of the problem. Consumers were telling us they thought the product wasn't very different from other products. They would buy it if a need existed but they had no special interest in it because they had no commitment or loyalty to *any* brand in the category.

Since this product was designed with some unique features to help it stand apart from its competitors, it was clear that these features were not being clearly communicated. As a result of this question, we recommended that revisions be made to emphasize the unique benefits of this concept to strengthen Overall Interest and translate it into even higher brand preference.

119

IN CONCLUSION

On balance, a good concept test does much more than help pick a winner. It provides lots of clues on how to improve the concept being tested. A diagnostic tool like the forced-exposure question helps to identify specific elements that must be replaced or expanded. Questions that measure Perceived Cost, Advantages and Disadvantages, Honesty, Believability, and Similarity to Other Brands can also help to identify problems and suggest solutions.

And sometimes, merely by asking consumers how to change or improve a concept, you can uncover valuable insights. All you have to do is remember to ask the question.

7
Predicting First-Year Volume

Top management listens to most proposals to market a new product with one question in mind: "How many units will we sell?" New-product people talk about opportunities, competitive strategies, unexploited niches. "All well and good," thinks the chap in charge. "But how many cases can we move?"

To answer this question, many companies are experimenting with mathematical models that forecast first-year sales volume from concept test data. This is a recent research innovation. Lots of claims have been made by the first few research companies to jump into this business. Some of the promises were, to be charitable, a bit exaggerated.

THE STORY OF FORECASTING SYSTEMS

To help you understand the true capabilities of these forecasting systems and let you separate the wheat from the chaff, let's do a brief review of how these forecasting systems evolved and how they now operate.

Simulated Test Marketing

During the 1970s, the art of simulated test marketing (STM) received widespread publicity. STM provided users with estimates of actual sales volume without the need for in-market testing. By omitting the test market phase of a product's introduction, a marketer could save millions of dollars and 6 to 18 months of time, and not tip his hand to competitors. In many instances a traditional test market could be replaced with a statistical simulation that cost $30,000 to $40,000 and required only six to eight weeks to complete.

Concept Testing

STMs were not suitable for every product and they could not answer every question answered by a traditional test market, but in many instances, the savings in time and money, coupled with the secrecy advantage, were significant tradeoff benefits to marketers.

To estimate sales volume by STM, the marketer had to produce three things: final production-model products, actual packaging, and a finished commercial. Different STM models used variations of the following basic system.

1. A sample of consumers was shown commercials for the test product and its main competitors.
2. Consumers were then invited to "shop" for one product from the test category, either at a real or a simulated store. They were usually provided with "seed money"—discount coupons, play money, or actual cash.
3. The number who "bought" the test product provided the STM model with an estimate of the first-year trial rate, the percent of the population that would buy the product at least once within the first 12 months. In some cases the "buy" rate uncovered in the survey was statistically adjusted to compensate for survey bias.
4. Those who "bought" the product were then invited to take it home and use it for a short trial period. A followup telephone reinterview then measured interest in repurchasing the product as well as the respondent's forecasted frequency and volume of future purchase. These estimates were plugged into the STM model (and adjusted to compensate for consumer tendencies to overstate their future volume).
5. The resulting first-year volume estimate was a pretty good approximation of volume for a product that achieved 100 percent consumer awareness and store distribution. Since new products do not immediately achieve these levels, the estimate was then adjusted downward to compensate for the expected level of awareness and distribution.

Experience repeatedly showed that the resulting forecast was pretty accurate. And even when an STM did not *precisely* predict first-year volume, it still was quite useful in suggesting the general likelihood of success or failure.

Predicting First-Year Volume

Secret Mathematical Models

In the early 1980s some STM practitioners began to sell forecasts based solely on concept tests. In other words, they attempted to forecast first-year volume before the advertising, the package, or even the product actually existed. Each of the companies claiming to provide this "expertise" developed proprietary mathematical models using secret formulas, private assumptions, and confidential estimating procedures. Often the techniques were kept secret to ensure that the sponsoring company kept its unique lock on the market.

Reaction was mixed. Some early clients expressed great disappointment about the accuracy of these predictions. Others felt they were useful as rough guides. But all parties did agree on one point. At best, a concept-based volume forecast can provide you with a very rough approximation of market potential—and the risk of being wrong is quite high. Needless to say, client opinions differed widely from the claims made by the marketers of these predictive models.

Computer Models

By the time the mid-1980s arrived, several new models became available. They are products of skilled computer software companies that have gone public with very precise descriptions of what they do and how they do it. Anyone still using a company that issues forecasts from a model using secret "black box" methodology is foolish, given the new realities of the marketplace.

These new computer programs allow every company to prepare volume projections without relying on overpriced services or confidential methods. All that is needed is raw data from a concept test, which can be conducted by any reputable research organization. Merely plug the concept test data into the model and the analyst is off and running—faster, more accurately, and at lower cost than ever before.

But before you use this kind of data, a word of caution. Be very careful. While the accuracy of these models is improving, they are still imprecise estimating tools. It is not surprising, given the lack of product, package, and advertising. In effect, all of the final production values that differentiate one product from another are factored out by the model.

As *rough* volume forecasts, models can be useful. But as *precise* predictions of first-year volume, they are highly suspect. A brief review of how these models work will help you use these models more effectively and avoid a few traps and pitfalls.

HOW CONCEPT FORECASTS WORK

Step One

The first piece of information required by most models is an estimate of the percentage of the population that will try the product at least once in its first year on the market. If the product and package existed, a simulated shopping experiment could provide this data. Since no product or package exists, most companies use the Purchase Interest score from a concept test to derive a first-year trial estimate. One company uses the "definitely will buy" score. Another takes 90 percent of the "definitely will buy" score and 15 percent of the "probably will buy" score. Another uses 80 percent of the "definites" and 20 percent of the "probables." Still another uses 75 percent and 25 percent. Others use different scale weightings. Each weighting system is passionately defended by its creator. All seem to work well.

Step Two

Step two is to estimate the number of one-time triers who will make at least one repeat purchase during year one. As before, the best way to calculate this information is to let consumers actually try your product and measure their repeat purchase likelihood. Unfortunately, no product yet exists.

The way around this problem is to make an estimate based upon your company's experience with the category. If the typical product is repurchased by 50 percent of the people who bought it last time, then 50 percent is the number to plug into the forecast model. If you have no knowledge of the category, some models will provide an estimate based upon previous experiences with other products in the category.

Obviously, the repeat-purchase estimate is a weak link in the predictive process, regardless of how it is derived. You never know for sure if your concept will stimulate more or less than average repeat buying once it reaches the market.

Step Three

Step three is to plug two additional volumetric factors into the model: the number of weeks between each purchase, and the number and size of the unit typically bought on each purchase occasion.

Most models take data on purchase frequency and amount purchased directly from questions included in the concept test, and adjust each estimate in some manner. The reason for the adjustment is that consumers usually cannot accurately provide volume and frequency information; they tend to overstate their intended consumption. Adjustment factors are calculated by examining historical relationships. One technique is to correlate responses to similar questions in previous concept surveys versus actual diary panel or store scanner data for those same products. The resulting deflation factor is applied to the test concept.

Step Four

Based on step three, it is possible to forecast year one volume assuming 100 percent consumer awareness and 100 percent product distribution. Step four deflates this forecast by the level of distribution and consumer awareness you anticipate that your product will achieve. Some models allow you to plug in advertising weight estimates and convert them to appropriate awareness levels. And if your budget has not yet been set, some models can provide you with typical awareness and distribution patterns, based on their experience with related products.

Step Five

As a final step, some models allow you to plug in special factors like seasonal variations in category sales, anticipated trade deals, coupons, and other special factors to help you refine your prediction. The more sophisticated the model, the more it accommodates special treatments and allows you to adjust your prediction by the size of the treatment as well as the point in the year that the event will occur (for instance, delaying advertising will delay awareness buildup and result in lower year one volume).

SHORTCOMINGS OF FORECASTING

As you can see, the model is based on assumptions that previously observed relationships and interactions will be applicable to your concept. And the truth is that, in most cases, these relationships *do* apply. But all you need is one relationship to act atypically, and the entire volume forecast is miles off target.

The bottom line: Using a volume forecast for anything more than a very rough preliminary guesstimate is quite foolhardy. Unfortunately, top management in some client companies force the new-product marketing executives to produce volume estimates early in the development cycle, causing a greater-than-deserved emphasis on these models.

The risk of a poor forecast varies from product to product. In some categories where the marketing practices of various competitors follow "typical" patterns, accurately predicting first-year volume is easier. In other categories the task is more difficult; snack food, for example.

Snack food brands make extensive use of off-shelf displays, such as a bin at the end of an aisle or a display rack near the check-out counter. According to the Point-of-Purchase Advertising Institute, consumers are 250 percent more likely to buy an item when it is located in an off-shelf display. And if the item is located in an off-shelf display *and* consumers remember having seen an ad for it, they are 600 percent more likely to buy it. Clearly the leverage associated with off-shelf displays is awesome.

Unfortunately, off-shelf displays vary widely in their effectiveness. Some are larger, more colorful, or placed in better locations. Consequently, it is harder to predict first-year volume for a snack food that makes extensive use of off-shelf displays than for, say, a shelf-bound carpet freshener product.

It is especially hard to estimate first-year volume for a new product in a new category that consumers never used or heard of before. The immensely successful Post-it line of memo pads from 3M is a case in point.

Post-its are pads of small colored memo sheets with a sticky adhesive strip along one edge. The user can write a note and stick it directly onto another sheet of paper, eliminating the need for a paper clip. A memo from a Post-it pad can also be attached to a wall, telephone, chair, or any place you would like to leave a visible message. The benefit of Post-it is that the adhesive is not permanent; the memo sheet can easily be removed, with no damage to whatever it was attached to.

When Post-it was first developed, there was a great deal of uncertainty about its true market potential. Executives from 3M admit that the decision to market it was "a bit touch and go." On the one hand, many in the company believed Post-it was worth the added cost and that consumers would flock to the product once they experienced the ease and convenience of using it. However, some of the preliminary investigation yielded several red flags. Consumer comments suggested that the idea of a product that would eliminate the need for a paper clip (big deal!) and would not mar the surface of the underlying document (can't be true!) was not persuasive. It took seeing, living with, and trying the product to convince many consumers to purchase it regularly. Had 3M relied on a typical print concept test and first-year sales forecasts to make a go/no-go decision, Post-it probably would not be on the market today.

Post-it is not the only product for which first-year volume forecasts are suspect. The problem occurs quite frequently. Another example: Back in the early 1970s a young man by the name of Fred Smith had the ridiculous idea of an overnight delivery company that linked the entire country through a central depot in Memphis. First-year volumetric forecasts from concept data for new business-to-business products didn't exist in those days. But even if they had existed, they couldn't have been accurately applied to a new category that offered no norms, ratios, or deflation factors to hone and sharpen estimates with.

Smith put his money where his mouth was and started Federal Express Corporation. In the space of just one decade, his ridiculous idea grew to a company that generated more than $1 billion per year in revenues.

Ten years later Smith, who never did learn the lesson that untestable ideas should be killed, came up with another one. This time it was to provide businesses throughout the country with the ability to communicate instantaneously with each other, using something he called ZapMail. He offered to pick up a letter, take it to a local Federal Express office for transmission, and have a high-quality copy of it delivered to the recipient in another city, in less than two hours. And for those with sufficient ZapMail volume, he would even put a transmission machine right in their office for still faster and less expensive service. Once again, no magic research numbers to rely on. At best, a forecast could have provided Smith with a guesstimate of initial usage. But there was no way to determine if the idea would take off in the long run, or what level of growth could be achieved. Smith could only act on a clear vision of his company's mission, an investigation of the marketplace to identify consumer needs compatible with his mission, and his capacity to design a product that would satisfy those needs.

Although Smith was assisted by a number of bright and talented executives, the final decision was a judgment call that he alone had to make. With hundreds of millions of dollars at risk, he took the chance. Unfortunately for Smith, the ZapMail idea failed and the product was withdrawn from the market. The bigger issue, from a concept tester's point of view, is that volumetric forecasts have very critical limits. If you want to market a safe product, different but not too different, it is safer to use them (as long as you keep in mind that the results are only rough guesses). But completely

Concept Testing

new products give big headaches to those who like to rely on volumetric forecasts, because they must forego the security of a model and put their own credibility and judgment on the line.

Some theoreticians describe the issue in terms of continuous versus discontinuous innovation. A continuous innovation might be a basic telephone with new push-button calling feature (back when a rotary dial was the only option) or a red instrument (when black was the only available color). An example of a discontinuous innovation is the telephone itself, back in the days when the only other communications alternative was a letter or a personal visit.

Unfortunately, the real world is not always so precisely neat and tidy. It is not always clear if a new product is continuous or discontinuous, or if it is very discontinuous or just slightly discontinuous. I prefer to think of the issue as points on a continuum. The closer you are to the discontinuous end of the scale, the less likely that volumetric forecasts can be accurately calculated.

Regardless of the terminology, the point is clear. Volumetric forecasts are not always possible. I liken it to a baseball game. If your goal is to aim for singles, a volume forecast model *might* help you achieve your goal. But to hit a home run, a model often cannot help. You must come up to the plate all alone, like Fred Smith did.

III.

Extra Dimensions to Maximize Effectiveness

8
Study the Respondent, Not Just the Concept

Many of the techniques described in earlier chapters show how to focus directly on the concept and the consumer's reactions to it. This chapter deals with another category of diagnostic questions—the values, opinions, and characteristics of the consumer. Sometimes you can significantly improve a concept idea based on the characteristics and needs of consumers rather than their reactions to the concept itself.

STUDY AWARENESS AND USAGE OF COMPETITIVE BRANDS

Early in the 1980s, John DeLorean was arrested in a now-famous "cocaine bust." His advisers were concerned about his ability to get a fair trial because of the extensive media coverage: Stories in all the major weeklies and on all the national network news programs, covering all aspects of the case as well as his wealth and flamboyant lifestyle, continued for several weeks.

I was asked to conduct a research survey to measure his ability to get a fair trail. From the research, I learned that a very large proportion of the general population either did not know who John DeLorean was (after weeks of headlines) or had heard the name DeLorean but were not sure in which context. With awareness this low, it was a safe bet that media contamination was not going to prevent his getting a fair trial.

You might be wondering what in the world John DeLorean's trial has to do with concept testing. Plenty. Just as the public's awareness of De-Lorean's encounter with federal agents was of concern to his advisers, awareness and usage of competitive brands should be of concern to the concept tester. In most cases, prior knowledge and experience can affect the situation, be it a criminal trial or a concept test. For this reason the best

Concept Testing

concept tests often measure awareness and usage of competitive brands, with questions like this:

For Awareness:

(Unaided) When you think about products in the dog food category, what brands have you seen or heard of? [*Probe:*] Any others?

(Aided) Have you ever seen or heard of the [*Blank*] brand of dog food?

For Usage:

(Usual brand) When purchasing dog food, what brand do you usually buy?

(Brand ever used) Have you ever purchased or used the [*Blank*] brand of dog food?

Surprisingly, some researchers do not measure awareness and usage of competitive brands in their concept tests. Their position is that identifying the major competitors in a category is an issue that has already been explored. Since the information is already available, asks the cost-conscious researcher, why bother to waste valuable time in a concept test by collecting repetitive information, especially when the time could be better spent by asking other questions?

There are two important diagnostic reasons to collect competitive brand awareness and usage data as part of a concept test. For one thing, consumers who are aware of or who use various competitive brands often have unique reactions to the test concept. Knowing who these people are and what they think allows you to identify target subgroups most responsive to your concept's reason for being.

For another, when brand awareness for all the products in the test category is especially low, that may provide a useful clue on how to modify your concept in order to better exploit the opportunity. Let's examine each of these ideas in some detail.

Competitive Users Have Unique Reactions

In one study of the overnight package delivery industry, the idea of a service that will pick up your package within three hours of your call stimulated *some* positive interest among overnight delivery customers in general, but *very* high interest among UPS customers (see Chart 8–1). That's not surprising when you consider that UPS agents usually make just one pickup

Study the Respondent, Not Just the Concept

Chart 8-1. Interest in three-hour pickup for an overnight package delivery service.

	Total
Very Interested	
All users	26%
UPS customers	41

per day, late in the business day. Since UPS dispatchers cannot easily contact drivers out in the field, an occasional customer who is not on the driver's preset route structure usually cannot get a pickup the same day its request is made. But a regular customer with no packages being sent out that day is still visited by a driver as part of the daily pickup route.

If you are in the air freight business and your target is UPS's extensive customer base, this piece of information might become a valuable concept development tool.

Another side of the coin is illustrated when overnight package delivery consumers are asked how interested they are in a service that delivers before 11:00 the following morning. As noted in Chart 8–2, interest is relatively high among all overnight air freight users except those who use Federal Express.

Once again, these results are not surprising when you consider that Federal Express already promises its customers a delivery before 11:00 the following morning. From a concept development point of view, the data suggest that an 11:00 A.M. deadline is not much of a benefit if your intent is to compete against Federal Express.

Chart 8-2. Interest in receiving delivery before 11:00 A.M. the following morning.

	Total
Very Interested	
Federal Express customers	16%
All other customers	39

Concept Testing

Low Brand Awareness Can Be a Powerful Hook

In some product categories, brand awareness is especially low. Take the toothbrush category, for example. Virtually everyone owns at least one toothbrush. Many people own two. And some people who travel a great deal or have second homes own more than two. Many of these brushes are worn out and should be replaced. Trade statistics suggest that a brush should be replaced after three to four months of continued use but that most brushes are used a good deal longer.

If you ask typical consumers what brand of toothbrush they own, the answer in most cases is a rather rueful "I'm not sure." One of the reasons, of course, is that consumers don't really see meaningful differences between the various brands in spite of manufacturers' attempts to differentiate by color, size, and shape.

What can you do to help your new product if you are competing in a category like this one, with little interbrand differentiation and low brand awareness? If you are a toothbrush manufacturer, you can band together with other manufacturers into a trade association to stimulate consumers to replace worn-out brushes more often. With brand awareness so low, an industrywide program would probably help everyone to the same degree, in proportion to their current sales. No single brand would be especially helped.

If you are a toothpaste manufacturer, you can come out with a new toothbrush that can be jointly promoted with your toothpaste, perhaps even directly on the toothpaste package. You can even remind consumers to replace their worn-down toothbrush with your brand the next time they purchase a tube of paste.

Another example, this time from the skin treatment segment of the cosmetics industry. The product in question is fade cream. Back in the late 1970s, fade creams were a tiny market generating perhaps $10 million per year at retail. The product was purchased mainly by older people or those with uneven coloring or dark spots caused by overexposure to the sun.

A concept was developed by one marketer that wished to expand its business. It was a new product, with several added benefits not currently available to consumers or available but not promoted by existing brands in the category. The target group was people with spotted skin who were currently nonusers of any brand of fade cream.

As part of the concept test, consumers were asked what product, if any, they had ever heard of to treat their problem. The majority were familiar with no product at all. Even among those who were aware of a product, most thought it wasn't intended to treat their kind of skin problem.

The concept itself scored very highly, although the new features themselves were not of especially high interest to consumers. Interest was quite high among those who indicated they were unaware of the existence of products that treat skin discoloration or blemishes.

The message was quite clear. The problem with the category had little to do with poor positioning. It was primarily an issue of nonawareness among relevant population segments. The solution was equally clear: Raise awareness.

Within four years a quiet little category quadrupled, to more than $40 million in annual sales, primarily on the strength of one simple question, which encouraged one manufacturer to promote more heavily, leading to higher sales, and in turn leading others to increase their own promotional spending.

MEASURE INTEREST IN TRYING NEW PRODUCTS

In your next test, ask consumers how interested (in general) they are in trying new products within the test category. The results are often quite useful. Here is one way to ask the question:

In general, how interested are you in trying a new line of frozen entrees? Would you say you are . . .

Very interested	☐
Somewhat interested	☐
Not too interested	☐
Not at all interested	☐

As a starting point, compare the level of interest that exists in your category with the level of interest that exists in other categories. This comparison gives you considerable insight into the ease of entry within your category.

In some categories, interest in trying new products is quite low. Computers, telephones with new features, and detergents are examples of low-interest categories, based on this question. And the difficulty of successfully marketing new products in these categories attests to the accuracy of this information. Specialty foods, oven cleaners, and insecticides are examples of product categories on the other end of the continuum. Consumers express an above-average interest in trying new products in these categories.

Where does your product category fit? This may be the $64,000 question, of greater value than any other question on the survey. The cost to you is just one tiny closed-end question.

The question also provides you with a useful diagnostic tool as you analyze the test concept's performance. Try this approach. Start by observing the level of Purchase Interest among those with high versus low interest in trying new products. As a rough rule of thumb, those with high new-product interest usually have higher Purchase Interest in your concept. If these high interest people don't have high interest in your concept, then something is wrong. It is your signal to start cross tabulating to find out what it is.

And when you start cross tabbing to pinpoint the problem, begin with the Main Idea and Reasons for Purchase Interest questions. Analyze responses to these questions among those with high versus low interest in trying new products. Find out what each group considers to be the product's main idea or the reason each group gives for buying or rejecting the product.

In a concept test for a new business office product, Purchase Interest was low. The main reason was that potential consumers didn't think they had need for the product. Among those who expressed high interest in trying new office products, Purchase Interest was also low. But their reason for rejecting the idea was different. Instead of just saying they had no need for the product, they said that the product was deficient and gave some very clear clues on how to fix the concept. Apparently, their greater interest or need for new, different products in the test category made them more sensitive to the concept's deficiencies, or more willing to verbalize these opinions.

STUDY SATISFIED AND DISSATISFIED CUSTOMERS

The most successful new products are those that exploit the deficiencies of existing products. One tool to help you benefit from current category deficiencies is the study of both satisfied and dissatisfied customers. Let's face it, those who are dissatisfied with their current brand are the best prospects for your new product. But the flip side of the coin is just as valid. Those who are completely satisfied with their existing product make pretty poor prospects for a new product.

Back in 1971, the S. C. Johnson Company was considering whether or not to market a moisturizing shaving product for women to use while shaving their legs. Women liked the product, a gel that turned to foam when rubbed on the skin. Unfortunately, the concept had one fatal flaw. Women were perfectly satisfied with the method they were currently using to shave

136

their legs. Many simply used bar soap; others used men's shaving products that were already in the home. The product went to market in 1972, marketed under the name Crazy Legs. It failed. The major reason: Women were resistant to buying it because they were satisfied with their current shaving preparation method.

Consumer satisfaction doesn't just kill products; it can also lead you to profitable new-product opportunities. In today's frozen breakfast category, one major problem is that many consumers think the quality and taste of products currently being sold is poor. As a result, many nonusers report they are quite dissatisfied with products in this category. How can you use this information to maximize sales for a new product in this category? That's easy: Deliver a credible taste and quality story.

Another example, this time from the window-cleaning category. According to *Advertising Age*, Miles Laboratories' consumer research efforts showed that consumers were dissatisfied with the smell of ammonia. Their solution: Glass Works, a new window cleaner with a vinegar-based formulation that eliminates the smell of ammonia.

A powerful tool to help you uncover potential winners or losers in the marketplace is to measure the degree of satisfaction or dissatisfaction that consumers have with the category. One way to measure it is to ask:

How satisfied are you with the products you normally use from this category? Would you say you are . . .

Very satisfied ☐
Very dissatisfied ☐
Somewhere in between ☐

[*If somewhere in between*] On balance, would you describe yourself as leaning more toward being satisfied or being dissatisfied with the products from this category that you normally use?

Satisfied ☐
Dissatisfied ☐

Clearly, studying dissatisfied consumers can be rewarding. But you can also learn a great deal about how to market your product from those who are satisfied with their present brand. In a concept test for a new food seasoning, I found that consumers who were highly satisfied with existing products were lukewarm to the test concept. They didn't think it offered a good taste benefit; see Chart 8–3.

Concept Testing

Chart 8-3. Degree of satisfaction affects concept attitudes.

	Low Satisfaction with Current Product	*High Satisfaction with Current Product*
Percent of Sample with High Purchase Interest	22%	14%
Major Benefit of Concept		
Good taste	61	36
Ease of preparation	35	41

The data suggested that the test concept could be helped by better communicating good taste. And I learned this with nothing more than a simple computer cross tabulation.

TRY OFFBEAT DEMOGRAPHIC QUESTIONS

Virtually every concept test includes a series of demographic questions dealing with age, income, occupation, and family size of the respondent. Unfortunately, these "standard demos" are an incomplete profile of the respondents and their values and lifestyle. Many times a perfectly fine concept test has produced inconclusive results because some other key demographic or classification question was omitted. As a result, an important aspect of the individual's values or behavior was undiscovered or a critical analytical variable was unavailable.

Searching for offbeat demographic characteristics sometimes provides the missing hook that makes a concept come alive or pinpoints the reason a concept is not performing well. Unfortunately, the inclusion of these questions in many concept tests is a very underused research step. The reason is obvious: It takes time. Lots of it. And the time must be spent at the very beginning of the concept test to think of all the right questions to ask. Sadly, many analysts first discover the data deficiency at the tail end of the assignment. No matter how good an analyst they are, if they forget to ask the right questions at the beginning, they cannot come up with the right answers at the end.

In one survey involving a line of fashion clothing, I added a battery of classification questions measuring the height and weight of the respondent.

138

Study the Respondent, Not Just the Concept

Based on readily available life insurance height-weight tables, it was easy to zero in on height-weight combinations that signaled the person was heavily overweight. A series of cross tabulations involving attitudes toward clothing among those respondents revealed that heavily overweight women have an above-average willingness to purchase expensive clothing that promises good fit.

One manufacturer used this information and launched a line of expensive fashion items for large women. He is having no trouble selling the line at a higher-than-normal price point. In the meanwhile, retailers are busy marking down high-priced merchandise by Ralph Lauren, Calvin Klein, and similar fashion leaders.

The automotive after-market category (parts and accessories normally purchased to improve or repair an auto) currently is being buffeted by change. On the one hand, domestic automobile manufacturers are making more and more effort to provide customers with better-built cars that malfunction much less often than models from earlier years. To some degree the manufacturers have been successful, thereby reducing demand for some after-market products. On the other hand, influenced by economic factors such as unemployment and the high cost of new car purchases, American consumers are keeping their cars longer. So the sales of some after-market products are growing.

Concept research in this category is tricky. In addition to standard classification questions about the respondent, the researcher must remember to ask about the age of the *car*, since owners of older cars are more likely to need repairs and replacement parts. Another special or offbeat issue to include in a concept test in this category is to determine how concerned individuals are about the automobile's operation and appearance. The more concerned they are, the more likely they are to purchase a car care product.

Turning to the topical analgesic category, the fitness craze that hit U.S. consumers in the late 1970s caused considerable soul searching by several manufacturers. While they were excited at the prospect of increased sales because of increased physical activity, they wondered if they should be changing how they marketed their products toward these health- and fitness-oriented people.

On the one hand, with estimates of up to 50 million runners annually and untold millions of tennis buffs, racquetballers, golfers, and handball players, some manufacturers projected huge marketing opportunities for a sleepy but profitable category that was then already generating more than $100 million in annual sales.

The issue that concerned them was that most of the then-current users of topical analgesics were arthritis sufferers, who tended to be older and nonathletic. In contrast, the newer target group of fitness enthusiasts were 30 to 40 years of age and upscale.

Makers of established brands worried about being left behind by competitive brands. They had to decide whether to market their current products to the new opportunity segment or whether to develop new products. And if the same product was to be marketed to all consumers, the company had to wonder if its advertising copy and strategy should remain the same for all user groups or if a supplemental campaign should be targeted to the emerging market.

Special "sports activity" questions added to a series of concept tests helped to clarify this issue. These questions found that the market among fitness-oriented individuals was much smaller than it first appeared to be. Many of these consumers exercised sporadically, and tended to tear or strain muscles or ligaments most often when they first began to exercise. Shortly thereafter, injuries stopped, either because the muscles were strengthened from repeated exercise or because the consumer lost interest and stopped exercising.

What these special questions really suggested was a huge number of potential one-time users, not a solid, long-term market segment. Hardly the reason for coming out with a new brand. The validity of these findings became even more apparent in the mid-1980s as the running boom peaked and then began to fade. The market became even smaller than earlier projections assumed.

Another instance of unusual demographic research: In a concept test for a low-calorie food, I collected a great deal of information about respondents, including the amount of weight they would like to lose. The information turned out to be quite useful. While analyzing some brand usage data, I found that the category's leading brand owned 20 percent of the market within the subgroup that the test concept was seeking to compete within. I then found that women who wanted to lose more than 20 pounds were the primary users of this brand. Within this heavily overweight segment, the category leader owned 33 percent of the market.

Overwhelming domination, you say? Not if you play with the numbers a bit. If a competitor controls 20 percent of the total market and 33 percent of one of its segments, it follows that another segment exists with much lower support. Sure enough, women who are happy with their weight have different food preferences and relate to themselves, their families, and the world about them in a unique way. They also purchase category products differently. Is the category leader vulnerable? You bet it is.

Study the Respondent, Not Just the Concept

Talking about food, a series of special questions reveals the following segments when consumers talk about their attitudes toward salt:

- About 20 percent are very concerned about the relationship between salt and health and are willing to make a taste tradeoff in the interest of better health.
- Another 40 percent are somewhat interested in the relationship between salt consumption and good health. They *may* be willing, under certain circumstances, to do with less salt in some parts of their diet.
- About 40 percent will not change their eating behavior with respect to salt, no matter what they are told or shown.

If you are a marketer of a salt-free or salt-reduced product, targeting your new product toward the first group is the easiest strategy to follow. However, this segment contains just 20 percent of the marketplace, and many of the individuals in this segment reside in older, smaller (one- and two-person) families. The harder but potentially more profitable strategy is to reach the second group and try to motivate them to buy your product. The starting place is recognizing that the public's salt-related attitudes are complex and including the correct special questions within your concept test to help you explore this issue. The third group, obviously, will not be a market for your product.

And finally, a concept test for a manufacturer of long underwear included a question on the degree of participation in outdoor winter sports. The test found that women are more likely to observe sporting events while men participate to a greater degree. Can you think of any design implications, packaging decisions, or distribution ideas from this finding? The bottom line: Expanding your list of "standard" demographic and classification questions can uncover big secrets.

9
Norms:
A Critical Resource

When you analyze the results of a concept test, it is helpful to have scores available from previous concept tests to act as a point of reference or benchmark. In effect, these data serve as a historical perspective against which the current concept's results can be compared.

These points of reference—called norms—are the most powerful tool a researcher can use to help interpret data. I consider them to be my most important resource, more important than any single question or technique. Some researchers agree. Others complain that norms merely perpetuate mediocrity. Which point of view is correct? Both, I think. It all depends on the quality of the norms used.

A USEFUL DATA BANK

Good norms can help immeasurably to evaluate a concept (or any survey, for that matter). Just what is a good norm? One based on a concept test for an idea that became fabulously successful. A good norm provides the analyst with a meaningful action standard, a goal for the current concept to surpass. Building a norm that is based on data from a general assortment of 30 or so previous concept tests (some strong, some average, and some weak concepts) creates a category average. Using this average creates a target that can easily be achieved, and provides a great way to develop mediocre products.

Minimum Requirements

Your norm data bank should be quite extensive. *At the very minimum* it should include:

1. Positive Purchase Interest. You need two scores: the number who "definitely will buy" and the total number who are positive. These two norms will tell you if your product is liked and the intensity of the preference.
2. Neutral and negative Purchase Interest. This information tells you if the reason for a concept's failure is just a passive lack of positive feeling or a strong rejection of the idea.
3. The number of consumers who think your concept has advantages or disadvantages compared with competitive products.
4. The number of consumers who think your concept offers *major* advantages or *major* disadvantages.
5. Information to help you measure if the concept is interesting, believable, persuasive, unique, important, easy to understand, and honest.
6. The number of respondents who suggest improvements to the concept idea.

The norms for items 3 to 6 should be collected for the total sample, for those with high Purchase Interest, and those with low Purchase Interest. Having norms for these different groups of people gives you a more powerful analytic tool. If your concept is performing poorly on some survey dimension, and the problem is mostly with people with high Purchase Interest, then it's not too important a problem. But if the poor performance is connected to those with low interest, the problem would be of greater concern.

I recently tested three concepts for a new financial service. The results of that test illustrate the value of good norms. Concept B scored the strongest of the three on several dimensions; even when it was not the best, its score wasn't far behind the winner's. But normative data showed that Concept B was not really as strong as it appeared to be (see Chart 9-1). In fact, it was only the best of three mediocre concepts. Without good norms, I never would have known that.

Chart 9-1. Reactions to new financial service.

	Concept A	*Concept B*	*Concept C*	*Category Norm*
Had high Purchase Interest	15%	19%	14%	(24)%
Recalled the key main point	25	47	34	(56)
Found at least one major advantage	36	(56)	49	(54)
Found hard to understand	14	17	14	(12)
Thought relevant to my needs	21	25	18	(36)

Test the Competition

Begin to build norms for your product category as soon as possible. Building them is easy. Each time a competitive product is introduced, test it immediately. If it's in test market, do your research in another market where advertising and promotion have not begun. And if it is being nationally introduced, search for consumers who haven't yet heard of the product. If you move fast, you may find that 90 to 95 percent of the population are unaware of the product and can be easily sampled at relatively low cost.

If your company's research budget doesn't normally allow for this type of expenditure, try to get the policy changed. These data are invaluable, and it doesn't have to be expensive to collect them. Conduct a stripped-down survey, collecting just the basic information needed for building norms. Necessary data can be collected through a short, closed-end questionnaire.

If the competitive product you tested succeeds, you have obtained a standard against which to compare your own new product.

VALUABLE DIAGNOSTIC AIDS

The value of norms goes far beyond serving as an action standard. They also are valuable diagnostic tools that can help you zero in on weaknesses within your own concept.

Norms: A Critical Resource

Chart 9-2. Reactions to a new computer program.

	Test Concept	Category Norm
High Purchase Interest	14%	⟨24⟩%
High ratings on selected attributes		
Easy to use	⟨62⟩	48
Reasonable price	⟨58⟩	51
Offers a benefit not available elsewhere	⟨44⟩	37
Awareness of the sponsoring company	22	⟨49⟩

A concept test for computer software showed that the idea scored well on a variety of measures but stimulated low Purchase Interest (see Chart 9-2). None of the obvious places revealed a clue to explain why Purchase Interest was low. Consumers thought the product was easy to use, fairly priced, and would satisfy a need not being fulfilled by other available products. Without norms, it would have been difficult to identify the source of the problem: low familiarity with the company.

For this software concept, having a rather offbeat awareness norm saved the day. An even bigger implication: The more detailed and complete a norm bank is, the more useful it becomes.

My own norm data bank is very detailed. It goes far beyond the bare bones minimum outlined at the beginning of this chapter. I collect norms on many different issues. In Purchase Interest, for example, I collect Purchase Interest norms for various demographic subgroups and use them to help pinpoint how each segment of the target group population reacts to the concept being tested.

Here's how it can work. In a test for a new food product, the concept stimulated high Purchase Interest among 24 percent of the target group. Analysis of Purchase Interest by age of respondent showed that those 18 to 34 had the highest Purchase Interest score (see Chart 9-3). In the absence of other information, I would have concluded that this product had a young age skew.

Similarly, a review of Purchase Interest scores among respondents of different educational and income levels would have revealed a middle-range tendency in both population subgroups; see Chart 9-4.

But the norms provided a completely different point of view about this product. Take a look at Chart 9-5. The norms show at a glance that a 24

Concept Testing

Chart 9-3. High Purchase Interest within various age groups.

	Test Concept
Total respondents	㉔%
Age breakdown	
18–34	27
35–54	22
55 or over	21

percent level of high Purchase Interest is merely average for this segment of the food business—nothing to write home about. Norms also reveal that all products in this category have a young age skew. There is no special magic that would make this test concept attract younger consumers; it is merely picking up its fair share of this market segment.

These age norms also raise some provocative questions. Why don't older consumers react well to products in this category? What is the industry doing wrong? What can we do to persuade the older, currently unexploited segment of the market to buy our product? The norms do not provide the answers, but they sure help raise the right questions.

The education and income normative data again create a totally different story. Instead of scores suggesting a product that especially appeals to the middle-range group, the data reveal that our concept is very deficient among higher socioeconomic individuals. This is a critically important piece

Chart 9-4. High Purchase Interest among key demographic subgroups.

	Test Concept
Total respondents	24%
Education	
High school graduate or less	23
Some college	㉛
College graduate	19
Income	
$19,999 or less	23
$20,000–$34,999	㉗
$35,000 or more	19

146

Norms: A Critical Resource

Chart 9-5. High Purchase Interest compared to norms.

	Concept Score	Category Norm
Total respondents	24%	23%
Age		
18–34	27	25
35–54	22	23
55 or over	21	20
Education		
High school graduate or less	23	19
Some college	31	26
College graduate	19	⟨27⟩
Income		
$19,999 or less	23	18
$20,000–$34,999	27	24
$35,000 or more	19	⟨28⟩

of data. It directs the rest of the analysis toward a population segment that is holding back potential sales for this product.

Once again, the data do not tell us how to solve the problem among upscale individuals. Other questions will do that job. But the norms help identify the existence of the problem.

NORMS FOR OPEN-END QUESTIONS

A rich and detailed norm data bank should also include responses to open-end questions as well as closed-ends. Normative data for open-end questions can help you sharpen your interpretation of responses to these questions.

After viewing the concept for a new food, consumers were asked to explain, in their own words, what the Main Idea of the product was. Those with high Purchase Interest were also asked what it was about the product that motivated this high level of interest. Their responses are shown in Chart 9-6.

Without norms, an analyst would probably conclude from the Main Idea question that the concept stressed convenience and elegance. Judging

Concept Testing

Chart 9-6. Diagnostic questions for a food concept.

	Test Concept
Main Idea	
Quick/easy/convenient	33 %
Fancy/elegant food	31
Tastes good	(14)
Reasons for positive Purchase Interest	
Quick/easy/convenient	(39) %
Tastes good	(32)
Fancy/elegant food	(13)

from the low level of playback for taste, it appears that taste was not stressed very much by the concept. Yet the large number of people mentioning taste as a reason for having positive Purchase Interest suggests that taste is an important motivator. The implication: Since good taste is a persuasive aspect of the concept, it should be stressed more heavily.

However, norms tell a completely different story. Chart 9-7 shows the same open-end data with norms added. The norms reveal that *all* food concepts have a hard time communicating good taste in the Main Idea question; only 18 percent typically think good taste is a major issue being communicated by a concept. This is not surprising when you stop to think about it. Communicating good taste requires high-quality photography and skilled production values. That is why companies spend $100,000 or more to film

Chart 9-7. Diagnostic questions for a food concept compared to appropriate norms.

	Test Concept	Category Norm
Main Idea		
Quick/easy/convenient	33%	35%
Fancy/elegant food	31	10
Tastes good	14	18
Reasons for positive Purchase Interest		
Quick/easy/convenient	39%	34%
Tastes good	32	(51)
Fancy/elegant food	13	11

a commercial. Because sophisticated production values are deliberately omitted in written concepts, it follows that the taste norm is low.

Within this context, the fact that 14 percent of those exposed to the test concept think the Main Idea is "good taste" is about average. The real problem is revealed in the lower portion of the chart. Although 51 percent of those positive to the *average* concept state that its perceived taste is the reason for high Purchase Interest, only 32 percent of those who want to buy *our* product mention taste. Conclusion: We communicated taste dominantly enough but not at all persuasively—exactly the opposite of what the conclusion would have been without norms.

I hope you are convinced. Norms are the place to start an effective analysis. I urge you to begin your norm-building program as soon as possible.

10
Procedural Guidelines

Up to now we have dealt with special questions and analytic approaches that can help you evaluate and improve your concept candidate. However, a skillfully executed concept test requires much more than asking the right question or doing the right computer tabulation. Drawing the right conclusions involves a large number of procedural issues dealing with sample design, sample size, respondent selection guidelines, questionnaire design, coding procedures, and the like. Perhaps the most important procedural issue of all is selecting the right company to conduct your concept test, unless you have the staff and time to proceed on your own.

This chapter will discuss some of the more significant procedural aspects of a concept test. My goal is to help you avoid many common pitfalls that can destroy the usefulness of an otherwise excellent survey. Please keep in mind that each of these issues is quite complex. Entire books have been written about each one. In most professional research companies, entire departments, each headed by a highly paid director, have been set up to deal with these issues. Obviously, the brief discussion here is far from the last word on each subject.

SETTING OBJECTIVES

The first step of any concept test is to set survey objectives. This is a very important step, for the objectives are the road map that provides the direction the concept test must follow.

A good starting place is to meet with various interested parties, both within your company and in outside advertising agencies and consulting firms, to identify the issues of importance to them.

Procedural Guidelines

General Objectives

There are general objectives that are appropriate for any concept test as well as specific ones applicable to just one test. The general objectives include these three critical issues:

1. Does the concept have sufficient appeal and sales potential to warrant further development?
   - If potential is high, the test should help you pinpoint the segments of the population that are most responsive to the idea.
   - If results are disappointing, the test should help you determine whether the concept, or some future variation of it, has potential if focused toward any demographic, behavioral, or attitudinal segment of the population.
2. Is the message that consumers take away after reading or viewing the concept (both factual direct statements and subjective hints or implied suggestions) the same one you think you are sending?
3. What are the concept's individual strengths and weaknesses?
   - Which concept elements play a major role in making the concept succeed?
   - Which elements play a minor role or provide no help at all?
   - Which elements create problems that hold back acceptance?

Specific Objectives

In addition to general objectives, you should be listing a series of specific questions and areas of concern unique to your concept. Be *quite* specific. The more specific, the better. For instance:

- Do consumers believe the sound quality of our long distance telephone service is as good as the sound quality they associated with AT&T?
- Is "good taste" communicated strongly or persuasively enough?
- Do consumers understand that our bank will provide homeowners' insurance, at a discounted price, to customers who get their mortgage through us?

The most frequent and most serious problem with setting concept test objectives is the tendency to make them too general. In preparing your list of objectives, keep in mind that the more issues you raise in advance of the test and the more detailed your list is, the more successful your concept test.

WHO SHOULD CONDUCT THE TEST?

Unless you have substantial in-house resources, the best way to obtain a fast, professionally conducted, and skillfully analyzed concept test is to engage a full-service consumer research firm that specializes in concept testing.

Choosing a Research Firm

Use only research companies that specialize in concept testing. As with any other technical skill or service, the more experienced the practitioner, the better the job you'll get. A skilled concept tester can help make your project succeed in many ways.

Here are four major advantages skilled concept testers can provide:

1. Merely by examining your concept, before the test even begins, they can recommend special diagnostic questions or respondent classification questions that you might not have thought of.
2. Knowledge of the special nuances of concept testing means the right computer tabulations will be prepared.
3. Experts in this area can perform a more professional, insightful, and useful analysis of the data.
4. They have the detailed norms derived from other tests within your category to help interpret your data. The existence of these norms has the potential to add great value to your test results.

You can find qualified companies in the *Green Book*, a directory of research companies published by the New York chapter of the American Marketing Association.* It lists most research companies in the United States with a brief description of each and a cross index of companies with unique skills in various specializations such as concept testing.

Compile a list of candidates, then screen them in an organized fashion. Your screening criteria should include questions in the following areas:

1. General experience of the company with concept testing.
2. Concept testing experience within your category.

*The mailing address of the New York chapter of the American Marketing Association is 310 Madison Avenue, New York, New York 10017.

3. The quality and quantity of their norms.
4. The skill of the senior researcher who will be assigned to your project.
5. The amount of time the senior researcher typically spends analyzing and interpreting survey findings for concepts similar in length to yours.

You should also determine whether or not the firm is a member of the Council of American Survey Research Organizations (CASRO). Approximately 130 full-service research companies, of all sizes, are members of this professional association, and all member firms agree to follow a Code of Standards and Conduct. In my opinion, any research company that chooses not to support CASRO is making a very clear statement, and I would not invite such a company to work on one of my projects.

Doing It Yourself

There are other ways of conducting a concept test. You can save money by doing some of the professional steps yourself. For example, you can write the questionnaire and hire a full-service research firm to execute the project for you. The final result will be a book of computer tabulations, which you then analyze and interpret.

For companies that have standard procedures about how to do a concept test and how to interpret data, this practice is perfectly sound. It can save several thousand dollars. However, if you are looking for fresh product ideas, this shortcut often does not work.

Companies that analyze their own data sometimes get into trouble, usually because:

1. The questionnaire missed some key issue.
2. The norm data bank was inappropriate, insufficient, or nonexistent.
3. The company analyst was distracted by other job responsibilities, and consequently the concept test analysis was quite superficial.

A concept test can be done even less expensively if the sponsoring company writes its own questionnaire, prints sufficient copies of it, and goes directly to different field, coding, and tabulating agencies to conduct the various phases of the project. In effect you are your own general contractor, buying parts of a project instead of hiring a full-service agency to do all the legwork. In this way you can save 40 to 50 percent of the cost of a concept test. The various "subcontractors" are listed in the *Green Book* mentioned earlier.

Unfortunately, there is a price you must pay to save this money. You must be able to select competent field, coding, and tabulating agencies. You must be able to write competent field instructions, give guidance to the code builder, and prepare accurate computer tabulating specifications. And most important of all, you must have the skills to supervise and evaluate the performance of each of these service companies.

SAMPLE TYPE

After deciding who should conduct the project, you must now decide on the type of sample to be used. Naturally, the research firm (if you are using one) will have a recommendation for you to consider. As you evaluate these recommendations, keep in mind that there are no right or wrong answers. The whole issue is merely comfort versus cost. Here are some observations to help you make the decision that is best for you.

To start with, there are three major types of sampling procedures used in market research: probability samples, purposive samples (also known as judgment samples), and quota samples.

Probability Sample

A probability sample is the most reliable form of sampling. Unfortunately, it is also the most expensive. You may have heard it referred to as a random sample, stratified sample, or cluster sample. Each is a type of probability sample and each has its place in market research, but because of space limitations I will spare you the task (and the pain!) of understanding the nuances separating each type.

The common element linking all probability samples is that each person in the total population (or "universe") being studied has a known probability of being included in the sample as one of the respondents. If you apply careful and rigorous definitions of the universe being interviewed, how the respondent is to be selected (randomly or by some other selection system that eliminates bias), and how many of the selected respondents are actually interviewed (the "completion rate"), a probability sample can quite reliably reflect the characteristics, behavior, attitudes, and future intentions of the population being studied.

A probability sample provides the researcher with a known and predictable range of sampling error. If you do a probability sample among 100 respondents and learn that 20 percent of the sample like your new product, you can conclude that the real-world figure is within a range of 10 to 30 percent because of sampling error. A probability sample allows you to widen or narrow the amount of sampling error by adjusting the sample size or the degree of risk you are willing to accept. (A fuller discussion on degree of risk follows later.)

The only problem with probability sampling is expense. A properly done survey using probability sampling techniques can cost two times as much as a survey that uses a different sample-selection procedure. For this reason, probability sampling is rarely, if ever, used by companies testing new-product concepts. Think of it this way. Surveys have a high potential for error. In addition to poor samples that do not accurately reflect the target population, survey errors occur because designated respondents refuse to be interviewed, questions are worded poorly, and interviewing is poor or biased. The list of things that can go wrong is endless, from poor codes to clerical coding errors, keypunch errors, computer instruction errors, and of course human analytic errors.

The amount of error caused by a deficient sample-selection system is just a *tiny* part of a survey's total possible error. And the cost of preventing many of these other errors is quite small. As a result, most researchers are quite willing to accept some sampling deficiencies by not using a probability sample, preferring instead to put their financial resources against other, larger sources of error.

Purposive Sample

The purposive (or judgment) sample is about as far away from a probability sample as it is possible to go. It consists of a group of respondents who have been interviewed because they have a specific characteristic that is of interest to the survey sponsor, typically usage of a specific brand or category, or interest in trying some new-product idea.

This type of sample is frequently used by new-product marketers, and that is unfortunate. The main problem is that the survey sponsor is defining, in advance, the target group for its new product. In effect, the sponsor is saying, "Our new product will primarily attract people who currently use Brand X." This kind of thinking presumes the new product is not capable of changing or expanding the market.

I consider this approach foolhardy. A better procedure is to conduct a quota sample—a compromise between the two extremes of a probability and a purposive sample.

Concept Testing

Quota Sample

Some industry wags refer to a quota sample as a poor man's probability sample. In quota sampling, the project manager selects the *number* of interviews that must be conducted among different segments of the population and leaves the selection of specific respondents to the interviewer.

Unlike a purposive sample, which focuses very generally upon the target group, a quota sample sets a number of specific guidelines about who to interview. The guidelines make the sample more representative of the target group being surveyed. But since the quota sample does not pre-select individual respondents and lets the interviewer select the respondents, the system is not as unbiased as a probability sample would be. Using this kind of sample helps you to avoid situations like the following:

- You are doing a concept test for a new office computer and have instructed your interviewer to interview individuals who play a role in the selection of a new office computer (a purposive sample). After the results are tabulated, you learn that all the respondents are technical people; none are vice presidents and none are administrative workers. You further learn that no respondents work for large companies, which purchase most of the computers used by American industry.
- A concept test is conducted for a new food product. The results reveal that none of the respondents interviewed is employed. All are full-time homemakers.

In each of these two examples, the researcher should be quite concerned—a large part of the potential market for the concept being tested is not represented by the sample.

One way around the problem is to set a quota for each characteristic you deem to be important. For a food concept, you might set interviewer quotas to match current U.S. census data on several demographic characteristics. Your instructions to interviewers might be along these lines:

1. Half of the interviews must be among women, one-half of whom are employed.
2. Half of the interviews must be with consumers under 45 years of age and half must be 45 or older.
3. A third of the respondents must have one or more children living at home.

Procedural Guidelines

Using this quota, an individual interviewer might be given an assignment by the project manager to do, say, 24 interviews following these guidelines:

1. Do 12 interviews among men and 12 among women; 6 of the women should be employed and 6 unemployed.
2. Do 12 interviews among consumers under 45 years of age and 12 among those 45 or older, with an equal number of men and women in each group.
3. Do 8 interviews among those with one or more children living at home and 16 among those with no children living at home.

Obviously, there is still some risk. You may not have covered all key variables. It may turn out, after the fact, that wealthier women have different opinions from poorer ones, and your sample contains an insufficient number of wealthy women. Other problems are also possible. In the interview quota of 24 just discussed, given the absence of further guidelines, the interviewer could conceivably have done all 6 of the interviews with unemployed women under 45 years of age. Obviously, this sample would be very unbalanced and unrepresentative, in spite of its superficial correctness. The likelihood of a problem is compounded by the fact that the interviewer is often a part-time worker paid at an hourly rate and may have a limited amount of technical training. To help reduce this problem, the quota can be broken down even further. One interviewer might be assigned 12 interviews among women, with the following instructions:

Number of Interviews	Respondent Characteristics
1	Employed, under 45, with a child
1	Employed, 45 or more, with a child
2	Employed, under 45, with no children
2	Employed, 45 or more, with no children
1	Unemployed, under 45, with a child
1	Unemployed, 45 or more, with a child
2	Unemployed, under 45, with no children
2	Unemployed, 45 or more, with no children

In spite of these precautions, it is important to remember that quota samples are not risk-free. There are two potential major problems:

1. No matter how many quotas you set, you cannot control the degree to which the sample is very different from the rest of the population on some other characteristic you did not set quotas for.
2. Since respondent selection is up to the interviewer, the chance exists that some bias is built into the sample. The interviewer may have selected people who seemed sympathetic. Or maybe they were the ones who happened to be at home on the day the interviewer worked that area of the city.

Given the tradeoff between cost and representativeness, a quota sample may still be your best bet. Don't be afraid to focus the sample somewhat, by eliminating population subgroups that you are absolutely certain have no possibility of ever using the product being tested. In effect, this is admitting that some degree of "purposiveness" is acceptable. However, my philosophy is this: If in doubt about any population segment, include it.

TYPE OF INTERVIEW

Related to the issue of sample type is the kind of interview you do. Researchers use four different procedures for concept testing: mail, telephone, personal interviews door-to-door, and personal interviews with people recruited at shopping centers and other high-traffic locations. Let's look at how each works.

Interviews by Mail

The least expensive method of conducting a concept test interview is by mail. The researcher mails a copy of the concept and the questionnaire to a sample of consumers (perhaps randomly selected from telephone directories or subscriber lists). They complete the questionnaire and mail it back to the sponsor in a postage-paid return envelope.

Unfortunately, there are some problems with this technique. For one thing, the percentage who return a completed questionnaire is quite low—often 5 percent or less. You must therefore worry about the extent to which nonresponders differ from responders. You can eliminate this problem by including a cash incentive of $1 or $2 with each questionnaire. Of course that presents another problem: The incentive eats away at the cost advantage.

You can also do a mail survey with a research company that has already recruited a group of consumers willing to respond to mail surveys. This procedure generates a high response rate without the need for cash incentives. However, some researchers worry that consumers who volunteer to be interviewed frequently are different from the rest of the population.

A second problem is that it is very hard to get useful responses to open-end questions like the Main Idea or Reasons for Purchase Interest. Without interviewers to probe and coax the answer out of respondents, these questions—which otherwise would be extremely valuable diagnostic tools—are often unproductive.

Another difficulty: Since the respondents open the envelope in the privacy of their home, they can read the entire questionnaire before answering any question. If the questionnaire contains information that affects responses to other questions, the responses will be flawed. For example, early in the questionnaire a respondent is asked what the main idea of the concept is. A short time later the questionnaire lists 12 attributes and asks respondents how important each one is. This listing calls attention to all the points that potentially could be mentioned as main ideas.

Finally, of course, there is the time factor. It takes several weeks for completed questionnaires to be mailed and received by the main office for processing.

For these reasons, a mail questionnaire is not always a useful concept testing tool unless the purpose of the test is to collect information from a few closed-end questions.

Interviews by Telephone

Another technique is to conduct interviews by telephone. The main problem is that a telephone interview does not allow the respondent to inspect the concept statement or to review a printed list of attributes before answering a question. For this reason, the telephone interview is not effective with most concept testing efforts.

Some researchers have attempted to get around this limitation of telephone interviewing by mailing concept statements and other interviewing material to qualified respondents and then interviewing them by telephone once the material has arrived and is sitting in front of them. There are three problems with this technique:

1. Two interviews are required, one to ensure that respondents are qualified and to enlist their cooperation, the second to get reactions to the concept.
2. Extra time is required; you must wait for the mail delivery to the respondent.

3. Some respondents misplace the material or do not have it readily available at the time of the telephone interview.

This interviewing procedure is usually not cost-effective or time-effective for concept testing.

Personal Interviews Door-to-Door

The third type, personal interviews conducted door-to-door, eliminates many of the problems associated with mail and telephone interviewing. Personal interviews can be done quickly. Material can be given to the respondent to study. Questions can be asked in a predetermined order; the respondent isn't biased by peeking at questions designed to be exposed later in the interview. Interviewers can easily probe for clarification or amplification on open-end questions.

The main problem is cost. Door-to-door interviewing often is more expensive than other kinds of interviewing. For this reason, most companies do the fourth type of interviewing.

Personal Interviews at High-Traffic Locations

Personal interviewing among consumers recruited at shopping centers and other high-traffic locations is the most common technique.

These interviews are also known as central location test (CLT) interviews. A CLT interview is usually conducted in a private interviewing booth set up in the general area where respondents are recruited. A CLT interview offers all the benefits of door-to-door recruitment and is also less expensive to do. It has the added advantage of allowing the interviewer to work directly under the supervisor, providing greater control over the quality of the work performed.

The only problem is sample representativeness. Obviously, the only people who get interviewed in this type of study are those who are in the vicinity of the interviewer. One wonders how these people differ from others who are not in the area of the interview.

However, most researchers ignore this factor. Their main concern is the *total* survey error, not just the bias introduced by a weak respondent-selection procedure. Their position is that respondent selection is just one component of the total survey error, that the use of a quota sample reduces the seriousness of this sampling problem, and that all other problems associated with mail and telephone surveys are resolved with this technique. Most researchers use a CLT interview for concept testing.

SAMPLE SIZE

Your next decision concerns the size of the sample that should be exposed to your concept. Once again, there are no right or wrong answers. It's a judgment call, and the tradeoff is between the precision of the resulting estimate and the cost. The smaller the sample, the lower the cost and the less precise the estimate. Your ability to do diagnostic cross tabs is also affected by a smaller sample size.

Before deciding what sample size per concept to sponsor, you should keep in mind that an estimate derived from any sample, regardless of its size, must have some degree of error or uncertainty associated with it. The only way to avoid this problem is to do a complete census of the entire universe being studied—an unaffordable option.

Don't fret too much about the problem of survey error. Although 100 percent accuracy is impossible to achieve in the real world, it is also quite unnecessary. Knowing whether 20 percent or 65 percent of a group of consumers plan to buy a product in the next year is certainly an important distinction for a survey to make. But does it really matter if the survey produces a 20 percent trial estimate that turns out to be 18 or 21 percent in the real world? The simple truth is that most marketing decisions do not require a very high degree of precision.

Allowing for Sampling Error

In selecting a sample size that is accurate enough for your purposes, there are two issues to consider: degree of confidence and sampling error.

Degree of confidence. The confidence you have that a survey finding reflects the real-world event being estimated is called Degree of Confidence. Most executives use a 95 percent level of confidence, meaning that they want a survey statistic to accurately reflect the real-world event 95 percent of the time. They accept the fact that 5 percent of the time the survey will produce an incorrect portrayal of the universe being studied.

The degree of confidence affects the sample size. The greater the degree of confidence desired, the larger the sample must be. For example, consider two business executives who both think that flipping a coin when faced with uncertainty will result in being right 50 percent of the time. But, rather than flipping a coin, each decides that his knowledge, intelligence, and general business skill will allow him to "guess" right 70 percent of the time.

Concept Testing

Each does a survey to improve his decision-making accuracy. One decides that a 95 percent confidence level is perfectly acceptable and authorizes a survey with a required number of interviews. The other decides that a 90 percent level of confidence suits his needs. His survey requires fewer interviews. Who is right? They both are. It's merely a risk and sample size trade off.

Sampling Error. A sampling error refers to the extent of deviation between the data produced by a survey sample and the real-world statistics that the survey predicts. If you interview 100 people about a new product and 20 percent of them say they would purchase it, the sampling error would be plus or minus 10 percent at the 95 percent level of confidence. This means that the real-world level of interest in the product is within a range of 10 to 30 percent, with just 5 chances in 100 that the true level is outside this range.

Working in Tandem. The two factors, degree of confidence and sampling error, work together to affect your sample size needs. As noted above, interviewing 100 people about a new product yields a sampling error of plus or minus 10 percent at the 95 percent level of confidence. You may decide that a spread of 20 percent is too imprecise. One option is to double the sample size to 200, so that the sampling error drops to plus or minus 7 percent, a spread of 14 percent. Or you could keep the sample size at 100, yet still produce a smaller, tighter sample error by accepting a lower level of confidence that the results reflect the real world, say 90 percent instead of 95 percent.

On balance, no magic number is "right" for sample size. Nor is there just one way of reaching your goal. The final answer is ultimately based on your budget and your tolerance for risk. When I conduct a concept test, I typically use a sample size of 150 respondents per concept. I am comfortable with this sample size. It works for me.

From an analytic point of view, a sample size of 150 per concept usually gives about 100 people with high Purchase Interest, enough to do the kinds of cross-tabulated diagnostic analyses described in this book. And if a concept is so poor that it is liked by an insufficient number of people, you usually have a clear answer about reasons for its low efficacy without these special cross tabs. Also, your subgroup of nonacceptors becomes more important *and* coincidentally has risen in size to a usable number.

Allowing for Market Realities

One final sample-size issue to consider. If you have a clear idea about who your new product will be marketed to, a sample size of 150 is probably adequate. But if your market definition is fuzzy or unclear, you may need a larger sample size.

As an example, let's look at the market for toothpaste specifically designed for people with sensitive teeth. Surveys reveal that just a tiny percentage of the general public uses this product, about 4 million people. If you intended to market a new product to these people, a sample size of 150 would do the job for concept testing. However, in addition to the 4 million, there are 12 million more who used such a product in the past but not at present. And there are 24 million more who have sensitive teeth but never used any product specifically designed for people with sensitive teeth. They presumably are suffering in silence.

Clearly, the market potential for a new product in this category is a lot bigger than just the 4 million current users. Equally clear: A different kind of product appeal is needed to reach people who suffer in silence and the former users not currently using any product in the category. For a concept test, a sample of 150 probably would not be sufficient. You would want a larger sample so that you could study each user group separately.

When choosing a sample size, you must think through the problem as it relates to your own plans and opportunities, as well as your budget. Think of the subgroups you must analyze and the analytic problems unique to your industry. For example, in many categories an analysis of the Reasons for Positive Purchase Interest question can be done among everyone with high Purchase Interest. This analysis tells the full story, because for those product categories all consumers, whether rich or poor, male or female, have similar reasons for high interest.

But in other categories, patterns of response to this question differ by subgroup. In the do-it-yourself home repair category, women react differently from men. Women are much more likely to be concerned about the appearance of the repaired item. A man might say, "Ah. Now it works." A woman might add, "But look how sloppy the repair looks." Women are also much more concerned about cost in this category. In this environment, a larger sample size is needed to look at reasons for acceptance or rejection by sex.

THE QUESTIONNAIRE

There is no such thing as a typical concept questionnaire. Various researchers use questionnaires that range in length from 5 to 35 minutes to explore different aspects of a concept and the consumers' reactions to it. My typical questionnaire requires 30 or 35 minutes to administer. The questions fall into the following eight areas:

1. Demographic characteristics of the respondent
2. Socioeconomic characteristics of the respondent
3. Attitudes toward the category
4. Knowledge of the category
5. Actual category behavior
6. Information about the concept retained by the respondent
7. Attitudes toward the concept
8. Future purchase intention toward the concept

Specific questions for those areas have been discussed in the preceding chapters. In addition, an actual example of a concept test questionnaire can be found in the Appendix.

Some researchers fear that a concept questionnaire that takes 30 minutes to administer is too long. But length-related problems can be avoided if you take steps to hold respondent attention for the complete interview. The secret is in preparing an interesting and varied questionnaire. Try switching around among different kinds of questions. Give respondents the opportunity to choose answers from preprinted scales, allow them to express opinions in their own words, ask them to check off answers on self-administered checklists, and have them reread the concept and circle key words or sentences. If you juggle the questions and the kind of responses required, you can maintain a high level of interest and involvement.

Most of the questions you will ever need for a concept test are included in the Appendix. However, there are occasions when you will have to write additional questions to explore or measure consumer reactions to issues that are unique to a specific concept. For the most part, writing an additional question requires a small bit of research knowledge and a large dose of common sense. If you must write additional questions, follow the pattern set by the questions in this book. You might also consult Stanley Payne's

Procedural Guidelines

book, *The Art of Asking Questions.* * This book, published in 1951 and still in print, is one of the best ever written on the subject of question writing. It's short, fun to read, educational, and as actionable today as it was almost four decades ago.

CODING

Once the questionnaire is written and the interviewing is completed, the data are ready to be coded. This is basically a clerical operation and will probably be done by someone other than you. Nevertheless, an understanding of the process of coding could help you improve the quality of your concept test.

Coding is the process of classifying the responses to open-end questions into a series of logical groupings. To illustrate: In a concept test for a window cleanser with a special ingredient that helps to clean windows faster and better, a code was prepared summarizing the various comments people gave to the Main Idea question. A portion of that code was:

Reference to Special Ingredient

1. Cleans fast because of a special ingredient.
2. Cleans more easily because of a special ingredient.
3. Leaves no streaks/smudges because of a special ingredient.
4. Leaves no grease because of a special ingredient.
5. Cleans good/well because of a special ingredient.
6. Only product available with a special ingredient.
7. Contains a special ingredient (no reference made to the cleaning benefit that the special ingredient provides).

Reference to Cleaning Ability But No Mention of Special Ingredient

8. Cleans fast/faster.
9. Cleans more easily/means less work for the person doing the cleaning.
10. Leaves no streaks/smudges.
11. Leaves no grease.
12. Cleans good/well.

*Stanley Payne, *The Art of Asking Questions* (Princeton: Princeton University Press, 1951); see especially pp. 228–37.

Concept Testing

In their own words, four of the respondents gave the following answers to the Main Idea question:

1. "They were telling us that this product cleans windows fast and streaklessly because it has a special ingredient in it."
2. "The only window cleaner on the market with a special ingredient."
3. "Gets rid of streaks and dirt from the window so that the sun shines in."
4. "It's got some special chemical in it that keeps the glass from streaking."

Coding the answers given by these respondents involves reading them and selecting the item from the code that best captures the essence of what the respondent said. In this example, respondent 1 would be coded as having said response 1 and 3. Respondent 2 would be coded as having said 6. Respondent 3 would be coded as having said 10. And respondent 4 would be coded as 3 even though the language used was different from the language used by respondent 1.

The first step of the coding process is to build a code. To do that, read through all or most of the answers to a question and then list a series of categories within which all the answers could be classified. Each code category contains similar kinds of comments and each is clearly different from other code categories. In the window-cleaning example, you would not put comments relating to fast cleaning and to the elimination of grease in the same category. In a concept for food, you would not put comments about good taste and speed of preparation in the same code category.

The most frequent problem with code building is that codes are often too detailed and too complex. The code builder defines too many different categories, and then gets caught up in nuances that have no marketing significance. For example, in the window cleaning concept test, one respondent talked about the product cleaning better than other products on the market while another talked about it cleaning best of the products on the market. These comments are similar; each is a reference to relative superiority. But some code builders might be tempted to have a "cleans better" category and a "cleans best" category. To me this is overkill. Often the problem occurs because the code is built by a junior member of the staff who may not have experience analyzing survey results or applying them to real-world marketing problems.

TABULATING

Once code building and coding of the open-end questions are completed, the data are ready to be tabulated. Tabulating, as used here, refers to counting the number of times a specific answer was given and organizing the results in a more meaningful way. Since this book contains many, many examples of how to optimize the tabulating phase of a concept test, we need not spend much time on the subject here.

There is one further point, however, to be made about tabulating open-end questions. It is often valuable to look beyond the responses to individual questions while attempting to measure respondents' understanding of a concept's main points or benefits. The process, called global tabulating, counts the number of consumers who are aware of some fact or who have some opinion, regardless of where on the questionnaire the information is expressed.

Global Tabulation

Unfortunately, many researchers are too myopic. They look at responses on a question-by-question basis without getting an all-encompassing overview of how the respondent truly feels. A researcher might attempt to evaluate the ability of a concept to communicate key product benefits by separately analyzing responses to the Main Idea question, the Advantages question, and other open-ends. This question-by-question approach occasionally distorts the communication strength or weakness of a concept.

Chart 10-1 illustrates the results from a recent concept test evaluating two different ways of describing a new food product that offered the twin benefits of good taste and ease of preparation. The chart shows answers to four different questions. If a researcher tabulated the results of only the Main Idea question, he would incorrectly conclude that Concept A communicated the main product benefit somewhat better than Concept B. The last line of the chart shows the conclusion would be wrong. By doing a net count of individuals who exhibited *some* sign of understanding the main benefit, regardless of where on the questionnaire such an indication appeared (see responses in italics), we found that both concepts communicated the main product benefit equally well.

True, the quality of the communication stimulated by each concept differs. However, both are equally effective in communicating the product's

Concept Testing

Chart 10-1. Global Tabulating.

	Concept A	Concept B
Main Idea		
Taste	34%	47%
Convenience	28	21
Taste plus convenience	(18)	13
What Were They Trying to Tell About Product? (Comprehension)		
Taste	63	75
Convenience	52	49
Taste plus convenience	(37)	31
What Is Hard to Believe?		
Good taste	4	3
Easy to prepare plus good taste	3	6
Price I can afford	3	1
What Is Hard to Understand?		
How it can cost so little	3	1
That my kids would like it	3	6
Easy to prepare yet tastes so good	1	2
Total communication of *"taste plus convenience"* any place on questionnaire	(41)	(40)

reason for being to the consumer. And this point would have been missed without global tabulating.

The longer the concept, the greater the need for global tabulating. The more elements a concept has, the harder it becomes for a respondent to pick them all up. The problem is most prevalent among concepts for products in highly competitive categories. It seems that marketers attempt to differentiate their products with small "cosmetic" benefits or improvements. Faced with a long concept that stresses both general category benefits and specific product attributes, it's not surprising that consumers become confused and miss the main strength of the concept, or play back different elements in response to different questions.

Procedural Guidelines

Analytic Tool

Tabulating the percentage of respondents who show evidence anywhere on the questionnaire of understanding the concept is an important first step. Once you've done this tabulation, you have provided yourself with a valuable analytic tool. Use it to evaluate the internal consistency of your data. If your concept scores high on Purchase Interest but communicates its main benefits to only 3 percent of the sample, you've identified a danger signal. Globally tabulating your open-end data opens the door to interesting and valuable special analyses that can help you improve your concept and its performance in the marketplace.

The toothpaste industry provides one pertinent example. For years, Procter & Gamble's Crest had monopolized toothpaste sales. Various competitors failed when they tried to unseat Crest, using approaches suggesting either that they too contained fluoride or that their product was good-tasting. Finally Aim came along, and succeeded. Its original basic premise was also that it was a good-tasting fluoride toothpaste. When consumers were asked to describe the concept, many talked about the good taste of the product. The opinions of one respondent were expressed in various ways, within various questions.

- *Main Idea.* "The product tastes good and it contains fluoride."
- *Major Advantage.* "I'll brush with it a little longer if it tastes good."
- *Reason for Purchase Interest.* "It contains fluoride so I'll brush with it for a longer time each morning in order to take care of my teeth."

Globally tabulating the responses of this person and others exposed to the concept established that many people heard three claims: "has fluoride," "tastes good," and "you will brush longer." The next step was a cross tabulation among those with high Purchase Interest versus those with low Purchase Interest in the concept. The tabulation found that consumers with high Purchase Interest were especially likely to have heard all these claims: that people would brush longer with Aim because it's a fluoride that tastes good.

The resulting advertising campaign was for a fluoride-based toothpaste with a superior good-taste claim—that Aim would be used more *because* it has a good taste. It turned out to be a strong position with which to compete against the Crest monopoly.

TIME AND COST

The two questions most frequently asked about concept tests are "How long will the test take?" and "How much will it cost?"

Both depend on the length of the questionnaire, the number of concepts being evaluated, the sample size, and the difficulty of finding qualified respondents. Let us invent specifications for a hypothetical test.

1. *Questionnaire*: Long and thorough enough to explore all aspects of the concept and the consumer's reaction to it. It requires 30 minutes to administer.
2. *Number of concepts being evaluated*: Three.
3. *Sample size*: 150 per concept, or 450 interviews in total.
4. *Difficulty in finding qualified respondents*: No problem. Any adult females can be interviewed.

Given these specifications, the 1986 price might be in the area of $10,000 per concept. Plan for the assignment to take six weeks. You might be able to get it done faster, but you run the risk of having less time available to analyze and interpret the findings.

SCREENING MULTIPLE CONCEPTS

Most of this book has discussed the evaluation of a single concept. As you have seen, a thorough and all-encompassing concept test requires conducting a lengthy and relatively expensive interview, coding many open-end questions, preparing a large number of computer tabulations, and devoting many analytic hours to digesting and interpreting the results.

What do you do when there are 25 to 50 new-product concepts to screen? Do you use the same research approach? I think not.

For one thing, the cost would be incredibly high to test all of them intensively, including those that could quickly be eliminated with a few key questions.

Even if cost were not an issue, an intensive evaluation of all concepts might be a case of overkill. When there are *many* different new-product concepts to screen, the initial goal should be to winnow down the candidates to a manageable number. We want to eliminate the obvious dogs and hone in on those with the potential for further development. We can eventually go back to the winning concepts for a more in-depth review of their strengths and weaknesses.

While an intensive review of each concept is not advisable, some researchers go too far in the opposite direction and do a simple screening, often involving just one or two closed-end questions per concept. The benefit is an extremely low cost to screen each concept, but this approach has two problems:

1. Many concepts follow the distressing pattern of scoring in a narrow range. As a result, it is hard to discriminate between winners and losers if you rely on one question.
2. Concept statements sometimes do not clearly communicate to respondents. A potentially winning idea can die because a simple-to-fix communications flaw was not discovered.

In solving these two problems, you run the risk of completing the circle by reverting back to the initial approach—a long (and expensive) survey. This problem becomes more significant as you increase the number of concepts tested. Here's a procedure for a middle position:

1. Measure Purchase Interest to help predict the future potential of each concept.
2. Ask some tie-breaker questions, since Purchase Interest does not always discriminate.
3. Include some diagnostic questions to help identify obvious and easily fixed problems.

The goal here is to do more than a typical two-question concept screener that basically seeks a single magic number. This procedure will not provide *final* positioning insights, but it will collect sufficient diagnostic data to tell you if there are any serious problems that caused an otherwise potentially successful candidate to fail.

A QUESTIONNAIRE FOR MULTI-CONCEPT SCREENINGS

The questionnaire discussed here is intended to be quickly administered, produce sensitive, discriminating data, and provide you with some insight into how to fix a deficient concept. It consists of six sections.

1. Each concept should be evaluated on Purchase Interest and Reasons for Purchase Interest. To make maximum use of the Purchase Interest ques-

tion, use Purchase Interest norms to help you determine how much potential your concept has.

2. Each concept should also be rated on an Emotional Reaction Battery. This is a group of questions covering such issues as the concept's ability to be:

- Interesting
- Important
- Unique
- Relevant to the consumer's needs
- Believable
- Clear

These questions can help you pick concept winners when other "overall" questions like Purchase Interest are too insensitive.

Norms will help you to maximize the usefulness of this battery. They will allow you to pinpoint which element of the battery is below par.

This battery of questions is also very useful in a diagnostic sense. Valuable insights have been uncovered when responses to various open-end and closed-end questions are tabulated by, say, those with high and low Uniqueness scores.

3. It's important to identify the main idea about the product that is communicated by the concept. Analyzing this question tells you what concept elements are successfully or poorly communicated. Use this data to tell you if the benefits you think you are communicating are the same ones that consumers are hearing. This will help you to identify concepts whose poor performance was related to the fact that consumers didn't "get" the message you thought you were sending.

You probably recall from Chapter 4 that I recommend that you analyze the Main Idea question in conjunction with Reasons for Purchase Interest. This will tell you the degree to which various benefits were unsuccessful either because they weren't heard or they were heard but were unpersuasive. This type of analysis will give your marketing people good advice on how to fix the concept.

4. You should also determine if the respondents think there are any advantages or disadvantages about the concept that they consider major. This is a useful closed-end question for diagnostic purposes. Once again, having good norms will help you to make this data quite useful.

5. Be sure to find out how the product described by each concept could be improved. This is a useful diagnostic question when compared with appropriate normative data.

As indicated earlier, you must use some imagination when you interpret this issue. Look for patterns of response rather than literal comments. For example, if a few respondents complain about, say, the color of an appliance while others complain about the shape or the size, don't be too concerned about each individual complaint. But do notice that they are all complaining about design or style issues.

6. Appropriate questions of product usage (including Occasions of Use and expected Frequency of Use), classification, and demographic data also belong in these questionnaires.

Considerations for Multi-Concept Tests

I recommend that you conduct 250 interviews per concept. This is larger than my normal concept test sample size of 150. This expansion is sufficiently large to tell you which population segments you are attracting. It is important for you to know early in the product's development if it has broad or narrow appeal.

Interviewing can be completed in shopping centers at several dispersed markets acceptable to you. Each interview will require about 25 minutes to administer, since a given respondent can evaluate four concepts.

When you analyze the data, do more than just operate like a "field and tab" agency. Build your own customized norms, following the guidelines suggested in Chapter 9. Make a special effort to clearly identify the strong candidates worthy of further development, and "dogs" with no redeeming qualities. Use the techniques described throughout this book to help you accomplish this goal.

Keep in mind that this approach just gives limited help to fix "so-so" concepts that have some strength but also have a major problem that can be easily fixed. Accept the fact that you are not doing as intensive and detailed an examination as you normally do. Nevertheless, the preliminary look will help you avoid the problem of killing a potentially great idea just because a simple revision was never made.

IV.

Concept Testing in Action: A Case History

11
The Case History:
Collecting the Data

The previous chapters of this book have shown how many different survey questions and analytic techniques can unlock secrets that lead to successful new products. The unfortunate side effect of separately discussing each concept testing tool is that you cannot appreciate how the interaction of various questions and analytic approaches fleshes out and enriches the analysis. It is akin to analyzing Mona Lisa element by element and describing her as having a beautiful chin, interesting eyes, and thin lips that hint of a smile. Without seeing all parts of her face, working in tandem, you cannot properly appreciate her beauty.

The case history described in the final section of the book will show how the lessons of the earlier chapters can be applied in a real-world situation. The case history is based on a concept test I conducted for a frozen food product. Although the category here is food, the analytical approach is applicable for concept tests in all product categories.

Let's begin with some background information about this segment of the food business. This information will clarify why this concept test had to be conducted and will provide a context within which some of its major findings can be better understood. Every concept test should begin with this type of category review.

BACKGROUND

The frozen meal segment of the food industry grew quite rapidly after World War II as rising incomes and increased numbers of working women caused drastic changes in the values and lifestyle of the typical American family. The lifestyle changes were voluminous but two had a major effect on the frozen food category:

Concept Testing

1. The availability of large home freezers.
2. Reduction in time available for food preparation.

Early frozen dinner products (excluding specific menu items such as a frozen vegetable or frozen dessert) tended to be reasonably priced and convenient to serve. They were full meals like chicken pot pie and TV dinners, complete with roll, vegetable, and choice of meat, chicken, or turkey. These meals may not have tasted so great, but who could tell for sure with the heavy gravy topping?

In spite of many changes and additions to the cast of industry players and the products they offered, consumers did not think the industry was changing very much in the years after World War II. Ask a 1970s housewife to talk about frozen dinners or frozen entrees and she would tell you they were low-cost, convenient foods to keep on hand for emergencies and informal family eating, especially for nondiscriminating children. This response was quite similar to the one you would have been given by a 1950s housewife.

A Segmented Market

But in the mid-1970s, noticeable changes suddenly began to rock the industry from many different directions.

1. America's food tastes and preferences began to change. A market emerged for more exotic, interesting, and varied choices.
2. Consumers began to become more calorie-conscious. They looked to food marketers to provide them with dieting help in tasty, low-calorie items. Companies like Weight Watchers jumped in with product lines aimed directly at the dieting segment of the American public.
3. A second health segment began to emerge, this one consisting of consumers who, while perhaps not actively dieting, were interested in eating wholesome and healthy foods. Suddenly, natural foods were in and salt, sugar, additives, and preservatives were out. Marketers quickly responded to these changing tastes. Lean Cuisine emerged around 1980 with a slew of very tasty low-calorie entrees. While perfectly suitable for the dieter, they also successfully attracted an even larger number of health-conscious, weight-conscious, calorie-conscious individuals.
4. The microwave oven began to enter America's homes, stimulated by a desire for faster, easier, more convenient food preparation. Mar-

keters responded with new-product formulations designed to be microwaved.

5. The category fragmented further. Benihana introduced exotic frozen meals and Campbell Soup marketed Le Menu, frozen meals with a sophisticated, upscale imagery and menu choices to match. Along came Budget Gourmet, which competed on price. Each of these companies in turn attracted its own competitors. This practice of segmenting the market into smaller and more focused product lines shows every sign of continuing.

6. Concurrently, the cost side of the business also was in a state of change. By the mid-1980s, inflation had fallen. The public's tolerance for price hikes ended and companies were increasingly prevented from passing additional costs on to the consumer. At the same time, increasingly competitive marketplace conditions required more and better menu selections. Advertising and marketing expenses constantly rose so that drastic budget increases were required each year merely to maintain the same relative presence (or share of voice) in the marketplace.

Two Big Changes

As we approach the 1990s, two other major changes in America's food consumption habits are occurring, each one so big that it threatens to shake the very foundation upon which the frozen food industry is based. So far the food industry has not responded effectively to either, although both are life-and-death issues for the current product lines of various manufacturers.

1. The popularity of "grazing," the custom of eating more lightly and more frequently during the day. In effect, grazing reduces consumption of traditional lunch and dinner items.

2. Increasingly, members of a family eat separately—different foods at different times, in different locations. Here too, the process of eating separately reduces consumption of traditional lunch and dinner items manufactured by existing companies in the food industry.

This is the environment within which a major food company with no meaningful presence in the frozen meal business wanted to launch a new frozen dinner line. The company had set some tough requirements:

1. The line had to be different, that is, somewhat unique from other lines, to win its share of business.

179

2. Yet it had to be close enough to current consumer needs to attract a reasonable level of sales in the short term.
3. It had to be launched as soon as possible to have a better chance against rapid category fragmentation and drastic increases in marketing costs.

This background review, however brief and superficial it seems to individuals already in this business, is quite useful and necessary for the analysts with no knowledge of the category. It provides a context for understanding, interpreting, and effectively using the survey data.

Unfortunately, background reviews are frequently not done, which could explain why so many executives are dissatisfied with the results of concept tests. After all, if analysts don't know the full background, how can they know what special questions to ask, what special tabulations to execute, or how to best interpret the data?

THE NATURE OF THE ASSIGNMENT

The manufacturer had been considering many different alternatives with which to enter the frozen dinner category. The one I will discuss here was an idea for a line of tasty entrees, a bit more interesting, fancier, and more sophisticated than competitive lines, and a bit less in bulk, volume, and calories. The goal was to provide a balanced and complete but less filling meal. It would be priced competitively. A concept describing this line is shown below.

Candidate Concept for New Frozen Dinner Line

A healthy and nutritious light meal complemented with a refreshing medley of chilled fruits. A unique treat that offers a balanced meal to meet today's lifestyles.

Here's the perfect meal for the light way you like to eat today— delicious light entrees, accented with fruit for a fresh, sophisticated touch.

You might choose delicate turkey and asparagus crepes with a side dish of kiwi fruit and red and green grapes. Or broccoli quiche, served with avocado wedges and a chilled medley of blueberries, strawberries, and honeydew melon balls. Or lemon chicken with crispy pea pods and seasoned rice with cashew slices, accompanied by chilled peaches with melba sauce. Three varieties in all.

They're healthy and elegant taste combinations for today's life-

style—perfect any time you're in the mood for something light and nourishing.

Each comes frozen on a handsome plate ready for your microwave
or conventional oven. The chilled fruit medleys come in a pop-out dish,
and thaw on your counter in minutes while your main course heats. The
three varieties range in price from $1.79 to $2.99.

Before the company proceeded with actual product, advertising, and
package development, it authorized a concept test to determine whether the
idea had sufficient potential to warrant additional expense and effort. The
objectives of the concept test were to answer four questions.

1. Was the message communicated to consumers by the concept (both
direct statements and emotional or subjective implications and suggestions)
the same message the sponsor wished to communicate? In case of concept
failure, these data would tell us if the problem was caused by our poor
communication of the product's positioning or an inherent weakness in the
idea itself.

2. Was the positive appeal stimulated by the concept of sufficient depth
and intensity to warrant further development? If insufficient appeal was
apparent, the test should identify if there were any pockets of strength within
small segments of the population once consumers were classified into ho-
mogeneous groupings based upon their demographics, attitudes, or behavior. Such pockets of strength could, of course, suggest further developmental
directions.

3. What were the individual strengths and weaknesses of the concept?
What elements made the concept succeed? Which ones held back acceptance? What was said or shown that should have been said or shown louder,
better, or not at all? Information in this area could help us to identify appropriate changes or improvements that would strengthen the concept.

4. What marketing insights could be uncovered that could be translated
into the creation of better advertising, packaging, and promotional programs?

PROCEDURAL CONSIDERATIONS

To test this concept, a sample of consumers was invited to read it and answer
a battery of questions that required about a half hour to administer. (The
complete questionnaire is in the Appendix.) The questionnaire is long and
detailed, covering many aspects of how respondents react to the concept as

well as background information about them that would help us analyze their reactions.

Sample Size

A sample of 150 female household heads or spouses of household heads was interviewed. The sample was equally distributed over six geographically dispersed areas. The sample size of 150 was a compromise. There was a $10,000 research budget. Given this budget, I had to choose between giving a short questionnaire to a large sample size (with the resultant small sampling error and the opportunity to do lots of special subgroup analysis) and giving a much longer questionnaire covering more special issues to a smaller sample size.

I concluded that a sample size of 150 was a suitable compromise. It provided me with a sampling error that was small enough to work with. It also afforded me the opportunity to do a number of special subgroup analyses to help me to understand the data better and milk it more thoroughly. (Chapter 10 discussed sample sizes and tradeoffs in some detail.)

Composition of Sample

All interviews were conducted among female household heads (or spouses of household heads) who were between 18 and 65 years of age and had purchased frozen entrees or frozen dinners within the past three months. A great deal of thought went into this rather simple specification, including these four considerations.

1. Since females purchase more than 75 percent of all frozen entrees, this group definitely must be represented in the sample. I also considered including men in the sample, but decided that if I were to include some men (in proportion to their share of frozen food purchases) their number would have been too few to allow me to analyze their attitudes and opinions separately. And if I included a small number of them in the sample and in my analysis, without breaking their results out separately, the relatively larger size of the female segment would overwhelm and hide their reactions. So I decided that the male portion of the sample was too small to be analytically useful and elected to focus all resources on the concept's primary target, females.

2. A decision to interview household heads or spouses of the household head was made for essentially the same reason. Most of the purchasing in this category is done by women who run their households. If I broadened the sample to include children living at home who shop for their family and

buy products in this category, I felt I might water down the number of female household heads—the prime target group—while providing an insufficient number of other females for analytic purposes.

3. The age of an eligible respondent was deliberately limited to a maximum of 65. The general experience of companies who market products in this category is that older consumers account for a small percentage of category sales and have an above-average number of special diet requirements or desires (for example, no salt or reduced cholesterol). I concluded that older consumers' opinions about our proposed product were worth studying separately if the concept got a passing grade on this first test.

4. The decision to require each eligible respondent to have purchased a frozen entree or dinner product within the last three months was tricky. When a category is newly developing, I look at this type of restriction as a dangerous constraint. My rationale is that much of the initial trial of a product comes from people who have not yet tried a competing product, perhaps have not even heard of one.

But as a category matures, and sales for a new entrant come increasingly from other brands, the danger associated with this exclusionary practice becomes less serious. In fact there comes a point when a prior nonuser has such a low likelihood of being swayed into the category by a new candidate that it doesn't pay to devote any of our limited resources to study this person.

In my judgment the frozen entree and frozen dinner category is a lot closer to full development than to being a newly developed one. For this reason I leaned toward focusing my limited budget on current category users. I felt that conducting a few interviews among noncategory users would weaken the precision of my estimate among the prime target group.

A Subjective Question

You should keep in mind that each of these decisions is based on subjective judgment, not unassailable fact. Another analyst could take an opposite tack and refute all my recommendations. He or she might argue to include children who are responsible for their family's food shopping, or women 78 years of age since they too represent part of the marketplace. If they are a small part of the potential market, so the argument might go, they should be included in their correct proportion, a small part of the sample.

My rejoinder: I am interested in specific population segments, in finding out what makes them tick and how to motivate them. Muddying the water with other segments gets in my way analytically, the research equivalent of a fuzzy television screen. My opponent's counterargument might be that I should be interested in the total marketplace as a starting point and worry about individual segments later. My response: Having these people in the sample with possibly lower interest in the test concept may broaden the size of the potential market but may also cause the premature death of an otherwise fine idea.

Back and forth the debate could go. Who is right? That is a judgment call that you must make. My goal here is to tell you what I did and why I did it. You are invited to question these judgments, as well as those to come, and decide for yourself what you would have done given the same issue to resolve.

12
The Case History: Analyzing the Results

The objectives are clear. The sample size and composition have been determined. The questionnaire has been written (see Appendix) and administered. The responses have been coded and tabulated. Everything is in place. We are now ready to discuss consumer reactions to the test concept.

As you read this chapter, note how the analysis proceeds in an organized and systematic way, yet is constantly open to unexpected twists and hints that pop up from time to time. The fact is that these surprises exist in virtually every concept test. Finding them, figuring out why they occur, and developing appropriate marketplace responses are often what converts an average, unexceptional concept test into an insightful and exciting management tool.

OVERALL REACTIONS

Purchase Interest

My usual starting place is the Purchase Interest question. Analysis of these results provides a good estimate of the concept's level of effectiveness. The information was collected via the following question:

A producer of frozen foods is thinking about some ideas for new frozen food products. I would like to show you a description of one of these products, and then I would like you to tell me your reactions to this new product. Please read the description for as long as you like and tell me when you have finished.

[*Hand respondent concept statement. When she indicates that she is finished, take back concept.*]

185

Concept Testing

[*Hand respondent Purchase Interest card*] Which phrase on this card best describes how likely you would be to buy one or more products in this line if it were available for a price ranging from $1.79 to $2.99 in the store where you usually shop for frozen dinners?

> Definitely would buy it 5
> Probably would but it 4
> Might or might not buy it 3
> Probably would not buy it 2
> Definitely would not buy it 1

As Chart 12-1 shows, just 17 percent of all consumers in our prime target group express a strong positive interest in the product. At first glance, this level of response is quite unimpressive. My normative data show that the typical new-product concept in this category stimulates strong positive response in 19 percent of the public exposed to it. In other words, the test concept is barely average. And we must keep in mind that this norm is based on *all* concepts, including low-scoring failures that hold the average down.

A second perspective about the concept's performance is provided by the norm for "winners," which is the minimum score of concepts that eventually went on to become winners in the marketplace. This norm is a rather high 26 percent, demonstrating that the test concept is substantially below par, as it now stands.

In many companies the concept would be killed because of this "top box" or "definitely would buy" score. But that would be a very poor decision. Other data from this same question are signaling that the product has some potential in spite of the low level of intense positive interest that it stimulated.

The third line of Chart 12-1 contains a useful clue. On average, 44 percent of those exposed to the typical concept in this category state they "probably would buy it"—a positive but weaker commitment to a product. But our concept received a 55 percent "probably would buy it" score, well above norm for all concepts as well as for winners.

Adding these 55 percent to the 17 percent who tell us they definitely plan to buy the product gives us a total of 72 percent who indicate some level of positive interest in our concept, well above all norms for the category. The data are simultaneously showing us a problem and an opportunity. The message being sent by the data is not to kill the concept, but to try to fix it by identifying the key issues that can raise the intensity of

The Case History: Analyzing the Results

Chart 12-1. Purchase Interest.

	Test Concept	Frozen Entree and Dinner Norms	
		All Concepts	Winners
Definitely/Probably would but it	(72)%	63%	66%
Definitely would buy it	17	19	(26)
Probably would buy it	(55)	44	40
Might or might not buy it	21		
Probably would not buy it	4		
Definitely would not buy it	3		

Purchase Interest. In effect, the task at hand is to uncover the sparks or "hot buttons" that can convert mild positive interest into intense interest.

A very significant amount of time and effort is required to intensively analyze the data from a concept test to identify these hot buttons. Before embarking down this road, the analyst should know with as much certainty as possible if this effort will be a worthwhile one. So far, all I know is that one question, Purchase Interest, merely suggests that the concept has some additional potential. But Purchase Interest is just one question and not a magical one, at that. I also do not know for sure if the "definitely would buy" score, disappointing to start with, has been affected by statistical sampling error because of a small sample size. The same for the "probably would buy" score. Again, it is just one number from a multi-point scale.

Benefits and Shortcomings

In view of this uncertainty, the next step in my analysis is to seek corroboration from other survey questions that the concept has some additional potential and that it contains no major flaw that makes it unworthy of further development. One battery of questions that is quite useful in this regard measures the benefits and shortcomings that consumers associate with a product idea. The questions are:

Concept Testing

Do you think this line of products would have . . .

> Major benefits 1
> Minor benefits 2
> Or, no benefits at all 3

Do you think this line of products would have . . .

> Major shortcomings 1
> Minor shortcomings 2
> Or, no shortcomings at all 3

As with so many other survey indicators, the usefulness of these questions is largely influenced by the availability of norms that provide a context within which to interpret reactions to the test concept.

As shown in Chart 12-2, 84 percent of the total sample believe the product described by the concept offers one or more benefits. At first glance, this score seems quite impressive considering that many of the people in this group merely had neutral or negative Purchase Interest. However, the norm for the category, again based on an average of all concepts tested (including weak ones), reveals that 84 percent is a substandard score.

Chart 12-2 also shows that the number who believe our concept offers a *major* benefit is also substandard. In contrast, the number who report that the product offers one or more *minor* benefits is well above average. This information supports the hypothesis suggested by the Purchase Interest question, that the concept stimulates a great deal of mild interest but the absence of hot buttons holds back its performance. The Shortcomings question provides further confirmation of this theory. Few consumers think the concept contains any shortcomings, major or minor.

Total Emotional Profile

Before putting this issue to bed I turn to one more battery of questions to help corroborate the tentative hypothesis that the concept is worth saving in spite of its low Purchase Interest score. The battery, which I refer to as the concept's Total Emotional Profile, measures different emotions stimulated by the concept.

The battery consists of a series of seven-point bipolar questions that allow respondents to react to the concept on a series of specific dimensions. The question is self-administered, an interviewing method that keeps respondents interested and involved in the interview. The question and the self-administered answer sheet are shown on page 190.

Chart 12-2. Benefits and shortcomings.

	Test Concept	*Frozen Entree and Dinner Norms, All Concepts Tested*
Has Benefits	84%	(90)%
Major benefits	33	(48)
Minor benefits	(51)	42
Has Shortcomings	29	(36)
Major shortcomings	5	6
Minor shortcomings	24	(30)

Chart 12-3 shows the results of this question. Comparing the data with appropriate norms shows that consumers think the concept describes a very believable and interesting product idea. Consumers also apparently think the concept says important things and contains unique ideas.

Unfortunately, the concept is just average with respect to its general persuasiveness; see the scores for "talking to me," "relevant to my needs," and "persuasive." And this question reveals one problem: Something about the concept is confusing or difficult to understand. I will try to identify the cause of this problem shortly. But for the moment, I am quite comfortable with the direction suggested by the data.

What We Know So Far

In sum, the evidence suggests that:

1. Purchase Interest in the concept is low. The number who "definitely will buy it" is substantially below the norm of previously tested winning concepts.
2. However, it does generate significant amounts of mild positive interest.
3. The mild interest, coupled with the results of the Benefits/Shortcomings questions and the Total Emotional Profile, suggests that the problem may be insufficient excitement or enthusiasm caused by the lack of a hot button of value to the respondent, rather than a fatal flaw caused by poor or inadequate benefits or features.

Total Emotional Profile

The paper I'm handing you is a rating sheet for the description you just read. You can see a series of boxes between sets of various phrases. We would like you to "X" one box on each line to describe how you feel about the description.

Let's suppose you were asked to describe the weather this week and you found the phrases "Extremely Unpleasant—Extremely Pleasant." If you thought the weather was extremely unpleasant, you would put an "X" on the far left like this: [*Point to box.*]

If you thought the weather was extremely pleasant, you would put an "X" on the far right like this: [*Point to box.*]

However, if you felt the weather this week was somewhere between the two extremes, you would put an "X" in a box somewhere between the two phrases, depending on what you thought the weather was.

Do you see how it works? [*If no, repeat.*] Remember to think in terms of the description you just read.

Respondent Self-Administered Rating Sheet

Please check one box between each pair of statements to indicate your opinion of the description you just read. The more strongly you feel a phrase describes your feelings, the closer to the phrase would be the box you check.

EXAMPLE:	Today, the weather was:	
Extremely unpleasant	□ □ □ □ □ □ □	Extremely pleasant

The description is:

	1 2 3 4 5 6 7	
Boring	□ □ □ □ □ □ □	Interesting
Not at all believable	□ □ □ □ □ □ □	Very believable
Not talking to me	□ □ □ □ □ □ □	Talking to me
About an ordinary product	□ □ □ □ □ □ □	About a unique product
Relevant to my needs	□ □ □ □ □ □ □	Not relevant to my needs
Persuasive	□ □ □ □ □ □ □	Not persuasive
Not saying important things	□ □ □ □ □ □ □	Saying important things
Easy to understand	□ □ □ □ □ □ □	Not easy to understand
Saying something unique	□ □ □ □ □ □ □	Saying something ordinary
Something rubs me the wrong way	□ □ □ □ □ □ □	Nothing rubs me the wrong way
	1 2 3 4 5 6 7	

The Case History: Analyzing the Results

Chart 12-3. Rating of concept on specific characteristics.

	Test Concept	Frozen Entree and Dinner Norm, All Concepts Tested
Very believable	⟨74⟩%	56%
Saying important things	⟨71⟩	52
Interesting	⟨65⟩	44
About a unique product	⟨57⟩	36
Nothing rubs me the wrong way	70	74
Talking to me	55	50
Relevant to my needs	45	44
Persuasive	35	40
Easy to understand	69	⟨86⟩

I now feel more comfortable about the concept's potential. The evidence suggests that is it worthwhile to invest additional time and effort in this concept. I plan to continue the analysis, with the remaining phases aimed at isolating the concept's strong points. First I will work on identifying who is most likely to buy the product, and second, on learning how to restructure and improve the concept in order to create greater buying interest.

POCKETS OF STRENGTH

The next step is to complete a large number of different computer cross tabs to isolate segments of the population that are most responsive to the concept—in other words, to identify the concept's pockets of strength. Even though the sample size of 150 respondents does not allow me to do a *very* detailed analysis within various population subgroups, I can still get a rough qualitative feel for the way different segments react to the concept. Even though much of this analysis will not produce statistically significant differences, it often produces clues or stimulates hypotheses that can be tested or confirmed by other data from the survey, or from pursuing further research efforts.

191

Concept Testing

Chart 12-4. Positive Purchase Interest by
selected demographics.

Total respondents	72%
By employment status	
Employed	66
Full-time housewife	(79)
By household size	
1–2	67
3 or more	(78)
By household composition	
Have children at home	(81)
Do not have children at home	63
By age	
18–44	68
45 or more	(82)
By education status	
Graduated high school or less	(81)
Some college or more	66

Demographic Breakdown

Chart 12-4 shows the level of support for this concept among consumers within various demographic subgroups. Wide differences in Purchase Interest are observed when respondents are subdivided by employment status, household size, and the presence of children. The chart appears to indicate that full-time housewives with children are especially responsive to the concept.

This slant toward full-time homemakers does not correlate with norms or with actual category sales. Apparently, something about our concept may be attracting full-time homemakers instead of the more typical working woman. The issue interested me, so I did a number of special computer tabulations. They suggested that full-time homemakers are responsive to the notion that the product is especially appropriate for someone eating alone or in the mood for something light or different. The data offer no clue, as yet, to explain this finding. I make a mental note to explore this issue further as my analysis unfolds.

But even though we don't yet know *why* full-time homemakers are especially responsive to the concept, the fact that they are is very valuable for media scheduling. Knowing that your target audience is at home all day suggests the value of traditional women's service magazines and daytime television as a means of reaching them.

Other interesting demographic differences are also apparent in Chart 12-4. It appears the younger and better-educated consumers have a lower interest in the concept than do their older and less well-educated counterparts. This is noteworthy because it is the opposite of category norms and the sales profile enjoyed by many brands currently on the market. I first assume that these older, less-educated women are the full-time housewives just discussed. But a few simple cross tabulations quickly dispels this assumption. There is just a small correlation between the two groups. In effect, the high interest of older, less-educated women is a separate and unrelated issue.

As a tentative hypothesis, I wonder if their interest is providing us with an opportunity to reach a population subgroup not being adequately reached by products currently on the market. I also wonder what elements of the concept cause these women to be more responsive to it. Some additional computer tabulations suggest that older, less-educated women seem to react more positively to the concept's overtones of elegance and sophistication. Why are they responding more positively to these two elements?

Perhaps women with lower educational levels do not encounter much glamour or elegance in their usual meals, a problem that this product addresses. Or perhaps their positive reactions to elegance may not be the true motivating issue. It may be that because of their lighter usage of other frozen food brands, this concept is more interesting because it seems new. In other words, the gut issue might really be their relative inexperience with the category.

The specific reason causing their positive reaction is unclear, but it is quite important that we isolate it, since it affects how the product will ultimately be positioned, packaged, and advertised when it reaches the marketplace. Unfortunately, we cannot milk the current question any further to answer this question. All we know for sure is that older women, who use frozen foods less often than other population groups, are especially responsive to the test concept. It is an issue that must be clarified in other questions in this survey.

Chart 12-5. Positive Purchase Interest by
usage of competitive brands.

Total with high Purchase Interest   17%

Brand Ever Used

    Le Menu   ㉖
    Lean Cuisine   ㉕
    Benihana   16
    Armour Dinner Classics   14
    Budget Gourmet   13

Use of Competing Brands

In addition to the demographic analysis, I also completed a special tabulation correlating Purchase Interest with usage of various frozen food brands. This information is potentially quite valuable. It provides a strategist with the tools he needs to decide whether to compete in the current segment of strength, go after other brands instead, or develop a more generally acceptable position that appeals to everyone. There is no single correct answer. The specific decision depends on many marketing, product, and competitive issues well beyond the scope of this research. Nevertheless, even partial information is of obvious benefit.

Chart 12-5 shows that the concept does draw its strength from some brands more than others. The concept has an affinity with Le Menu (probably because of its overtones of elegance and sophistication) and Lean Cuisine (probably because of its "light" positioning, which is suggestive of low calories). On the other hand, the middle-of-the-road positioning of Armour Dinner Classics, the more exotic offerings of Benihana (often with heavy sauces to match), and the low prices of Budget Gourmet clearly do not deliver as many users to our product.

Once again, I cannot tell from this question alone whether these results are optimal. Should we be doing a better job of reaching Armour users? Are we appealing to Le Menu users too heavily? I resolve to use data from upcoming questions to clarify this issue.

Keep in mind that the differences in preference among users of the various competitive brands are much larger and more meaningful than the numbers in Chart 12-5 suggest. The problem is caused by our use of the

Brands Ever Used question. A better question is Favorite Brand or Brand Used Most Often. Unfortunately, with a total sample size of 150, the number who use each brand most often would be too small for analytic purposes. For this reason I often work with Brands Ever Used.

In view of the fact that there is a great deal of brand switching in this category, it is likely that many of the same people are in two or more brand user groups. Consequently, differences in preference among the various groups tend to be narrowed in a chart like this. Knowing of this narrowing effect allows the analyst to be more respectful and appreciative of a difference when it occurs.

13
The Case History:
The Search for Hot Buttons

The final purpose of this analysis is to identify the issues that are capable of holding back acceptance of the product. What are the things we should have said but didn't? What should we have said better or differently? What did we comment on that was better left unsaid? This is the section of the analysis in which I spend most of my time.

MAIN IDEA QUESTION

The place to start a search for hot buttons is the responses to the Main Idea question. Respondents were asked this question:

Other than trying to sell you the product, what do you think was the main idea in the description you just read? That is, what was the main thing they were trying to communicate about the product?

But first, it is important to remember that the data only report what consumers regard as the *major* ideas communicated by the concept. The question does not measure whether an idea is actually communicated or not, but whether it was communicated with enough importance and emphasis to cause the respondent to mention it in response to this question. It is possible, for example, for a consumer to hear five benefits but mention just two of them in response to this question.

It is also important to remember that the value of the Main Idea question is created by the analyst, not the interviewer. The analytic process is slow and laborious. If you spend just a minute or two on it, you simply are not doing the question justice.

Before reviewing the data you should reread the concept statement slowly and carefully. As we discussed in Chapter 4, using your own personal opinions and judgments, pick out the sales points or benefits that are the product's main reasons for being. Then select the benefits of lesser importance, and lastly, the benefits that are window dressing—the kinds of things one would say to provide credibility or support a more important benefit.

Your overall goal is to list all the elements and benefits actually given to consumers in the concept, not just the ones management meant to provide. The key to this analysis is to make personal judgments, in advance, of what to expect. Then, if the actual data are different from expectation, you have the basis for making assumptions and developing hypotheses on how to solve problems and create opportunities.

In this test, I listed the following series of primary, secondary, and tertiary benefits.

Primary

1. Light meal
2. Healthy, nutritious, balanced meal
3. Good taste
4. Three varieties
5. Elegance, sophistication
6. Chilled fruit side dish

Secondary

1. Convenient and easy to prepare
2. Modern food for today's lifestyles

Tertiary

1. Appropriate for microwaves or conventional ovens
2. Unique
3. Reasonable price points
4. Handsome plate
5. Fruit comes on a pop-out dish
6. Fruit thaws in minutes

Even before we inspect responses to the Main Idea question, this special step of listing out benefits in order of apparent importance pays a major dividend. While I was not especially bothered by the large number of secondary and tertiary benefits, the fact that the concept provides six primary benefits troubles me. The problem is that the more primary benefits you offer, the harder it is for an impartial and relatively uninvolved individual to keep track of them all and be motivated to purchase the product. In my experience, when you offer more than three primary benefits, the concept often does not perform well. Consumers get confused. Their ability to remember or become excited about one of these special features is reduced, so their desire to purchase the product tends to be lower.

The obvious solution: Rewrite the concept so that primary attention is focused upon a smaller number of major benefits.

Primary Benefits

Let us now turn to Chart 13-1, which summarizes the main ideas communicated by the concept. This chart provides a great deal of very valuable information. To start with, just two of the six primary benefits—lightness and health—are considered to be main ideas by large numbers of respondents. The other four, which deal with good taste, three specific varieties, the product's elegance and sophistication, and the chilled fruit side dish, make a significantly smaller impact. The consumer is already confirming, on this opening diagnostic chart, that she cannot, or will not, keep track of all six primary benefits. The number must be reduced, and the data will help us to accomplish this task.

Lightness. It's clear from the nature of the comments in the "lightness" category that consumers do not equate lightness with dieting or weight loss. Few of their light-related comments pertain to calories. Most focus on the product's nonbulky, nonfilling nature. I cannot tell from these data alone whether a low association with weight loss and dieting is a problem. It's an issue that I have in mind to follow up with some of the other diagnostic questions.

Health. I also wonder about the frequent mention of various health-related comments. Is this frequency of mention good for the concept or does it minimize the impact of other benefits? Once again, these data give me no insight. Other questions must provide that answer. However, it is the Main Idea question that helps me to raise the issue.

Good Taste. I am very troubled with the low level of mention for "good taste." Let's face it, the reason most people buy a food product is because it tastes good. It may be healthy, filling, convenient, or inexpensive, but if consumers do not think it will taste good, most will not buy it. Given the

Chart 13-1. Main Idea of test concept.

	Test Concept
Light (Net)	37%
Light/not filling	29
Less calories	12
Health (Net)	31
Balanced meal	19
Healthy/nutritious	15
Convenience (Net)	31
Quick/fast	16
Easy to prepare	15
New/different	16
Good taste	16
Variety (Net)	16
Good variety/like the varieties	13
Reference to one of the specific varieties	5
Elegant/sophisticated	12
Has fruit	9

relatively high level of mention for lightness and health, the fact that only 16 percent think the main idea of the product is "good taste" is a danger signal.

The performance of taste is also weak from another point of view. According to my normative data bank, the average number of "good taste" responses to the Main Idea question in the frozen dinner category is 18 percent. So our 16 percent is barely average. Consequently, even though I am at a very early point in my analysis, I already know that one of my recommendations will be to strengthen the communication of "good taste" so that it becomes a more dominant and persuasive copy element.

Invariably when I make this recommendation, someone in the audience argues back that the test stimulus is "just a concept, without all the bells and whistles" created by skilled food stylists, quality photography, high-powered production values, and so on that go into a final print advertisement or commercial. Once the folks in the creative department get their teeth into the assignment, so the argument goes, the "good taste" story will become more powerful. It is a seemingly persuasive argument. Unfortunately, it is 100 percent wrong.

Here is my response to this argument.

1. I first ask if the company's best effort went into the development of the concept. The usual response: The concept is a pretty good effort, although "if we had a little more time, it probably could have been a bit better."
2. I then point out that their response is typical. Most companies test their best or near-best effort. Therefore, my taste norms are based on concepts with similar degrees of effort.
3. My conclusion: The concept is deficient on the taste dimension when compared with other concepts of a similar degree of finish.
4. Of course, skillfully applied production values can eventually improve perceptions of good taste, but from a low base. In the meanwhile, competitive concepts also get the benefit of skillfully applied production values, but from a higher base.
5. My clincher: If your creative team is vastly superior to the creative teams that work for your competitors, then don't worry about the low taste score. But if your team is merely "excellent," like many of your competition's creative teams, there is a high probability that the low level of taste communicated by the concept is signaling the existence of a potential problem.

The bottom line: A food concept that does not strongly communicate a "good taste" story is a troubled concept. Of course, final production values might save the product. But why gamble? Doesn't it make more sense to figure out how to communicate these taste issues at the beginning of the product development cycle, not after all the major strategic and executional decisions have already been made?

I reread the concept in an attempt to figure out what went wrong with the "good taste" communication. I noticed that good taste was hinted at just one time, in the second paragraph, when reference was made to a "delicious" product. No wonder taste mentions are low. We forgot to mention the benefit to consumers!

The Case History: The Search for Hot Buttons

Varieties. The small number of people (16 percent) who make any reference to the individual product varieties described in the concept also concerns me. On the one hand, I realize that the consumer cannot possibly mention every single product feature as being a Main Idea since the very nature of the question forces her to focus upon elements most important to her. Therefore, a feature could be important or valued yet receive little mention because it is not valued to the same high degree as other, more frequently mentioned benefits.

The other side of the coin is that relatively few people make references to any of the varieties in spite of the fact that more than 25 percent of the concept is devoted to describing them. This lack of response to a very dominant feature is disturbing. Why is the response so low? Could the problem be that consumers simply do not like the varieties we offer? Might they like them in theory but not the way we describe them? Is there an ingredient that is turning consumers off? Or could it be that consumers are not interested in reading about individual varieties because their prime interest is in more general product benefits?

I cannot make a decision about the source of the problem from these data alone. However, the low level of mention is a danger signal that must be watched and examined at other points in the analysis when appropriate data becomes available.

Elegance. The fifth primary benefit, elegance and sophistication, is considered to be a main idea by just 12 percent of the sample. As I noted earlier, playback of this issue is higher among older, low-income women.

Once again, I remind myself that consumers can appreciate a benefit but not comment on it because of the presence of an even more important or valued benefit. On the other hand, I wonder if the low level of mention comes from the fact that an elegant, sophisticated connotation is inappropriate for a meal that comes out of a supermarket's freezer section. Could this be the reason why older women, who buy frozen dinners less often than younger women and who have fewer preconceptions about the category, hone in on this issue more often?

To investigate this issue further I re-examine special computer tabulation which correlated playback of sophistication and elegance with Purchase Interest. Reviewing this data in a new context helps me see that I have made a serious analytic error. I had originally concluded that the concept performed better among older women because it was associated with sophistication and elegance. I now realize that the data were misleading and I had emphasized the wrong half of the equation. The more important finding was that this benefit had weak performance among young women, not strong among older women.

I conclude that elegance and sophistication should be dropped as a primary benefit as a way of improving the product's appeal among current category users of all ages.

Fruits. The final primary benefit, the presence of fruits, is mentioned by just 9 percent of consumers exposed to the concept. Is it a good benefit but dominated by even better benefits? Did we give it an incorrect level of emphasis? Or is the low level of mention telling us that the offer of fruit is a strategic error?

Once again, I cannot resolve the issue from this question alone. Fortunately a special battery of questions on the presence of fruit has been included in the survey and will be analyzed shortly. The Main Idea question is useful, nevertheless, for identifying this issue as one that must be investigated in greater detail.

Secondary Benefits

Turning to the concept's secondary benefits, comments pertaining to the ease and convenience of using the product are mentioned as a main idea by about one-third of the sample. In general, a large "convenience" score for frozen food products scares me. The fact is that *every* frozen food is convenient to use. That is the reason the category was invented. It is the category's main reason for being.

If "convenience" is all consumers take from a concept, it is clear that we have not done a good enough job of differentiating ourselves from other products and presenting other product benefits in a meaningful way. Even when consumers do mention other features and benefits, if "convenience" is too high a proportion of all reactions, I interpret this as a sign of weakness.

Obviously, there are exceptions. Some products are *solely* intended to be a convenient substitute for "the real thing." Canned iced tea, powdered spices, and frozen juice concentrate are good examples of this phenomenon. But the current concept does not fit into this category of exceptions. So what is an acceptable level of convenience mentions? The first part of my test of acceptability is to compare the level of response against available norms. My norms from other main meal frozen food concept tests finds that convenience-related comments are generally made by 30 to 60 percent of consumers. So the 31 percent level of mention for this concept is quite reasonable.

The second part of my test for acceptableness is to see if other benefits are also mentioned with reasonable degrees of frequency. It is a judgment call. In my opinion, the low frequency of mention of various primary benefits in Chart 13-1 is a cause of concern to me. I don't think that the problem is caused by undue emphasis on "convenience." The real problem is the quantity and actual delivery of these other benefits. Nevertheless, the data are giving us a useful benchmark with which to evaluate future tests with this concept. Our future goal will be to improve communication of other benefits so that "convenience" receives less emphasis.

The other secondary benefit, a modern food for today's lifestyles, is not mentioned as a Main Idea by anyone. While we cannot conclude from this question alone that the "today's lifestyles" theme should be dropped, an unusually clear signal is being given by the data. Once corroborating evidence is found, we will recommend that this benefit be dropped.

Tertiary Benefits

The concept offers six other low-level support benefits. Five of them are not mentioned at all as a main idea. This is fine with me, for it indicates that consumers are reacting to these aspects of the concept in a predictable fashion. They are paying little attention to them.

The sixth support benefit, uniqueness, is mentioned as a main idea by 16 percent of the sample. Is this a problem or not? Unfortunately, there is no single objective answer to this question. The fact is that almost every concept for a new product contains at least one element that is new or different in some way. Therefore, some portion of the consumers seeing it for the first time will report that the Main Idea communicated by the concept is the availability of a new or different product. The problem is not the presence of this kind of comment, but its frequency.

Unfortunately, there is no magic number defining the acceptability of "newness" or "uniqueness" mentions when they are presented as a tertiary benefit. The key is the relativity to other comments. I would think highly of a food concept that communicated to 60 percent that the product is good tasting, and to 20 percent that it is new or different. I would think poorly of that same concept if the percentages were reversed.

Why? I have repeatedly seen that when *large* numbers of people report the main idea of a product is its newness and *small* numbers mention other product benefits, the result is low Purchase Interest. Apparently, a focus on newness (without being sufficiently convincing) causes lower levels of Purchase Interest. Obviously, there are exceptions to these rules of thumb. But I carefully observe this issue, nevertheless.

In the current concept, the relatively low number of references to the product being "new" or "different" is a positive sign; it serves as a signal to me that consumers are focusing on other, more important issues and benefits.

Nine Possible Hot Buttons

At this point in my analysis I have identified nine issues that could conceivably be playing some role in holding back success or might be the hot buttons we are searching for to improve the concept's performance if used correctly. The tentative position on these nine points is:

1. *Lightness.* The focus is on not being filling, rather than on low calories. We don't know yet whether this is a problem or not.
2. *Health and nutrition.* We don't know if the heavy emphasis on this benefit minimizes the impact of other concept benefits.
3. *Taste.* The level of mention is too low.
4. *Availability of variety.* The number of consumers mentioning this benefit is quite low given the amount of space the concept devotes to it. We don't know the reason why the level of response is so low. Other questions from this survey will help to answer this question.
5. *Elegance and sophistication.* Playback of this benefit is quite low and seems to be correlated with low Purchase Interest among younger consumers. If the concept's strategy is to aim for the broad market of all category users, this benefit should be dropped.
6. *Fruit.* The level of mention is quite low. As yet, we don't know why. But other questions will shed some light on this issue, including a special battery that directly addresses the fruit issue.
7. *Convenience.* There is no problem with the amount of emphasis placed upon this issue.
8. *For today's lifestyles.* This benefit is probably quite unimportant and is a candidate to be dropped.
9. *New/different.* There are no problems with the amount of emphasis placed upon this issue.

As you can see, the Main Idea question is quite useful in terms of identifying critically important issues. It is now up to other questions to provide a basis to further develop the hypotheses that the Main Idea question helped to initiate.

REASONS FOR PURCHASE INTEREST

The next question I usually analyze is Reasons for Purchase Interest. As noted earlier, the question works best when consumers with high Purchase Interest are segregated and analyzed separately.

The reasons consumers give (or don't give) for having high Purchase Interest in a concept provide available insights about the concept and its strength and weaknesses. Used in this way, the question is an excellent tool to identify potential problem areas, which data from other questions can then help to resolve. Here is the Reasons for Purchase Interest question:

Why do you say that you [*Insert answer to Purchase Interest question*]? [*Probe:*] What other reasons do you have for feeling this way?

Comparison to Main Idea Question

To gain maximum value from this question, I like to compare responses to it with response to the Main Idea question. In general, a frequently mentioned main idea should also be frequently mentioned as a reason for positive Purchase Interest. If 60 percent believe the main idea of a new food product is its suitability for snacking, but only 11 percent state this as their reason for having high Purchase Interest, something may be amiss. Three possibilities come to mind.

1. Perhaps the benefit is of little interest to consumers even though it dominates the concept. If so, we should drop it or reduce its dominance.
2. It may be that the benefit was delivered dominantly but not persuasively. If so, it is a signal that we should try again and improve the delivery of the benefit.
3. Or, it may be that appropriateness for snacking is a fine benefit but some other benefit, of even greater interest to consumers, is diluting the apparent value of this benefit. This might be a signal to leave things as they are.

The reverse is also true. If only 9 percent believe that the main idea of a food product is that it contains nuts, but 43 percent state that the presence of nuts is their reason for having high Purchase Interest in the product, it is a clear signal that we should stress nuts to a greater degree.

Chart 13-2. Reasons for positive Purchase Interest.

	Reasons for Positive Purchase Interest	*Main Idea*
Good taste	㊲%	16%
Convenience (Net)	35	31
Can pop in microwave	⑱	5
Quick/fast	16	16
Easy to prepare	11	15
Has fruit/like the fruit	㉖	9
Variety (Net)	20	16
Good variety/like the variety	18	13
Reference to one of the specific varieties	2	5
Light (Net)	15	37
Less calories	15	12
Light/not filling	—	㉙
Health (Net)	41	31
Balanced meal	㊴	19
Healthy/nutritious	4	15
New/different	5	⑯
Elegant/sophisticated	3	12

Chart 13-2 shows the Reasons for Positive Purchase Interest in the test concept. The results are quite interesting.

Good Taste. We had seen earlier that just 16 percent think "good taste" is one of the concept's main ideas. We now see on the first line of Chart 13-2 that 37 percent of those with high Purchase Interest say they will buy the product because of its perceived good taste. In fact, taste is the reason most frequently mentioned for having high Purchase Interest.

The implications are clear. Taste is an important benefit and must be communicated more loudly and more persuasively—not just one time, buried in the second paragraph. Responses to the Main Idea question had already caused me to hypothesize that taste was poorly or inadequately communicated. These data substantiate the theory.

Fruit. Chart 13-2 also shows that 26 percent of those with high Purchase Interest plan to buy the product because of the fruit. In contrast, just 9 percent thought the presence of fruit was a main idea of the product. Once again, the data are sending a signal that fruit-related elements of the concept should be strengthened. How to strengthen the fruit story still remains a question. Should the concept talk about fruit freshness or high quality, the fact that it is the only brand offering fruit, or the variety of different fruits offered in the line? Are there health or nutritional advantages that should be noted? Followup questions will provide these answers. However, it is clear from this question that the presence of fruit can be a useful hook with which to increase Purchase Interest.

Lightness. In the Main Idea question we had seen that "lightness," or more specifically the notion that the product is not too filling, was strongly communicated. Unfortunately, no one mentions "lightness" as a reason for having high Purchase Interest. This is a very sobering piece of information. Lightness was one of the concept's key reasons for being. Management's strategic goal was to slice out a segment of the frozen dinner category by appealing to those who wanted to eat a light, nonfilling meal. We now discover that a light, nonfilling meal is not wanted at all by consumers.

There are several possible explanations for this occurrence, each leading to a different course of action. It may simply be that "lightness" is of no special interest to consumers. For this reason the concept merely scored in the average range on Purchase Interest. If so, it is a signal to terminate further development of the concept. A company could tinker with the concept and perhaps marginally improve it, but why bother if its underlying reason for being simply does not exist?

A concept test cannot, by itself, provide enough information to fully sort out this issue. The marketer must understand the marketplace through observation of consumer needs, lifestyles, and changes in marketplace behavior. A thorough investigation of these issues is well beyond the focus of a concept test. Nevertheless, some insight into these issues is provided by the current test. Data from some of upcoming questions will provide clues to ensure that the lightness niche really does exist. If no such clues are forthcoming, it would lend credibility to the hypothesis that "lightness" is of no special interest to consumers.

Another explanation could be that consumers do have a need and desire for "lightness" but our execution of this benefit is poor. If this is the case, upcoming data will support this hypothesis. The consequence of this alternative would be to revise the concept and then state the benefit more persuasively.

A third possibility is that even though the "lightness" benefit receives no mention as a factor stimulating Purchase Interest, it is, nevertheless, a valuable concept element because its presence supports other benefits. If this is the case, this element of the concept might best be left as is, in spite of the low level of mention. Once again, an analysis of upcoming questions will provide some clues.

Health. Another inconsistency on Chart 13-2 that disturbs me concerns the "health" benefit. An astounding 39 percent plan to buy the product because of the promise of a balanced meal. Clearly, the claim of a balanced meal is of high interest to consumers. Unfortunately, just 19 percent mentioned it as a main idea. The implication: The concept must be revised to communicate this benefit much more clearly.

Other Benefits

The data from Reasons for Purchase Interest do not allow me to evaluate every single primary, secondary, and tertiary benefit. But they do send a few signs of value relating to some of the remaining benefits.

Primary Benefits. The Main Idea question had shown that comments relating to nutrition made the same impact on consumers as did the "balanced meal" claim. We now see in Chart 13-2 that nutrition is not as powerful a motivator as the "balanced meal" claim. Just 4 percent tell us they would buy the product because of connotations of good nutrition. The implication: Focus all health-related communications on the "balanced meal" claim, not on the more general "good nutrition" story.

Elegance and sophistication, which were not frequently mentioned as main ideas, were also not mentioned as Reasons for Purchase Interest. The implication: This is additional evidence suggesting this benefit be dropped.

Secondary Benefits. The "today's lifestyles" claim received no significant mention as a main idea or as a reason for Purchase Interest. The implication: Drop this benefit from the concept.

Tertiary Benefits. The product's appropriateness for microwave ovens is mentioned by 18 percent, suggesting that the concept should continue to give support to this benefit.

"Uniqueness," which was not frequently mentioned as a main idea, is also not mentioned as a reason for Purchase Interest. The implication: If the claim is needed to support some other benefit, it should remain in the concept. But if concept writers included it as a separate and distinct benefit to stimulate consumer interest in the product, the data are clearly signaling that the benefit should be dropped. It may not be hurting the concept, but it's not helping it either.

PROBLEMS AND DEFICIENCIES

On balance, the reasons consumers give for wanting to purchase a product are quite useful. Unfortunately, the question does not identify all the problems. Other questions must also be used.

Criticisms About the Concept

My next analytic step is to examine responses to a series of questions that encourage consumers to voice all their negative comments and criticisms about the concept. These responses often provide useful insights leading to modifications that improve the concept's sales potential. My starting point is to zero in on those consumers with neutral or negative Purchase Interest and to review the reasons they give for having this level of interest in the product. The results are shown in Chart 13-3.

Aversion to the Category. Chart 13-3 shows that 41 percent of all consumers with low Purchase Interest in our concept state that they will not buy it merely because it is a frozen food. Note that the concept is not being rejected because it has a unique deficiency. These people are rejecting *all* frozen foods. They claim to use them infrequently, perhaps in an emergency. In my opinion, there is not much a company can do to attract these people to its product.

The large number of people with low Purchase Interest giving this response suggests that we have not done a good enough job of defining the concept's prime target group. Because of the small sample size used in this survey, we are not able to precisely identify the demographic and lifestyle characteristics of these frozen-food rejectors. Future efforts should be made

Concept Testing

Chart 13-3. Reasons for neutral/negative
Purchase Interest.

	Test Concept
Frozen (Net)	41%
Don't buy frozen food too often	24
Like to prepare fresh food	22
Price	20
Specific ingredients (Net)	7
Don't care for fruit	5
Don't care for some vegetables	3
Concerned about the amount of calories	4

to identify them and to remove them from our target group because a sharper prime-prospect definition will enable us to focus our marketing and advertising efforts more effectively.

Problem with Price. The next category of complaint, price, is mentioned by 20 percent of all rejectors. Obviously, a company does not set a price solely from a concept test. Nevertheless, the number of price comments does get my analytic juices going. I wonder if we can profitably increase volume by lowering the price. Can any steps be taken to increase perceptions of value? Are these 20 percent from the group of 41 percent who said they don't like to buy frozen foods? If so, a lower price might be the hook we are looking for to move these people into the frozen food category.

This last hypothesis is easy enough to test by a special tabulation that correlates category rejection and price rejection. The correlation is positive. Price rejectors are largely the same people who are category rejectors. It seems then that price is an important problem for many rejectors but that a reduction of our prices by a few cents probably will not bring these rejectors into the mold.

At the beginning of my analysis I had noticed that users of Budget Gourmet, a new and rapidly growing brand featuring very low prices, expressed very little interest in the test concept. This latest tabulation explains why. It also shows why Budget Gourmet sales are growing so rapidly. Un-

Chart 13-4. Total shortcomings.

	Test Concept
Frozen (Net)	22%
Frozen food not as good as fresh	15
Frozen food tastes artificial	6
Not enough food	19
Price: too expensive	15
Variety (Net)	16
People wouldn't like the varieties	13
Dislike the combination	2
Not healthy	11
Not unique/lots of competition	6

fortunately, it may be a market segment out of our reach, given the current pricing structure.

Shortcomings

The second question in the series to identify problems and deficiencies measures perceived shortcomings in the product. The question is worded as follows:

What are the *major* shortcomings it would have? [*Probe:*] What other shortcomings are there?

Responses to this question are shown in Chart 13-4. Some of the complaints are similar to those discussed earlier, so we need not dwell on them again. But two new ideas do come up. They are mentioned with sufficient frequency to cause me to wonder if each is part of the solution to significantly improving the concept.

As indicated in Chart 13-4, 19 percent of those who report a shortcoming tell us they think there is an insufficient amount of food in each portion.

Concept Testing

Could this explain why the idea of a light, nonfilling meal is so unpersuasive? The data, thus far, are too sketchy to allow for a firm conclusion. It must be investigated further in upcoming questions. Fortunately, if this issue does turn out to be an important one, it is easy enough to fix.

Chart 13-4 also shows that 16 percent complain about the varieties of product described in the concept statement. Apparently there is a problem, either with some of the individual varieties, with the small number of varieties being offered, or with some of the elements that are included within each individual selection. This could explain why so few consumers mentioned anything about the varieties in the Main Idea question in spite of the fact that so much space was devoted to them. Once again, the source of the problem cannot be identified from this question. But fortunately, data from questions to be analyzed shortly will help to resolve this issue.

Improvements

The third question in this series, which asks the respondent to recommend changes or improvements in the concept, is worded as follows:

In what ways, if any, could this line of products be changed or improved? I'd like you to tell me anything you can think of, no matter how minor it seems.

The results of this question, shown in Chart 13-5, partially clarify the nature of the "variety" problem revealed in Chart 13-4. Many consumers complain that not enough choices are being offered. More than one out of every three suggested that improvements address this issue. Their language is varied. Some simply request additional varieties. Others ask for more meat dishes. Still others want items of interest to their children. Although the comments may vary, the big picture is clear: They want more menu choices.

This is a useful diagnostic insight but not the Big Idea I am seeking. The real-world problem is that retailers will not stock a complete line of 20 to 30 items until the line proves itself at the cash register. This means that even if the manufacturer were willing to market a wider line initially, consumers would not be exposed to all of it. It is not practical to consider this issue to be the Big Idea that improves concept performance, since we cannot initially execute it in the marketplace. Nevertheless, it is a useful piece of information to act upon as soon as possible.

Chart 13-5. Recommended improvements.

	Test Concept
Needs improvements	43%
Variety (Net)	16
Wider variety	7
More meat dishes	3
More items for children	3
Increase quantity/give larger portions	9
Food substitution (Net)	5
Change fruit	2
Change vegetable	2
Reduce cost/too expensive	5
Serving dish/fruit in separate dish	5

Benefits

The final question in the sequence, this one positive in nature, sheds additional light on problems that consumers have with the concept. The information is collected by asking people what benefits they associate with the product described by the concept:

What are the *major* benefits it would have? [*Probe:*] What other benefits are there?

At first glance, the results shown in Chart 13-6 are quite similar to the Main Idea question. In fact, when I first examined the data I almost chose to ignore it, thinking that it added nothing to my knowledge. But when I examined responses to the question after dividing consumers into two groups—those with high Purchase Interest and those with neutral or negative Purchase Interest—some interesting information emerged.

Within the "health" section of Chart 13-6, 42 percent of those with high Purchase Interest comment favorably on the "balanced meal" benefit; only 18 percent of those with lower Purchase Interest make a favorable comment on this issue.

213

Concept Testing

Chart 13-6. Total benefits, by Purchase Interest.

	Total	Positive Purchase Interest	Neutral/ Negative Purchase Interest
Convenience (Net)	62%	65%	52%
Convenient/easy to prepare	36	35	40
Quick/fast	34	34	36
Can pop in micro-wave/oven	9	10	4
Good for working/ busy people	5	6	—
Health (Net)	54	58	38
Healthy/nutritious	22	22	20
Balanced meal	37	(42)	18
Variety (Net)	32	33	28
Has fruit	24	25	20
Good variety	11	11	12
Has vegetables	4	5	—
Has meat	3	3	—
Reasonable price	31	(36)	8
Good taste	22	24	12
Light (Net)	20	21	16
Light/not filling	17	17	16
Less calories	7	8	4

How curious. We have already observed that a "balanced meal" benefit is an important Purchase Interest influence. We now see that those with low Purchase Interest hardly mention the "balanced meal" theme at all. What is going on? Why aren't low Purchase Interest individuals more interested in a balanced meal? Isn't everyone interested in good nutrition?

As I ponder this issue, I reread the concept and notice that the "balanced meal" benefit is mentioned just one time. I wonder if respondents with low Purchase Interest simply didn't see the benefit. I cannot support this hypothesis from the Benefit question alone. Fortunately, some upcoming questions will allow me to evaluate this issue. If the problem with the "balanced meal" benefit turns out to be merely a visibility problem, we may have discovered an important tool with which to raise Purchase Interest among those currently uninterested in the concept.

A second point of interest in Chart 13-6 relates to price. While 36 percent of those with high Purchase Interest volunteer that the price is reasonable, just 8 percent of those with low Purchase Interest share this opinion. Price clearly is a problem for some people. We saw evidence of this in the section discussing Reasons for Low Purchase Interest and we see it again here. This information validates an earlier hypothesis that the price structure for this product (as well as most competitive brands) eliminates some segments of the population from the prime prospect group.

PURCHASE FREQUENCY

A major problem with the concept was revealed when consumers were asked the expected frequency with which they would buy this line:

Assume that you tried this product and liked it. Which statement best describes how often, if ever, you think you would buy this product if it were available where you shop?

Once a week or more often	☐
Once every two or three weeks	☐
Once a month or every four weeks	☐
Once every two or three months	☐
Once every four to six months	☐
Once or twice a year	☐
Less often than once a year	☐
Never	☐

Responses to this question, when compared against appropriate normative data, suggest that most consumers, even those very positive to the product, would purchase and use it at a below-average frequency. At this point in the analysis I cannot determine for sure why this is happening. I have already observed that many consumers consider "lightness" to be a main idea of the concept, but not a very motivating one. I wonder if the low expected frequency of purchase and the infrequent mention of lightness as a reason for positive Purchase Interest are in any way related.

I further hypothesize that if the two issues are related, the problem may be caused by the wording in the concept, which tells consumers that the product is "perfect any time you are in the mood for something light." Perhaps, in an attempt to establish a point of difference from other products, we may have inadvertently caused consumers to think this product is appropriate *only* for unique occasions when they do not want to eat a full meal.

If my hypothesis is correct, the problem can easily be solved. One approach could be to refocus "lightness" into a virtue that health-conscious individuals always strive for. Another possible approach: Hook the concept to a lunchtime positioning, since lunch is an occasion where people often look for a lighter meal. There are lots of other possible solutions to the problem. The underlying point is that if a "light" positioning is causing low frequency of purchase, it is an easy problem to resolve.

The first step is, of course, to confirm that lightness and low Purchase Frequency are related. To test this theory I conduct a series of computer tabulations designed to uncover which of the respondent's attitudinal and behavioral characteristics correlate with a low frequency of intended purchase. This analysis reveals that perceptions of lightness are, in fact, correlated with a likelihood to purchase the product relatively infrequently.

The analysis also finds that those who plan to purchase this product frequently associate it with a lunchtime consumption period. Those with a low frequency of intended purchase are likely to regard the product as appropriate for snacks. Might the solution be to better communicate that the product is a full meal (especially a luncheon meal) and not a snack product?

Putting this issue aside, we see that an even bigger issue is now apparent. It is becoming increasingly clear that the lightness issue is related to many different problems, such as low Purchase Interest, low frequency of intended purchase, and various other complaints such as the product not providing a sufficient amount of food in each portion. Could "lightness" be related in any way to the Big Idea I am searching for, the hook I need to drive up the Purchase Interest and frequency of consumption? It's a tantalizing issue that I plan to address via some of the upcoming data.

MEAL OCCASIONS ASSOCIATED WITH THE CONCEPT

As part of my analysis of anticipated purchase frequency, I found that many individuals with a low frequency of expected purchase thought the test concept was a snack item. It piqued my interest in the whole issue of meal occasions most closely associated with the concept. This information was collected via the following two-part question:

216

The Case History: The Search for Hot Buttons

Chart 13-7. Occasions when most
likely to eat product.

	Test Concept
Breakfast	5%
Lunch	32
Afternoon snack	3
Dinner	43
Late-night snack	17

1. For what type of meal [*show meal card*] would you be most *likely* to eat the products you just read about?
2. Now let's suppose you had ten packages of these products in your freezer. Please tell me for what meal or meals on this card you would use these ten packages. You might use them for a number of different meals. You might also use them for some meal occasion that is not on the card. Now, how do you think you might use these ten packages?

	Most Likely	Number of Times Used
Breakfast	☐	_____
Lunch	☐	_____
Dinner	☐	_____
Afternoon snack	☐	_____
Late-night snack	☐	_____
Something else (specify)	☐	_____
_____	☐	_____
Total		_____

The question was deliberately designed with two parts. The second part was intended to be a tie breaker in the event that the first part of the question did not produce a winning occasion. It turned out to be unnecessary, as you shall soon see.

For Lunch

Since most frozen entrees and frozen dinners are consumed at dinnertime, I am not surprised to note in Chart 13-7 that the most frequently mentioned consumption occasion for the test concept also is at dinnertime. What does surprise me, however, is the large number of lunchtime men-

217

Chart 13-8. Most likely occasions, by Purchase Interest.

	Positive Purchase Interest	Neutral/ Negative Purchase Interest
Breakfast	4%	7%
Lunch	⑧⑧	14
Afternoon snack	4	—
Dinner	39	㊺
Late-night snack	15	㉔

tions. One out of three consumers claims to be most likely to eat this product for lunch.

This finding, coupled with the previously noted insight that a high frequency of purchase correlates with perceptions that the concept is for lunchtime consumption, causes me to wonder if lunchtime consumption can be the unique hook needed to separate our product from the rest of the pack. To help evaluate this idea, I retabulate responses to this question among those consumers with high versus low Purchase Interest. The results are eye-opening. While 38 percent of those consumers with high Purchase Interest tell us they are most likely to eat this product at lunchtime, just 14 percent of those with low Purchase Interest associate the product with lunchtime.

Dinnertime consumption and snack consumption show a reverse pattern (see Chart 13-8). Those with low Purchase Interest are most likely to eat this product at night.

Clearly, lunchtime is looking more and more like the hook we are seeking, the high-potential opportunity to make our concept stand apart from the rest of the pack. Perhaps it can be used as a stand-alone benefit. Or perhaps it must be joined with another benefit—in the health and nutrition category, for example—to explain and legitimize this feature. The issue can, by no means, be completely resolved here but the Occasions of Consumption question has nevertheless made a big contribution to my analysis.

For Dinner

As I ponder the opportunity of positioning this product as being appropriate for lunchtime, I remind myself that dinnertime remains an important consumption occasion. Most consumption of frozen meals occurs at dinnertime. Furthermore, consumers with high Purchase Interest in our concept are still more likely to eat it at dinner than at lunchtime. Therefore, if we strengthen the concept's luncheon positioning, we may be pulling consumers away from dinnertime consumption, a high-volume segment of the market.

My tentative conclusion: While I am excited over the possibility of a lunchtime hook for this product, the concept statement must continue to encourage consumers to use the product at dinnertime.

For Snacks

There is still one element of Charts 13-7 and 13-8 that concerns me. One out of every five consumers (including those with high Purchase Interest) think they would eat this product as a snack, not a main meal. Unfortunately, we already know that the amount of snacking that consumers do on a regular basis that involves actual food preparation, and that also requires them to sit down at a dining room table with a knife and fork, is quite low. This suggests very low-volume potential for the product and partially explains why the anticipated frequency of consumption is so low.

The bottom line: The product's apparent appropriateness for snacking must be addressed before this product can achieve its maximum sales potential.

QUADRANT ANALYSIS

One of the most valuable steps in the analysis of a concept's test results is correlating the importance that consumers place on various product benefits with the concept's perceived ability to deliver these same benefits. The two questions are:

1. Now, I would like you to rate this line of products on several characteristics. Although you have evaluated the line on an overall basis, you may feel differently about some characteristics. Since you may not have used these products before, please base your answers on what you've just read.

   On these cards are various characteristics. I'd like you to read each card, then place the card on the rating board under the word or phrase excellent, very good, good, fair, or poor that best describes how well you think these products would perform, for each of the characteristics.
2. Now I'd like to find out how important each of the same characteristics is to you. Using these same cards and this rating board, which goes from very important to somewhat important, neither important nor unimportant, somewhat unimportant, and very unimportant, please indicate how important each characteristic is to you for frozen dinners and entrees.

Concept Testing

When analyzing these data, the easiest way to grasp the relationship is to use a graphic presentation. Keep in mind that the specific percentages associated with each ranking and rating don't really matter. The key issue is the relative performance of each benefit or attribute. For this reason, I prepare the data as shown in Figure 13-1 without any percentages.

All Attributes

As you inspect Figure 13-1, keep in mind that the higher on the page an attribute is placed, the greater importance it has to consumers. The farther to the left, the better the rating for the concept in question. Therefore, attributes located in the upper left-hand quadrant represent important issues to individuals on which the concept performs strongly. Attributes located in the upper right-hand quadrant represent important issues to consumers on which our concept performs poorly.

At the very top of Figure 13-1 is the "balanced meal" attribute. The data are telling us that this issue is very important to consumers. However, we had previously seen that some consumers did not mention a balanced meal as a main product benefit. At the time I had hypothesized that they simply overlooked the benefit since it was mentioned just once in the concept. The importance now being shown to the idea of a balanced meal gives support to this hypothesis.

Individual Attributes

When a large number of attributes are included in a concept test, a busy graph like Figure 13-1 can be very difficult to analyze. One way of solving the problem is to divide the chart into separate elements, each containing several groups of related attributes. One such grouping, showing the performance of the "convenience" attributes, is seen on Figure 13-2.

Convenience. The cluster of convenience-related attributes in the upper left-hand corner clearly communicates that the issue of convenience is very important to consumers (because the attributes are plotted at the very top of the chart) and has been delivered strongly and believably (because they are plotted near the left edge of the chart). I conclude that in spite of the small amount of space given to the convenience story, the message got through clearly. Nothing need be changed. (If respondents had *not* rated these attributes highly, change might have been required, since frozen meals and "convenience foods" are virtually synonymous in consumers' minds.)

The Case History: The Search for Hot Buttons

Figure 13-1. Quadrant analysis of all attributes.

Concept Testing

Figure 13-2. Quadrant analysis of convenience attributes.

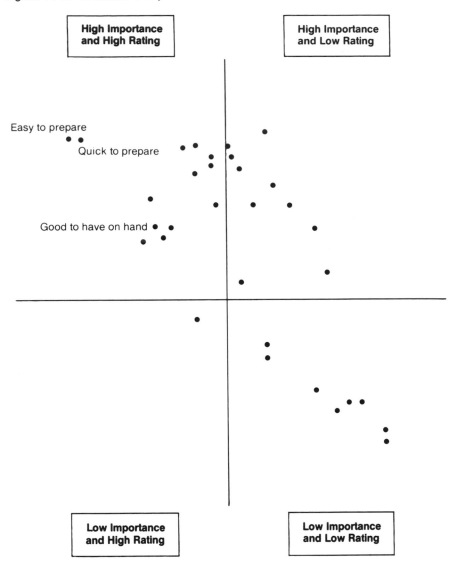

The Case History: The Search for Hot Buttons

Usage Occasions. Figure 13-3 shows that we did a strong job of communicating that the product is appropriate for lunch but were less successful in communicating its appropriateness for other meals and snacking occasions. Its strength as a lunch product is not surprising, given the insights derived from previously observed data.

The chart also shows that appropriateness for dinner is a more important issue to consumers than appropriateness for lunch. Once again, this is not surprising given the high level of frozen food consumption that occurs at dinnertime. It is a clear warning that too close an association with lunchtime consumption could cost lots of sales.

Perhaps most important of all, Figure 13-3 also demonstrates that the whole issue of "occasion" is simply not very important to consumers. There are many other issues of much greater importance. The data are confirming that the concept can support a lunchtime positioning (with some modification to solve the dinner problem), but in effect we are being told that as a Big Idea, a hot button to forcefully drive up sales, the issue is not suitable.

Fortunately, all is not lost. In Figure 13-4 the data provide one additional occasion-related insight that is breathtaking in terms of its ability to broaden the sales potential for this product. Even more important to consumers than appropriateness for a specific meal is the importance they place on a product that is appropriate for *various* occasions, such as a time when a light meal is desired or when the family members are not all eating together.

The consumer is apparently signaling that an even bigger issue than suitability for a specific meal is appropriateness for the housewife personally. That is why "variety of different occasions" scores highly on importance. And that is why the concept is rated strongly on being appropriate when the family does not eat together.

As a side note, I finally understand the elusive point, discovered at the beginning of my analysis, of why full-time housewives are especially interested in this concept. It hints at being suitable for when they are eating alone, an event that occurs every day as other members of the family are at school or work. I also now understand the apparent association between the concept and lunchtime.

Most important of all, the data are pointing to the critical answer. The hook is to design a product that is thought to be suitable for the potential user on all the various occasions when she is alone. The beauty of this idea, in addition to satisfying many problems with the existing concept, is that it responds to the new way that Americans eat—alone. Various family members are increasingly eating different foods, at different locations, and at

223

Concept Testing

Figure 13-3. Quadrant analysis of meals.

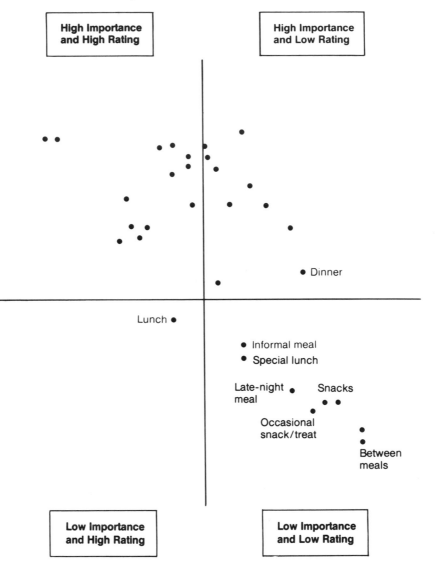

The Case History: The Search for Hot Buttons

Figure 13-4. Quadrant analysis of usage occasions.

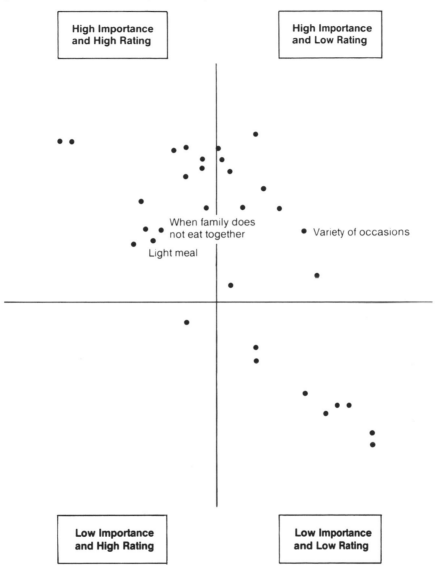

different times. The nation's food manufacturers have not yet successfully responded to the challenge of these changing consumption practices. This concept has the potential to get in on the ground floor. We may have come up with the Big Idea we have been searching for!

Don't break out the champagne just yet. The idea shows promise, but we are not yet ready to celebrate. There is a long way still to go. We still must resolve many problems with different concept elements such as lightness, taste, and presence of fruit. However, the Big Idea is in sight. We are seeing evidence that a frozen meal product—perhaps not the test concept as currently described—is of interest to women for those times when they are eating alone.

Confirmation of this hypothesis is seen in Figure 13-5, which shows that consumers place greater importance on a product that is appropriate for women than one that is appropriate for men or children.

We are far from having designed the optimum concept. Many creative judgments must yet be made. Should the product be described simply as being for women only? Or should it be slanted toward women for those occasions when they eat alone? Or when they are alone and want to pamper themselves? The possibilities are endless.

Lightness. And what should we do about "lightness"? The data have repeatedly been sending signals that "lightness" is a troublesome issue. Rather than functioning as a benefit to encourage consumers to use the product, it has been confusing them. The "hunger satisfaction" attribute shown on Figure 13-6 confirms the existence of the problem. It also shows us how to solve it. Lightness, as portrayed by the concept, causes consumers to think the meal will not be filling and will leave them somewhat hungry. The solution is easy. If lightness remains in the concept, we must communicate that the product may be light but it is a full, complete, and satisfying meal that will definitely satisfy someone's hunger.

The relatively high importance people place on hunger satisfaction and the relatively lower importance they associate with the product not being filling is puzzling to me at first glance. Might they be saying that they want their hunger satisfied and want to feel full? Or is the problem due to the looseness of our wording? Perhaps "filling" communicates different things to different people. Some who rate the attribute as unimportant may be telling us that they want the meal to fill them up. Others who rate the attribute as important may be saying that they do not want to feel stuffed or bloated.

As a side issue, I recall that at the beginning of my analysis I found that the concept had a poor "easy to understand" score. I wondered if there is

(text continued on p. 229)

Figure 13-5. Quadrant analysis of use, by sex.

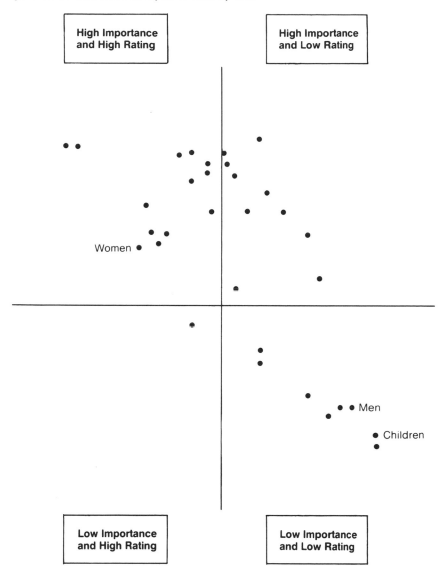

Concept Testing

Figure 13-6. Quadrant analysis of lightness attributes.

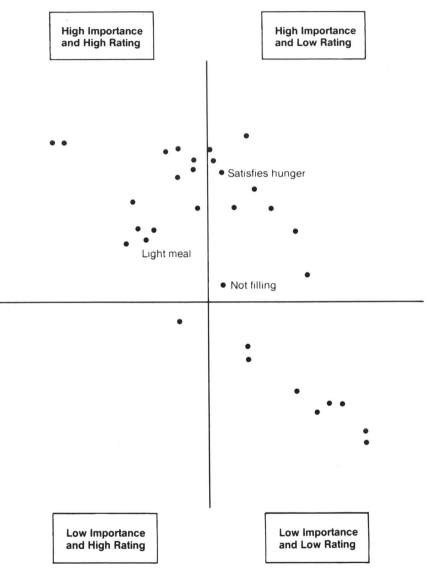

any correlation between that low rating and confusion on this issue of being filling.

To test this hypothesis, I isolated consumers who rated the concept highly on *both* hunger satisfaction *and* not being filling. A simple computer tabulation found that these people are especially likely to find something about our concept difficult to understand. Clearly, more work is needed to clarify this issue. For the present, we know that we have not done a good enough job in communicating the nonfilling nature of the product.

Fruit. It has been previously noted that the fruit issue is not being handled optimally by the concept. The presence of fruit was intended to be a point of difference from competitive products. Unfortunately, many consumers are not particularly impressed with our description of it in the concept.

Earlier data caused us to wonder how to solve the fruit problem. Should the concept talk about the fruit's freshness, its uniqueness in frozen dinners, the wide range of different fruits being offered? Figure 13-7 provides some hints on how to solve this problem. It shows that the presence of fruit and its quality are each important issues to consumers. However, quality ratings for our product are poor, suggesting the need to strengthen perceptions of quality.

Some of the earlier data contained clues suggesting that the "good taste" story is not being delivered persuasively. Figure 13-8 provides further confirmation of this hypothesis. The chart shows that taste, a very important issue, is perceived by consumers to be deficient. The fact that taste has not been stressed by the concept undoubtedly contributes to this problem. The obvious solution is to talk about it more often and more persuasively.

The other attributes shown on Figure 13-8 reveal an appreciation for the main course and for the taste of the fruit. The data suggest, then, that part of the taste problem may be with the side dishes of each variety. We cannot figure out exactly what is wrong with the side dishes from this question. Fortunately, an upcoming question will shed some additional light.

The problem with the side dishes correlates with another problem that was discussed earlier. You may recall that the concept communicated information about the varieties very poorly, in spite of a substantial amount of space devoted to it. The data shown on Figure 13-8 hint that part of the problem causing this poor performance is the side dishes offered with each choice. Since no attribute directly measures reactions to the side dishes, this conclusion is tentative. Fortunately, the forced-exposure question can provide confirmation.

Concept Testing

Figure 13-7. Quadrant analysis of fruit attributes.

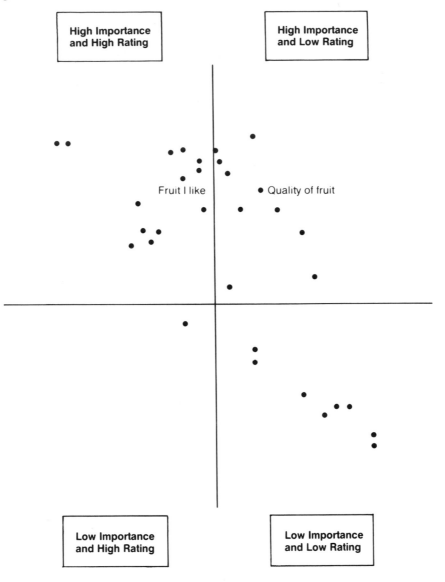

The Case History: The Search for Hot Buttons

Figure 13-8. Quadrant analysis of taste attributes.

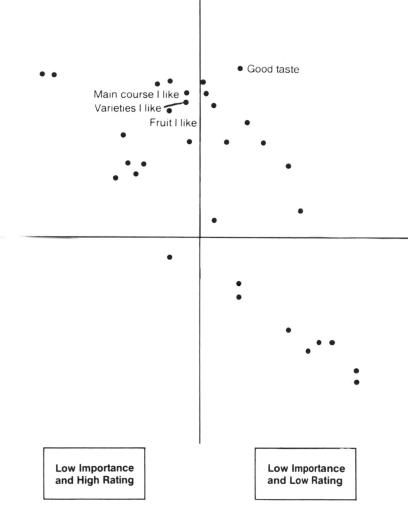

FORCED-EXPOSURE QUESTION

In the next step of the analysis, the concept is evaluated on a word-by-word basis, using a forced-exposure question. It allows a respondent to zero in on all elements that she finds to be of interest. This question involves asking the respondent to read the concept carefully and circle each word or phrase that she thinks is interesting or important. The instruction is:

Here is a copy of the description you have just read. I'd like you to circle any words, sentences, or ideas that you found to be especially interesting or important to you.

The results of this question are shown in Chart 13-9. The number over each word is the percent of the sample that expressed interest in that word by circling it.

Very useful information is provided by the chart. One issue it helps us to address is that of "lightness." Problems with this issue have permeated the data from the very beginning, where we saw communication problems associated with the main idea of a light meal. Consumers heard the benefit but were not especially persuaded by it.

We now see in this forced-exposure question that just 22 percent of the sample hone in on the word "light" in line one of paragraph one. And in the first line of paragraph two, just 27 percent express any interest in it. However, the level of interest shoots up markedly later in the second paragraph when "light" is hooked together with "delicious." The same phenomenon occurs at the end of paragraph four. When "light" is hooked together with "nourishing," 47 percent are interested in the lightness benefit.

Clearly, lightness can become a meaningful benefit but not if it stands alone. The implication is clear. To use "lightness" most effectively, it must be hooked to another benefit. Or looking at it from the other side of the coin, lightness—the issue upon which we attempted to build an innovative product—cannot stand on its own feet.

Paragraph one also shows that the idea of a unique treat is of little value. We had seen earlier that the "uniqueness" claim was not hurting the concept. We now see that it's not helping either. Virtually no one is interested in this benefit, even when we force them to read it. Obviously, it is not useful to us and can be dropped from the concept unless it is needed to support some other benefit.

Similarly, the idea of a product for "today's lifestyles" does not generate

Chart 13-9. Percentage who found words important.

```
9    14    9    19      22   19      11       11 13   20
```
A healthy and nutritious light meal complemented with a refreshing
```
20   18   33    33    7   11    9    9   10   18   53      51
```
medley of chilled fruits. A unique treat that offers a balanced meal
```
15  17   21      21
```
to meet today's lifestyles.

```
9    9    21     20  13  15   27   23   20  22  22 22   19      39
```
Here's the perfect meal for the light way you like to eat today—deli-
```
43   40      33      32   39  22 22   23      24        22
```
cious light entrees, accented with fruit for a fresh, sophisticated touch.

```
12   11    13     26      29    21      31      28    15 15 17
```
You might choose delicate turkey and asparagus crepes with a side
```
18  17  11   14   17  22  20    22      21   19   29      32      15
```
dish of kiwi fruit and red and green grapes. Or broccoli quiche, served
```
15    11    10    14 15  21     23   22     26        22
```
with avocado wedges and a chilled medley of blueberries, strawberries,
```
19    24    24   22  17   32     32   23   30   31  30   20
```
and honeydew melon balls. Or lemon chicken with crispy pea pods and
```
26    26   20    21     19       15      15   23      25
```
seasoned rice with cashew slices, accompanied by chilled peaches
```
15   13   15    33       33    25 25
```
with melba sauce. Three varieties in all.

```
19      27   23   35     29      24      21   19      19
```
They're healthy and elegant taste combinations for today's lifestyle—
```
28    37   37   26  41 41   43   21     29      47   38      49
```
perfect any time you're in the mood for something light and nourishing.

```
9     10     12    10 11    11      13    13   24 24      42
```
Each comes frozen on a handsome plate ready for your microwave
```
23      27      26    17     23    24     20      18  19 19    29
```
or conventional oven. The chilled fruit medleys come in a pop-out
```
27   13    17   15  15    15    16   17      12   12   13      13
```
dish, and thaw on your counter in minutes while your main course
```
13    13   14    17     17  17  19    22    52    50
```
heats. The three varieties range in price from $1.79–$2.99.

---

strong positive reactions. We had hypothesized earlier that this benefit is valueless. The current question supports this conclusion. The obvious conclusion is that this benefit should be dropped.

The "balanced meal" benefit of paragraph one received little mention in our Main Idea question or as a reason consumers give for having high Purchase Interest. Yet more than 50 percent of the sample think this benefit is interesting or important when forced to read it. Clearly, the benefit is worth saving. The data are suggesting it might be reworked and stressed more heavily in order to get through to the consumer.

In paragraph two, a "sophisticated" meal has generated no interest, compared with other benefits. Sophistication is not a worthwhile theme as far as this product idea is concerned.

One of the serious problems with this concept is the low "good taste" ratings. The problem, it has been hypothesized, is partially because the concept made just one reference to the taste when it referred to the product as "delicious" in paragraph two. Chart 13-9 shows that consumers react positively to the idea of a "delicious" product. In my opinion, it provides further support for the hypothesis that good taste must be stressed much more by the concept.

In paragraph three, each of the main courses seems to generate greater interest than the accompanying side dish. This correlates with data in the quadrant analysis, which suggested that the side dishes are creating a problem. The obvious conclusion: Greater efforts are required to develop side dishes of high appeal. Avocado wedges and melba sauce are especially weak elements. In the case of melba sauce, the low score may be signaling that the idea is at odds with an overall theme of nutrition and good health.

In paragraph four, there is a great deal of interest in the benefit that the product is "perfect for any time you're in the mood for . . ." It provides further confirmation for the hypothesis that making the product appropriate for a large variety of different consumption occasions is a genuinely good idea.

In paragraph five, the reference to a "handsome plate" is obviously an attempt to explain and enhance a rather boring and unexciting delivery system. Unfortunately, the communication does not work. Hardly anyone considers the plate a point of interest. There may also be a believability problem here, with few respondents willing to accept the notion of "handsome" tableware in an inexpensive frozen food package. Better to drop reference to the plate completely than leave it as it is currently stated.

SPECIAL INVESTIGATION OF FRUIT

As we've seen, one special feature about this product is the presence of fruit. It was included at significant expense in an effort to differentiate the line from competition, to support the idea of a light meal, and to stimulate greater consumer interest. Unfortunately, its presence also stimulated many marketing and financial concerns. It raised many questions: Is fruit a worthwhile addition to the line? Will the additional cost result in increased consumer interest? Do consumers view the specific fruits that we selected as an added benefit? Does the need to pop the fruit compartment out and defrost it separately present a problem to consumers? Do consumers like the idea of fruit in general, but dislike our presentation of it because of an easily changed executional element?

To answer these kinds of question, we asked consumers the following two-question battery:

1. As you may recall, the items in this line of products have a fruit side dish. How important is it to you that these items have a fruit side dish? Would you say it is very important, somewhat important, neither important nor unimportant, somewhat unimportant, or very unimportant that this product have a fruit side dish?

> Very important 1
> Somewhat important 2
> Neither important nor unimportant 3
> Somewhat unimportant 4
> Very unimportant 5

2. Why do you say that? [This was an open-end question.]

Responses to these questions show that consumers are quite interested in the fruit product feature. In Chart 13-10, we see that 81 percent think the benefit is important, with most thinking it is very important. Only two out of ten consumers don't think much of the idea.

Unfortunately, there are no norms to help interpret this question, so we must use our judgment. My opinion is that any product feature considered to be very important by more than half of the target group is, in fact, a very positive feature.

Concept Testing

Chart 13-10. Importance of having a fruit side dish.

	Test Concept
Important	81%
Very important	52
Somewhat important	29
Neither important nor unimportant	9
Unimportant	10
Somewhat unimportant	5
Very unimportant	5

Correlation to Purchase Interest

I attempted to confirm the value of this feature by doing a cross tabulation that correlated the importance of fruit by the level of Purchase Interest respondents expressed in the product concept. The results of this analysis are shown in Chart 13-11.

As you can see, not only is fruit viewed as important but those with

Chart 13-11. Importance of having a fruit side dish by Purchase Interest.

	Total Sample	Positive Purchase Interest	Neutral/ Negative Purchase Interest
Important	81%	90%	59%
Very important	52	62	28
Somewhat important	29	28	31
Neither important nor unimportant	9	6	16
Unimportant	10	4	25
Somewhat unimportant	5	3	9
Very unimportant	5	1	16

Chart 13-12. Reasons for rating fruit as unimportant.

Don't like/eat fruit	26%
Only like fresh fruit, not canned or frozen	26
Main course is what's important	7
Doesn't go with food offered	6
Not healthy (Net)	4
Has too much sugar	2
Loses vitamins when frozen	1
Not healthy	1
Fruit would get mushy	4
Wouldn't taste good	4

high Purchase Interest are especially likely to think so. Keep in mind that this is merely a correlation, not a statement of cause and effect. It does not prove that the presence of fruit causes high Purchase Interest. Nevertheless, I regard it to be a major plus in fruit's favor when 90 percent of those with high Purchase Interest think fruit is an important benefit.

However, there is a negative side of the coin. Not many of those with a neutral or negative interest in buying our product think fruit is a very important benefit. Furthermore, one out of four of them states fruit is unimportant. This causes me to wonder if the presence of fruit is turning off as many people as it turns on. I question if the same product concept, without fruit included, would do better in the marketplace.

The only way to know this for sure is to test both versions of the concept at some future date. However, for the present I attempt to use the current data to shed some light on the subject by identifying just what it is that causes some consumers to be negative to the idea of fruit. Chart 13-12, which lists the reasons given for rating fruit as unimportant (among those who feel the presence of fruit is unimportant), helps us to understand the negative aspects of fruit.

The first line of Chart 13-12 shows that one out of four individuals who rate the fruit side dish poorly do so simply because they do not like fruit. Without question, many of these people will not purchase the product because fruit is present.

Other Reasons for Opinion

Happily, a very positive side of the coin is revealed by the rest of the responses to this question. All the other reasons for holding the fruit side dish in low regard are completely or partially executional in nature. In other words, properly portraying or explaining the fruit can address many of the issues that cause these people to rate fruit poorly.

Take the second line, for example; 26 percent state they only like fresh fruit, not canned or frozen fruit. One solution to this problem is to explain to consumers that our fruit is freshly frozen, figuratively right off the vine. Also point out that the fruit has a health benefit that helps to make the meal balanced and well rounded. In addition, we should explain that some fruits lend themselves particularly well to flash freezing while others do poorly (lose taste and textural values), and that the fruit included in this product falls into the former category.

Without question, these arguments will never completely convince all these people. Some will continue to dislike our fresh fruit side dish. But some can be swayed, either completely or partially. On balance, we can significantly reduce the size of this group and the intensity of the feelings through a more skillful communication of fruit's values and benefits.

Each of the other reasons mentioned in Chart 13-12 for giving fruit a lower rating can be dealt with either directly or by implication. And many of these negative feelings can be addressed by the same few positive actions. For example, instead of offering a "medley of fruit" or "accenting" the meal with fruit as we currently do, we can talk about fruit being part of a healthy, well-balanced meal. That is, instead of treating it as a pretty accompaniment, we can treat it as a more important food value. The bottom line: We will never completely eliminate the loss of some individuals because of the presence of fruit, but we can do a great deal to lessen their number and the intensity of their feelings.

And lest we forget, the total number of consumers with a negative reaction about fruit is relatively small; the majority think the presence of fruit is an important benefit. And Chart 13-13 tells why.

In general, we know that people eat fruit at the end of a meal because they like it or believe it complements the earlier courses. Therefore, it is not surprising that the majority of people (54 percent) who think highly of fruit report that their main reason relates to end-use satisfaction.

But even more people (57 percent) tell us the reason for their high regard for fruit is the health benefit it provides. These people are telling us that fruit provides a nutritional balance and completeness to their meal. The

Chart 13-13. Reasons for rating fruit as important.

	Test Concept
Health (Net)	57%
Should include fruit for a balanced meal	25
Healthy/nutritious	23
Naturally sweet/ no sugar added	6
Less calories	8
End-Use Satisfaction (Net)	54
Like fruit	32
Like fruit with meals	9
Good addition to a fancy meal	9
Fruit is refreshing/tasty	9
Different from other desserts	19

naturalness, healthfulness, and small number of calories are of great interest to them. The implication of this finding is enormous. We are being told that the major benefit associated with fruit is one that we never mentioned, even once, in our concept. We never told consumers that we have offered fruit to them because it is a nutritious or healthy benefit, or that it was intended to flesh out their meal in a natural, balanced, and low-caloric manner.

The message is clear: We invented a great new weapon for the marketing wars but forgot to build a trigger on it. The idea of fruit is of great satisfaction to the great majority of people, and we can make this feature of even greater interest by talking about the benefits it provides.

14
The Case History:
Conclusion and Recommendations

As you can see, a concept test is more than a magic number or a pet question. It is an intensive analysis of a large body of information. Putting all this information together in a usable format is what a concept test is all about.

OBSERVATIONS AND ACTION STEPS

In this case-history test, the various facts, observations, hypotheses, insights, and guesses, taken together, tell the following story. We can think of it in 24 separate observations and action steps.

1. Purchase Interest in the concept is merely average. The concept, as currently worded, is not suitable for further development.

2. But killing the concept on the basis of a poor "Definitely Will Buy" score would be a serious mistake, for these reasons:

- Large numbers of consumers report they "probably will buy" the product. This suggests that a mild level of interest in the product exists.
- The Total Emotional Profile battery identifies a critical concept weakness: Consumers do not perceive that the concept is personally relevant to them and their needs.
- Responses to the Benefits and Shortcomings questions suggests there is some mild interest in the concept, but no excitement, enthusiasm, or passion for it.

The weight of evidence suggests that the concept's problem is the lack of a "hot button" to stimulate more intense levels of Purchase Interest. The solution to the problem is not to kill the concept but to fix it, by identifying key issues that can raise Purchase Interest intensity.

3. The product's competitive arena seems to be the premium-priced frozen entree and dinner segment of the industry. Its main competitors will probably be major premium-priced brands like Le Menu and Lean Cuisine. It doesn't compete as well against low-priced brands like Budget Gourmet or the more exotic offerings of Benihana.

4. The data also suggest that we did a poor job of defining our target group. A large number of concept rejectors state they do not buy *any* frozen food on a regular basis. This high level of rejection tells us that the definition of a prime prospect should be tightened. We should include just those people who regularly use frozen dinners and entrees. Exclude those who don't like products in the category, or who buy them very rarely for emergency purposes.

5. Turning to the diagnostic aspects of the test, industry observers have noted that family dining practices are moving toward a direction of separateness. Different family members tend more and more to eat different foods, at different locations, and at different times. America's food marketers have not yet successfully responded to this new direction.

This lack of response is a fortuitous situation for our test concept. The data suggest that a high-potential idea is to reposition the concept so that one of its key elements is its suitability for women to use when eating alone. In fulfilling this role, the product must be perceived as being appropriate for various occasions, moods, and meals. The main appeal should not be for a specific occasion or meal, but a general appropriateness for the consumer whenever she is dining alone.

6. Suitability for use when dining alone may be an extremely promising direction, but the issue is far from complete. Much work is required to learn the best way of explaining this idea to consumers.

- Do we position it primarily for women? For women only? For women who want to pamper themselves?
- The main theme involves appropriateness for various occasions when the consumer is eating alone. Is there any way of also keeping the door open for consumption by the whole family?
- Since lunch and dinner are the major food-consumption occasions, the concept must give some emphasis to the product's suitability for these occasions. How much emphasis on these traditional occasions is optimal?

Concept Testing

The questions are endless, and so are the possible answers. The point to keep in mind is that more thinking about this issue is still required.

7. There are six primary benefits offered by the concept:

- Good taste
- Several varieties
- Health
- Chilled fruit
- Elegance and sophistication
- Lightness

In general, research has shown that this number of benefits is far too high. Consumers exposed to many different benefits often fail to hear or appreciate all of them.

The current concept is no exception to the rule. Many of the primary benefits are not clearly heard or fully understood because respondents are overwhelmed by the complexity of our message. Furthermore, the strength of their positive reactions to those benefits that are heard is also lessened because of the complexity of the message.

The obvious solution is to simplify the concept by eliminating some primary benefits or reducing their dominance.

8. "Good taste" is a very important benefit for a food product to offer. Hardly anyone ever purchases a food for the first time unless she thinks it tastes good. For this reason, "good taste" should not be one of the benefits that is eliminated.

Unfortunately, the concept communicates its taste story very poorly. Taste is infrequently mentioned as an important product feature and is rated poorly in the quadrant analysis. Clearly, those who hear the "good taste" story are not persuaded by it.

Since the "good taste" theme was mentioned only one time by the concept, these results are not altogether surprising. Future versions of the concept must discuss the product's good taste in a more dominant and more persuasive way.

9. A great deal of space in the concept was devoted to the different menu varieties. This primary benefit was not very helpful in terms of persuading consumers to purchase the line. This leads to several ideas.

- Part of the problem is specific in nature. The number of complaints about some of the side dishes, especially avocado wedges, rice with cashew nuts, and melba sauce, suggests that a second look be taken at this aspect of the line.

242

The Case History: Conclusion and Recommendations

- Perceptions of fruit quality and freshness must also be improved.
- Consumers want more than three varieties. Their comments suggest we must expand the line as much as possible, given the obvious limits that retailers provide by virtue of their willingness to stock these items.

10. But even after solving the specific problems caused by our current treatment of the varieties, I suspect the issue will never, by itself, become the all-important hot button that causes consumers to purchase the product.

The data seem to suggest that the three varieties are actually a supporting benefit of the concept. In other words, the varieties can help support a taste theme, a quality theme, a theme of appropriateness for various occasions, and so on. Thinking about the three varieties in this new context significantly reduces the amount of space that should be devoted to it.

11. When consumers refer to the concept's health benefit, they seem to be talking about two different aspects of the issue and they seem to have different reactions to each one. The two aspects are good nutrition and a balanced meal.

The good nutrition story does not work well. Consumers are not responsive to the idea of a nutritious frozen entree. While they may like the idea in general, they do not think the test concept will provide this benefit to a greater degree than other products, nor will they buy it for that reason.

But the second component of health, a balanced meal, has high potential. It receives very little attention when consumers first see it. Few mention it as a Main Idea. However, when consumers are again exposed to the benefit in the forced-exposure question, reaction to it becomes very positive. It seems that the feature simply isn't noticed by consumers when they first read the concept. Given the large number of benefits contained in the concept and the fact that this one was briefly mentioned just one time, this result is not too surprising. The concept should be revised to stress its balanced meal benefit more dominantly.

12. Fruit has been included at great expense, in an attempt to differentiate the concept from competitive products. However, as used here, fruit is not a particularly persuasive benefit. Nevertheless, consumers like the idea of fruit, and this feature should remain in the concept. The data suggest several steps that can be taken to improve the value of this concept element.

The biggest problem with fruit is caused by our description of it. Most consumers perceive fruit to be a natural and healthy food. However, we never mentioned this benefit in the current concept. This is something to change in future versions. A related point: Fruit is considered by most consumers to a necessary element of a balanced meal. Once again, we never mentioned this reason to support the presence of fruit.

13. In addition to improperly positioning fruit, there are a number of specific comments that should be made about fruit to address some consumer complaints.

- Some consumers don't get the message that the fruits offered by the concept are fresh fruits, frozen "right off the vine." This issue should be clarified.
- A related issue is quality. We must better communicate that the fruits offered by the product are high-quality, top of the line.

14. A few of the changes and improvements about fruit are quite easy to make. Instead of talking about a "medley of fruit" or "accenting" the meal with fruit, talk about fruit as a "healthy and well-balanced accent to your meal" or a "natural and healthy medley."

15. Treating the product as elegant and sophisticated does not work. The claim is not believable or persuasive, except to older women, and should be dropped.

16. "Lightness" is also a major benefit that simply does not work. Instead of helping the concept, it holds back its success and causes problems in a number of different areas. At the heart of its problem is the perception that a light product will not be a filling and satisfying meal. The "lightness" benefit should be dropped.

17. Lightness causes confusion about some other elements of the concept. The concept tries to communicate the idea of a full meal that is not filling, yet satisfies hunger. Consumers do not think these ideas hang together. They tell us they don't understand how both these conflicting claims can be true. If we eliminate references to "lightness," most of this problem will dissipate.

18. A serious problem with the concept is the fact that it communicates there is an insufficient amount of food in each serving. Once again, part of the problem is caused by the "lightness" benefit. Dropping "lightness" will help to resolve this problem. In addition, we should address the quantity issue by telling consumers that each serving contains a satisfying amount of food.

19. Another problem partially caused by "lightness": Consumers tell us they plan to purchase the product relatively infrequently. Apparently, the presence of the "lightness" claim inadvertently suggests that the product should only be consumed when they are in the mood for something light.

Eliminating the "lightness" benefit will partially solve this problem. In addition, we can increase the intended frequency of purchase by clearly communicating the product is an everyday meal, and a meal that is full and complete.

20. One factor influencing the low frequency of purchase is that 20 percent think they will eat the product most often as a snack, not a meal. In view of the fact that Americans *regularly* consume relatively few snacks that involve extensive food preparation steps and are consumed while sitting down, with a knife and fork, this snack-oriented association is seriously affecting volume.

Undoubtedly, elimination of the "lightness" benefit will resolve part of this problem. But in addition, the concept must be clarified to communicate that this product is a full meal, not a snack.

21. Talking about consumption occasions, while our strategy should be to associate this product with a variety of occasions, it is important to keep in mind that women are especially interested in it for lunch (when full-time homemakers are most likely to be alone). On the other hand, a great deal of consumption in the entire frozen food category occurs at dinner. For this reason, the concept must "give permission" for the consumer to eat the product on both occasions.

22. "Uniqueness" does not appear to be a powerful motivator. Virtually no one shows any interest in this theme. If there is something unique about the product, it should be described by the concept in detail. Either we must actually show consumers what makes the product unique, or we must drop the benefit.

23. The idea of a modern food for today's lifestyles has no meaning, stimulates no curiosity, and generates no Purchase Interest in the concept. The benefit should either be dropped or significantly revised to make it more supportive of the "eat alone" phenomenon now occurring with increased frequency in many households.

24. Consumers make no reference to the handsome plate, either positively or negatively. Even after seeing this feature in the forced-exposure question, very few consumers show any interest in it. Apparently the plate is not a useful or believable benefit and should be dropped.

A CLOSING PERSPECTIVE

The purpose of this detailed case history—and of this entire book—is to help companies improve their concept testing procedures so they can pick winners early in the product development cycle, discriminate between similar alternatives, and fix or improve deficient concepts.

Many of the ideas are not magic—just common sense. They certainly are not foolproof. But, on balance, systematic usage of these procedures will help make an otherwise disappointing study come alive.

I have just scratched the surface. I invite you to look at your own concept testing system for better ways to analyze and improve it. All you need is some logical thinking and a bit of imagination. As you have seen, it takes so little to accomplish so much.

APPENDIX

Questionnaires for a Frozen Food Concept Test

SCREENING QUESTIONNAIRE

Respondent's Name _____

Address _____

City _____ State _____ Zip _____

Area Code _____ Telephone _____

Interviewed by _____ Date _____

Validated by _____ Date _____

Time Interview Began: _____

Time Interview Ended: _____

Total Time in Minutes: _____

(SIGHT SCREEN FOR FEMALES 18 TO 65 YEARS OLD.)

Hello, my name is _____ . I work for a nationwide market research company. We're conducting a survey and I'd like to ask you a few questions.

A. Do you or does any member of your family work for an advertising agency, market research company, a food retailer or distributor, or a manufacturer of food products?

    Yes to any......................... a → (TERMINATE. CIRCLE
    No .... b   NEXT NUMBER IN BOX
                                                           BELOW.)

TERMINATE: CONFLICT

01 02 03 04 05 06 07 08 09 10 11 12 13 14 15 16 17 18 19 20 21 22 23 24 25 26 27 28 29 30

B. Are you the female head of your household or are you married to the household head?

Yes .... a → (TERMINATE. CIRCLE
No .... b   NEXT NUMBER IN BOX
                                          BELOW.)

TERMINATE: NOT HEAD OF HOUSEHOLD

01 02 03 04 05 06 07 08 09 10 11 12 13 14 15 16 17 18 19 20 21 22 23 24 25 26 27 28 29 30

C. (SHOW AGE CARD.) My assignment is to obtain a certain number of interviews with people in various age categories. Into which age group do you fall?

Under 18 years old............... a → (TERMINATE. CIRCLE
                                         NEXT NUMBER IN BOX
18–24 years old 1   BELOW.)
25–29 years old 2
30–34 years old 3
35–39 years old 4
40–44 years old 5
45–49 years old 6
50–54 years old 7
55–65 years old 8

66 years or older .... c → (TERMINATE. CIRCLE
                                          NEXT NUMBER IN BOX
                                          BELOW.)
(TAKE BACK CARD.)

TERMINATE: NOT 18 TO 65

01 02 03 04 05 06 07 08 09 10 11 12 13 14 15 16 17 18 19 20 21 22 23 24 25 26 27 28 29 30

D. (HAND RESPONDENT BRAND CARD.) Which, if any, of the brands of prepared frozen dinners and single-dish entrees on this card have you yourself purchased at least once in the *past three months*?

Armour Dinner Classics 1
Benihana.. 2
Budget Gourmet 3
Green Giant Single Serving Entrees 4
Lean Cuisine Entrees 5
Le Menu Dinners 6
Light and Elegant 7
Stouffer's Single Serving Entrees.. 8
Weight Watchers Entrees 9
Classic Lite.. 0
Feast for One x

(TAKE BACK CARD.)

TERMINATE: NOT A CATEGORY USER
01 02 03 04 05 06 07 08 09 10 11 12 13 14 15 16 17 18 19 20 21 22 23 24 25 26 27 28 29 30

GO TO MAIN QUESTIONNAIRE.

Concept Testing

MAIN QUESTIONNAIRE

Respondent's Name: _____

A producer of frozen foods is thinking about some ideas for new frozen food products. I would like to show you a description of one of these products, and then I would like you to tell me your reactions to this new product. Please read the description for as long as you like and tell me when you have finished.

> HAND RESPONDENT CONCEPT STATEMENT. WHEN SHE INDICATES THAT SHE IS FINISHED, TAKE BACK CONCEPT.

1a. (HAND RESPONDENT PURCHASE INTEREST CARD.) Which phase on this card best describes how likely you would be to buy one or more products in this line if it were available for a price ranging from $1.79 to $2.99 in the store where you usually shop for frozen dinners?

Definitely would buy it...5
Probably would buy it..4
Might or might not buy it...3
Probably would not buy it..2
Definitely would not buy it...1

(TAKE BACK CARD.)

1b. Why do you say that you (READ ANSWER TO Q.1A)? (PROBE:) What other reasons do you have for feeling this way?

_____

_____

_____

_____

_____

252

2. (HAND RESPONDENT RATING CARD.) How would you rate this line of new products overall? Please tell me which phrase on this card is closest to your overall opinion.

Excellent 5
Very good 4
Good 3
Fair 2
Poor 1

(TAKE BACK CARD.)

3. Other than trying to sell you the product, what do you think was the main idea in the description you just read? That is, what was the main thing they were trying to communicate about the product?

_____

_____

_____

_____

_____

_____

4a. Do you think this line of products would have . . . (READ LIST)?

        Major benefits 1   (ASK Q.4B)
        Minor benefits 2   (SKIP TO Q.4E)
  or, No benefits at all 3   (SKIP TO Q.5A)

4b. What are the *major* benefits it would have?

_____

_____

_____

Concept Testing

4c. What other benefits are there?

_____

_____

_____

_____

4d. In what way, if any, are these benefits important to you?

_____

_____

_____

_____

SKIP TO Q.5A

4e. What benefits would it have? (PROBE:) What other benefits are there?

_____

_____

_____

_____

4f. In what way, if any, are these benefits important to you?

_____

_____

_____

5a. Do you think this line of products would have . . . (READ LIST)?

        Major shortcomings 1   (ASK Q.5B)
        Minor shortcomings 2   (SKIP TO Q.5D)
  or, No shortcomings at all 3   (SKIP TO Q.6)

5b. What are the *major* shortcomings it would have?

_____

_____

_____

_____

5c. What other shortcomings are there?

_____

_____

_____

_____

SKIP TO Q.6

5d. What shortcomings would it have? (PROBE:) What other shortcomings
are there?

_____

_____

_____

_____

Concept Testing

6a. How different is this product from other frozen entrees? Would you say it is . . . (READ LIST)?

        Greatly different 1

        Somewhat different 2   (ASK Q.6B)

        Not at all different 3   (SKIP TO Q.6C)

6b. In what ways is it different from other frozen entrees?

_____

_____

_____

_____

6c. What products or foods would this line replace?

_____

_____

_____

_____

6d. Assume that you tried this product and liked it. Which statement best describes how often, if ever, you think you would buy this product if it were available where you shop?

Once a week or more often 1

Once every two or three weeks 2

Once a month or every four weeks..................................... 3

Once every two or three months 4

Once every four to six months 5

Once or twice a year 6

Less often than once a year... 7

Never 8

7a. (HAND RESPONDENT DECK OF CARDS AND RATING BOARD #1.) Now, I would like you to rate this line of products on several characteristics. Although you have evaluated the line on an overall basis, you may feel differently about some characteristics. Since you may not have used these products before, please base your answers on what you've just read.

On these cards are various characteristics. I'd like you to read each card, then place the card on the rating board (POINT TO BOARD) under the word or phrase excellent, very good, good, fair, or poor that best describes how well you think these products would perform for each of the characteristics. By the way, the numbers on the cards are for identification purposes only.

> AFTER RESPONDENT HAS PLACED ALL THE CARDS ON THE RATING BOARD, GIVE HER THE CARDS UNDER THE "EXCELLENT" RATING.

Now I'd like you to read the numbers of the cards to me so that I can record your answers.

> WHEN ALL THE "EXCELLENT" CHARACTERISTICS HAVE BEEN RECORDED, PUT THAT PILE AWAY AND GIVE HER THE CARDS UNDER "VERY GOOD." CONTINUE IN THIS WAY UNTIL ANSWERS FOR ALL THE CHARACTERISTICS HAVE BEEN RECORDED. BE SURE NOT TO MIX THE CARDS UP.

Q.7a.

	#	Excellent	Very Good	Good	Fair	Poor
Being good for dinner	2	5	4	3	2	1
Being easy to prepare	3	5	4	3	2	1
Being a well-balanced meal	4	5	4	3	2	1
Being quick to prepare	5	5	4	3	2	1
Having high-quality ingredients	7	5	4	3	2	1
Being low in calories	8	5	4	3	2	1
Being appropriate for an informal meal	9	5	4	3	2	1

Concept Testing

	#	Excellent	Very Good	Good	Fair	Poor
Being good for lunch	10	5	4	3	2	1
Being appropriate for children	11	5	4	3	2	1
Being appropriate for a wide variety of occasions	12	5	4	3	2	1
Being suitable for my lifestyle	13	5	4	3	2	1
Being a good value for the money	14	5	4	3	2	1
Having a good taste	15	5	4	3	2	1
Being appropriate for adults	16	5	4	3	2	1
Being good for meals when not all family members eat together	17	5	4	3	2	1
Being appropriate for men	18	5	4	3	2	1
The quality of the fruit	19	5	4	3	2	1
Being nutritious	22	5	4	3	2	1
Satisfying your hunger	23	5	4	3	2	1
Being good for snacks	24	5	4	3	2	1
Being good for when you want a light meal	25	5	4	3	2	1
Not being too filling	26	5	4	3	2	1
Being appropriate for women	27	5	4	3	2	1
Being good for people who watch their weight	28	5	4	3	2	1
Has main courses I like	31	5	4	3	2	1
Being good for an occasional snack or treat	33	5	4	3	2	1
Being good for a special lunch	34	5	4	3	2	1
Being good to have on hand	36	5	4	3	2	1
Being good for a late-night meal	37	5	4	3	2	1
Being good for between meals	38	5	4	3	2	1
Has varieties I like	39	5	4	3	2	1
Has fruit combinations I like	40	5	4	3	2	1
Has unique varieties	41	5	4	3	2	1

Appendix: Questionnaires for a Frozen Food Concept Test

PICK UP ALL THE CARDS AND SHUFFLE THEM. REMOVE
RATING BOARD #1 AND BRING OUT RATING BOARD #2 AND
BLUE RECORDING SHEET.

7b. Now I'd like to find out how important each of the following characteristics is to you. Using these same cards and this rating board (POINT
TO BOARD), which goes from very important to somewhat important,
neither important nor unimportant, somewhat unimportant and very
unimportant, please indicate how important each characteristic is to
you for frozen dinners and entrees.

AFTER RESPONDENT HAS PLACED ALL THE CARDS ON THE
RATING BOARD, GIVE HER THE CARDS UNDER THE "VERY
IMPORTANT" RATING.

Now, as we did before, please read the numbers of the cards to me so
that I can record your answers.

WHEN ALL THE "VERY IMPORTANT" CHARACTERISTICS
HAVE BEEN RECORDED, PUT THAT PILE AWAY AND GIVE
HER THE CARDS UNDER "SOMEWHAT IMPORTANT."
CONTINUE IN THIS WAY UNTIL ALL THE
CHARACTERISTICS HAVE BEEN RECORDED. BE SURE NOT
TO MIX THE CARDS UP.

BEFORE YOU GO TO Q.8A BE SURE YOU HAVE ONE ANSWER
FOR EACH CHARACTERISTIC.

Q.7b.

	#	Extremely Important	Very Important	Somewhat Important	Not At All Important
Being good for dinner	2	4	3	2	1
Being easy to prepare	3	4	3	2	1
Being a well-balanced meal	4	4	3	2	1
Being quick to prepare	5	4	3	2	1
Having high-quality ingredients	7	4	3	2	1

Concept Testing

	#	Extremely Important	Very Important	Somewhat Important	Not At All Important
Being low in calories	8	4	3	2	1
Being appropriate for an informal meal	9	4	3	2	1
Being good for lunch	10	4	3	2	1
Being appropriate for children	11	4	3	2	1
Being appropriate for a wide variety of occasions	12	4	3	2	1
Being suitable for my lifestyle	13	4	3	2	1
Being a good value for the money	14	4	3	2	1
Having a good taste	15	4	3	2	1
Being appropriate for adults	16	4	3	2	1
Being good for meals when not all family members eat together	17	4	3	2	1
Being appropriate for men	18	4	3	2	1
The quality of the fruit	19	4	3	2	1
Being nutritious	22	4	3	2	1
Satisfying your hunger	23	4	3	2	1
Being good for snacks	24	4	3	2	1
Being good for when you want a light meal	25	4	3	2	1
Not being too filling	26	4	3	2	1
Being appropriate for women	27	4	3	2	1
Being good for people who watch their weight	28	4	3	2	1

Appendix: Questionnaires for a Frozen Food Concept Test

	#	Extremely Important	Very Important	Somewhat Important	Not At All Important
Has main courses I like	31	4	3	2	1
Being good for an occasional snack or treat	33	4	3	2	1
Being good for a special lunch	34	4	3	2	1
Being good to have on hand	36	4	3	2	1
Being good for a late-night meal	37	4	3	2	1
Being good for between meals	38	4	3	2	1
Has varieties I like	39	4	3	2	1
Has fruit combinations I like	40	4	3	2	1
Has unique varieties	41	4	3	2	1

8a. (HAND RESPONDENT MEAL CARD.) For what type of meal would you be most *likely* to eat the products you just read about? (RECORD UNDER COL. 8A.)

8b. Now let's suppose you had ten packages of these products in your freezer. Please tell me for what meal or meals on this card you would use these ten packages. You might use them for a number of different meals. You might also use them for some meal occasion that is not on the card. Now, how do you think you might use the ten packages? (RECORD UNDER COL. 8B.)

Concept Testing

	Col. 8a Most Likely	Col. 8b Number of Times Used
Weekday breakfast	1	_____
Weekend breakfast	2	_____
Brunch	3	_____
Lunch	4	_____
Dinner	5	_____
Late supper	6	_____
Afternoon snack	7	_____
Late-night snack	8	_____
Something else (SPECIFY)		_____
_____	0	_____
	Total	_____

> **THE TOTAL UNDER COL. 8B MUST BE 10.**

(TAKE BACK CARD.)

9a. (HAND RESPONDENT FAMILY CARD.) Who in your household do you think would eat this product most often? (RECORD UNDER COL. 9A.)

9b. Who else? (RECORD UNDER COL. 9B.)

	Col. 9a Most Often	Col. 9b Who Else
Self	1	1
Husband	2	2
Male teenager 13–17	3	3
Female teenager 13–17	4	4
Children 6–12	5	5
Children under 6	6	6
Other adult males (age 18 or over)	7	7
Other adult females (age 18 or over)	8	8
Don't know/no answer	0	0
No one would eat	x	x
No one else		y

(TAKE BACK CARD.)

10. In what ways, if any, could this line of products be changed or improved? I'd like you to tell me anything you can think of, no matter how minor it seems.

_____

_____

_____

_____

11a. (HAND RESPONDENT WHITE RATING SHEET.) The paper I'm handing you is a rating sheet for the description you just read. You can see a series of boxes between sets of various phrases. We would like you to "X" one box on each line to describe how you feel about the description.

Let's suppose you were asked to describe the weather this week and you found the phrases "Extremely Unpleasant—Extremely Pleasant." If you thought the weather was extremely unpleasant, you would put an "X" on the far left like this: (POINT TO BOX.)

If you thought the weather was extremely pleasant, you would put an "X" on the far right like this: (POINT TO BOX.)

However, if you felt the weather this week was somewhere between the two extremes, you would put an "X" in a box somewhere between the two phrases, depending on what you thought the weather was.

Do you see how it works? (IF NO, REPEAT.) Remember to think in terms of the description you just read.

> BE SURE RESPONDENT UNDERSTANDS BEFORE BEGINNING. WHEN RESPONDENT IS FINISHED, CHECK TO BE SURE THERE IS ONE AND ONLY ONE "X" ON EACH LINE. AT END OF INTERVIEW, STAPLE THIS SHEET TO THE BACK OF THE QUESTIONNAIRE.

263

11b. (CHECK WHITE RATING SHEET. LOOK AT PHRASES EASY TO UNDERSTAND—NOT EASY TO UNDERSTAND. IF RESPONDENT PUT AN "X" IN THE BOXES ON THE *RIGHT* MARKED 5, 6, OR 7, NEAR THE PHRASE *NOT* EASY TO UNDERSTAND, ASK:) What was unclear or hard to understand?

_____

_____

_____

_____

11c. (CHECK WHITE RATING SHEET. LOOK AT PHRASES NOT AT ALL BELIEVABLE—VERY BELIEVABLE. IF RESPONDENT PUTS AN "X" IN THE BOXES ON THE *LEFT* MARKED 1, 2, OR 3, NEAR THE PHRASE *NOT* AT ALL BELIEVABLE, ASK:) What was hard to believe?

_____

_____

_____

_____

| HAND RESPONDENT CONCEPT. |

12a. Here is a copy of the description you have just read. I'd like you to circle any words, sentences, or ideas that you found to be especially interesting or important to you. (HAVE RESPONDENT USE RED PEN.)

12b. Now, I'd like you to cross out any words, sentences, or ideas that you found to be especially uninteresting or unimportant to you. (HAVE RESPONDENT USE GREEN PEN.)

> WHEN RESPONDENT HAS FINISHED, TAKE BACK
> CONCEPT. AT END OF INTERVIEW, STAPLE TO
> BACK OF QUESTIONNAIRE.

13a. As you may recall, the items in this line of products have a fruit side dish. How important is it to you that these items have a fruit side dish? Would you say it is very important, somewhat important, neither important nor unimportant, somewhat unimportant, or very unimportant that this product has a fruit side dish?

Very important 1
Somewhat important 2
Neither important nor unimportant................................. 3
Somewhat unimportant... 4
Very unimportant 5

13b. Why do you say that? (PROBE:) What other reasons do you have?

_____

_____

_____

_____

14. (HAND RESPONDENT WORD CARD.) Thinking about food, what do these words mean to you? What is the difference between these two words? (PROBE:) Anything else?

_____

_____

_____

_____

(TAKE BACK WORD CARD.)

Concept Testing

15. What types of ovens do you own? (READ LIST.)

	Own	Don't Own
Gas oven	1	a
Electric oven	2	a
Microwave oven......................................	3	a
Toaster oven	4	a
Convection oven	5	a

16. What brand of frozen premium dinners or entrees do you ever buy, either regularly or occasionally? (DO NOT READ LIST.)

Armour Dinner Classics	1
Benihana..	2
Budget Gourmet	3
Classic Lite..	4
Feast for One	5
Green Giant Single Serving Entrees	6
Lean Cuisine Entrees	7
Le Menu Dinners	8
Light and Elegant	9
Stouffer's Single Serving Entrees...	0
Weight Watchers Entrees	x

17a. Counting yourself, how many people are currently living in your household? (RECORD EXACT NUMBER BELOW.)

_____

TOTAL IN HOUSEHOLD

17b. And, including yourself, how many household members are . . .
(READ LIST)?

	Number in Household	
	Males	Females
Under 6	_____	_____
6 to 12	_____	_____
13 to 17	_____	_____
18 or older	_____	_____
Total	_____	_____

(TOTAL OF MALE/FEMALE MUST EQUAL ANSWER IN Q.17A.)

18a. Do you, yourself work outside the home? (CIRCLE *ONE* ANSWER
BELOW.)

Yes 1   (ASK Q.18B)
No................................. 2   (SKIP TO Q.19)

18b. Is that . . . (READ LIST)? (CIRCLE ONE ANSWER BELOW.)

Less than 35 hours a week 1
35 or more hours a week 2
(DO *NOT* READ) Don't know/no answer 3

19. What was the last grade of school you completed? (DO *NOT* READ
LIST.)

Some high school or less 1
Graduated high school................................... 2
Some college 3
Graduated college or more 4

20. Are you . . . (READ LIST)?

Married 1
Divorced/separated 2
Widowed 3
Single 4

Concept Testing

21. (HAND RESPONDENT INCOME CARD.) For classification purposes only, we need to know your total family income, from all sources, before taxes. Please tell me the letter of the category in which your income falls.

    A. Less than $5,000 1
    B. $5,000–$7,999 2
    C. $8,000–$9,999 3
    D. $10,000–$14,999 4
    E. $15,000–$19,999 5
    F. $20,000–$24,999 6
    G. $25,000–$29,999 7
    H. $30,000–$34,999 8
    I. $35,000–$49,999 9
    J. $50,000 and over 0
       Refused x

(TAKE BACK CARD.)

22. (RECORD MARKET.)

Atlanta... 1
Boston.. 2
Chicago... 3
Los Angeles 4
Phoenix 5
San Antonio 6

THANK RESPONDENT.

Appendix: Questionnaires for a Frozen Food Concept Test

WHITE RATING SHEET

Please check one box between each pair of statements to indicate your opinion of the description you just read. The more strongly you feel a phrase describes your feelings, the closer to the phrase would be the box you check.

EXAMPLE: Today, the weather was:

Extremely unpleasant   ☐ ☐ ☐ ☐ ☐ ☐ ☐   Extremely pleasant

The description is:

	1	2	3	4	5	6	7	
Boring	☐	☐	☐	☐	☐	☐	☐	Interesting
Not at all believable	☐	☐	☐	☐	☐	☐	☐	Very believable
Not talking to me	☐	☐	☐	☐	☐	☐	☐	Talking to me
About an ordinary product	☐	☐	☐	☐	☐	☐	☐	About a unique product
Relevant to my needs	☐	☐	☐	☐	☐	☐	☐	Not relevant to my needs
Persuasive	☐	☐	☐	☐	☐	☐	☐	Not persuasive
Not saying important things	☐	☐	☐	☐	☐	☐	☐	Saying important things
Easy to understand	☐	☐	☐	☐	☐	☐	☐	Not easy to understand
Saying something unique	☐	☐	☐	☐	☐	☐	☐	Saying something ordinary
Something rubs me the wrong way	☐	☐	☐	☐	☐	☐	☐	Nothing rubs me the wrong way

1 2 3 4 5 6 7

Index

Index

Purchase Interest testing of, 46–47, 53
Clorox Company Fresh Scent liquid bleach, introduction of, 55, 110
closed-end questions, in user imagery, 88–89
code building, 88–89
coding, 165–166
Colgate-Palmolive Success campaign, 72
competition
  consumer's use of brands of, 131–135, 194–195
  evaluation of, 19–20
  and pricing, 113–114
  testing of, to establish norms, 144
completion rate, 154
computer models, 123–124
computer software, consumer attitudes toward, 145
concept
  core, 8–18, 32
  definition of, 3–4
  diagnosis of, 58–60
  examples of, 5–7
  filmed, 4–5
  fine tuning, with use occasion imagery, 89
  goal for, 142
  importance of, 66–69
  kinds of, 4–7
  as limiter of use by consumer, 91
  Main Idea of, 62–66
  multiple, 170–171
  persuasiveness of, 189
  pinpointing problems of, 22, 90–91, 97–102
  poor-performing, 22
  positioning of, 4–5, 6–18
  relevance to consumer needs of, 60–61
  revision of, 20
  sales potential of, 22
  strengthening of already strong, 97
  strengths of, 191–195
  uncovering of product advantages/disadvantages with, 22, 102–106
  uniqueness of, 54–60
  see also concept statements
concept failure, 98
  hidden problems that cause, 107–108
  reasons for, 21, 23, 63–64, 143
concept forecasts, 124–125
  shortcomings of, 125–128
  types of, 121–124
concept statements
  common errors in, 28–31
  communication failure of, 171

emotionally loaded words in, 31–32
examination of existing products for, 24–26
generation of ideas for, 23–24
headlines for, 32–33
illustration of, 33–35
lack of clarity in, 30–31
lengthy, 28–30
poorly written, 23
realistic approach in, 26–27
stating the obvious in, 30
concept testing
  Advantage question in, 104–105
  analysis of data from, 153–154
  asking the right questions in, 108–109
  benefits of, 22
  brand comparisons in, 106–107
  of core idea or positioning concept, 8–18
  cost of, 170
  definition of, 4
  Disadvantage question in, 103–104
  follow-up steps in, 20–21
  length of, 170
  for New York City's Metropolitan Transportation Authority, 40–43
  poor techniques in, 21
  preliminary steps for, 19–20
  procedural guidelines for, 150–173
  Purchase Interest question in, 43–46, see also Purchase Interest
  sample types for, 154–158
  selection of who should conduct the, 152–154
  unrealistic expectations from, 21
consumer(s)
  acceptance, 9–11, 22
  awareness, 125, 131–135
  brand use of, 194–195
  characteristics of, 85–86, see also user imagery
  complaints, 172–173
  demographic breakdown of, 192–194
  dissatisfaction, 137
  frequency of purchase by, 70–71
  height and weight, 138–139
  interest in trying new product, 135–136
  patterns of response, 163
  product improvement suggestions of, 143
  satisfaction of, 50–51, 136–138
  understanding of Main Idea by, 147–149
  see also respondent
consumer needs
  determination of, 19

271

Index

Index

Index

Index

Index